A CHAPLAIN

LOOKS AT

VIETNAM

A CHAPLAIN LOOKS AT VIETNAM

BY

John J. O'Connor

CHAPLAIN, UNITED STATES NAVY

Foreword by
SENATOR EVERETT M. DIRKSEN

Cleveland  New York

THE WORLD PUBLISHING COMPANY

Published by The World Publishing Company

2231 West 110th Street, Cleveland, Ohio 44102

Published simultaneously in Canada by Nelson, Foster & Scott Ltd.

First Printing 1968

Library of Congress Catalog Card Number: 68-26834

Printed in the United States of America

To all those who believe in the future of
Vietnam and have given something of
their lives to prove their belief

CONTENTS

Foreword

THE MORAL IMPLICATIONS of the conflict in Vietnam
and the United States' involvement there have not, to my
knowledge, been presented clearly to the American people—
until now. Nor are they likely to be presented at any future
time in such penetrating depth as within these pages.

Chaplain O'Connor's analysis of the tragic situation in
Vietnam is thoughtful and thorough in all respects—historical,
military, diplomatic, economic. From it he draws conclusions
of moral consequence and strength that are enlightening,
heartening, and of enduring significance.

The author's use of the word "involvement" is most appropriate. We are indeed involved in Vietnam. This reality
is one to which the pseudo-intellectuals, the sunshine patriots,
and the nay-sayers might well give heed. We are confronted
by a harsh fact, not a drawing-room theory. We had best
accept that fact if we hope to solve the problem implicit in
it—the winning of a decisive victory and of a just and durable
peace.

No mature American can deny that the best interests of
the United States must ever and unfailingly be our *first*
interest. But the best interests of this beloved country of ours
must ever have their root and base in moral strength as well
as in material resources.

"God willing," writes Chaplain O'Connor, "we Americans will always examine critically, if not, indeed, caustically,
our methods of waging war, will always demand that our
elected officials do everything reasonable to avoid war, and
if unsuccessful in this, seek ardently and intensely the road
to peace." There are those who disagree with, and those who
dissent from, our involvement in Vietnam. Between the two
groups lies a distance as far apart as the poles.

In *disagreement*—the thoughtful, temperate effort to find
answers and seek solutions—we have grown in wisdom and
stature as a free people. In *dissent*—the ear-splitting assertion
of personal identity and privilege—we hear today only the

quarrelsome and dangerous assertions of those seeking personal publicity, power, and privilege.

We welcome disagreement—sincere and searching. We condemn dissent for exactly what it is—a divisive, destructive force of evil origin and intent.

It is, then, of transcendent importance that, as we may disagree in our seeking of a way out of our complex involvement in Vietnam, we "read, mark, learn, and inwardly digest" the moral and spiritual aspects of that involvement as here set forth so well.

As without vision a people perish, so without moral concern and strength they cannot hope either to survive or to prevail. Firm and secure in our historic conviction that right *does* make might, we can be confident indeed that in this crisis, as in all others, we shall do both.

EVERETT M. DIRKSEN
MARCH 1968

Acknowledgments

I WANT TO THANK the countless numbers of officers and men of the Navy and the Marine Corps with whom I served in Vietnam. Their dedication and sacrifice alone would be enough to make me want to write a book. I wish I knew and could list all their names.

Certain individuals I can thank by name, and do so in the hope that they will serve as symbols of thousands of others in uniform. Lieutenant General Lewis W. Walt, now Assistant Commandant of the Marine Corps, formerly my commander in Vietnam, inspired me to write this book. I refer to him frequently throughout. General Wallace M. Greene, Jr., former Commandant of the Marine Corps, actively encouraged and supported my efforts. Lieutenant General James M. Masters, Sr., Commanding General, Marine Corps Development and Education Command, actually made the book possible, listening to my problems, urging me to complete the work. The Chief of Chaplains, United States Navy, Rear Admiral James W. Kelly, helped a great deal by recognizing the intent of the effort. Chaplains Robert C. Fenning and Milton U. Ray, successive staff chaplains of Marine Corps Base, Quantico, were most patient in helping me juggle my normal working hours. The present Commandant of the Marine Corps, General Leonard F. Chapman, Jr., presided when I first lectured to the Marine Corps Headquarters staff upon my initial return from Vietnam, and encouraged my continuing to make public presentations. Miss Hillary Masters was my indispensable associate in preparing the manuscript and in researching materials. Men like my present clerk, Lance Corporal Merle Clark, Purple Heart holder, sustained my determination to write in behalf of all the valiant.

My earliest introduction to the problems of Vietnam came in 1954 from Father Thomas O'Melia, an old China hand, of the Maryknoll Missions. My debt to him is immeasurable. Newsmen like Jim Lucas, of Scripps-Howard, and Eddie Adams, of AP, typify countless reporters whose professionalism motivated my own efforts. Many of my fellow chaplains have served in Vietnam far longer than I and under much more arduous circumstances than prevailed during my period of service. To them I am particularly grateful.

There are so many others who helped in so many ways, such as Brigadier General Frank E. Garretson, the Marine Corps Director of Information; his special assistant, Philip N. Pierce; and Lieutenant Colonel Richard S. Stark, the officer in charge of the Marine Corps Information Office in New York, that I could not begin to list all their names. Few people gave me more assistance than did the librarians of the Marine Corps command at Quantico. They are typical of the fine librarians of the Navy-Marine Corps family. I can and must in deepest appreciation list the names of Mrs. Manon Tingue and Mrs. Grace Shaw, of The World Publishing Company, who edited the manuscript, carefully and painfully. If this book is in any way readable, the credit is completely theirs.

A NOTE TO THE READER

THIS BOOK DOES NOT PURPORT, in any way, to represent any United States governmental or military authorities or agencies. The opinions expressed, the references used, and the entire content are solely the responsibility of the author.

No one in governmental or military authority directed me to write this book. No such individual requested that any material whatever be included. I alone am responsible for its content. If it offers any insights or is characterized by any strengths, these are the result of my associations with others, such as those mentioned in the Acknowledgments. Its many and obvious inadequacies are solely mine.

JOHN J. O'CONNOR

INTRODUCTION

IN DECEMBER OF 1967 I was asked to address the students and faculty of a liberal arts college on the moral and legal aspects of the conflict in Vietnam. The college official inviting me advised me that I could take as much time as I needed for my address, and that there would be one other talk on the subject. Upon arrival at the school, however, I learned that his plans had gone awry, and that I was to be one of five speakers, each to have a half hour or less, in what was obviously the general format of a debate.

When I discovered that of the three speakers opposed to U. S. involvement in Vietnam, two were Ph.D's in history from major universities, and a third was a lawyer from another major university, I must confess I felt uneasy. I had not come prepared to debate anyone. Moreover, I have never considered myself an expert about Vietnam, although I have been in South Vietnam, have read much of the literature available, and had, at that time, just completed the second draft of the manuscript of this book. But these gentlemen, presumably, were true "professionals." I was not at all sure that my experience and research would stand up under what I assumed would be a barrage of carefully documented facts beyond my ken, plus a series of tightly reasoned arguments that would make my presentation seem childish at best. So, while interested, of course, in the truth and anxious to learn, I felt less than enthusiastic about the probability of being publicly humiliated.

When the sessions ended, I was, indeed, sad—sad and frustrated—but not by having my expectations fulfilled. On the contrary, I was sad, frustrated, and not a little annoyed by the absurdities presented in all seriousness, by the misquotations offered as documentation, by the outright violence of the diatribes hurled against the President of the United States, by the quivering emotionalism of the unsubstantiated charges, and the sheer authoritarianism of allegations stated as facts. I had often witnessed this kind of intellectual weakness in "parlor debate," in political oratory, in the placards of many of the protest marchers, in the demonstrations of unreasoned hatred such as that displayed by those spitting in the faces of soldiers guarding the Pentagon. I had come across it in the writings of those with axes to grind. I had never experienced it in the writings of serious scholars, whether or not I agreed with the writings. I had not expected it from a Ph.D in a college auditorium.

As strange and unthinking as it sounds, I was appalled at "winning" a debate simply by presenting the facts, quoting accurately, and straightforwardly describing my personal experiences. I was appalled at discovering for the thousandth time how many sincere people are being misled, how much distortion is being accepted as truth. Even though I had spent so many hours of the previous year and a half studying the literature and trying to define the reasons for national confusion, it was still deeply disturbing to see confusion being generated before my very eyes.

I came home from that experience with the decision that I should make every effort to get this book published. If what I heard that day is illustrative of what college students are being told, or if the opinion of the general public is being formed by what I have read in so many places, then *something* is needed. Until someone fills the need adequately, I can only hope and pray that this book will help provoke a public recognition that there are far too many pied pipers abroad whose tune may sound very sweet in Hanoi, but who are playing very badly off key.

Wherever I have spoken about Vietnam, throughout the United States, I have found sincere concern about the morality of the conflict and of United States involvement. A certain number of articles have appeared on the subject, and various clergymen and church groups have addressed themselves to it. However, I know of few books in English concerned exclusively with the moral aspects of the situation. One is *Vietnam: Crisis of Conscience*, by Brown, Novak, and Heschel, and I treat it in some detail in this text. It is a strong indictment of the conflict and of United States involvement. I disagree radically with this book, but I am unfamiliar with any text but my own that counters the moral arguments it presents. Wherever I have lectured, people ask me for a reference text—something supporting the moral rightness of our position. I know of none. Hence, my own manuscript.

It is my earnest intent throughout this book to try to provide straightforward answers to questions about Vietnam and why we are there—questions being asked by people from all walks of life. But straightforward answers are not necessarily simple answers. In one of the strangest wars in history, with diplomatic, political, and military complexities that almost defy the broadest imagination and surely defy narrow classification, simple answers, simple solutions, simple conclusions can be frighteningly misleading. But there are answers. I have had to dig for the answers myself, and the realization that many thousands of servicemen's parents, wives, and sweethearts, as well as millions of other concerned Americans, have possibly been unsuccessful in finding these answers has been exceedingly frustrating to me. I have found my frustration shared by a large number of Marines who have returned from the conflict, as I have. Deeply convinced of the validity of our position, they have felt a sense of futility. Clear in their own minds, because of their own experiences, they respect the rights of critics and dissenters but are frankly puzzled. They find it difficult to discern precisely what the grounds of dissension are, exactly what the critics propose.

Because they are personally familiar with all facets of the situation, they simply cannot understand what people mean who demand that we negotiate now, or that we bomb here, mine there, don't bomb here, don't mine there, don't count dead bodies, prove we're winning the war, don't attempt a military victory, force the Saigon government to function differently, don't interfere in South Vietnam's political life, escalate, de-escalate, invade, withdraw, root out the Viet Cong, don't burn villages. Most military men who have served in Vietnam, I think, are as sincerely puzzled by what seems to them the oversimplification and the inherent contradiction of the critics, as the critics seem sincerely concerned by what seems to them to be the oversimplification and the inherent contradiction of our military and political position.

Perhaps I can speak in this book for some of my fellow servicemen, whose frustrations I have shared. Perhaps something of what I say will make enough sense to demonstrate that there *is* reason in what our country is doing, not madness; that there is much more honesty than there is duplicity, much more clarity than ambiguity, much more justice and sincere concern about the peoples of Vietnam and all of Asia and all the world than self-aggrandizement, or arrogance of power, much more humaneness than inhumanity, much—very much—more anguished determination to achieve a just, enduring peace than to protract war.

I

THE MORAL ISSUES

MONDAY, SEPTEMBER 4, 1967, was Labor Day in the United States. The returns had been coming in over the long weekend, and were now complete. A government had been elected by the people of South Vietnam in an election observed at first hand by the delegates of the President of the United States, invited to observe by the Premier of South Vietnam.

All-out Viet Cong terrorism attempted to prevent the Vietnamese people from going to the polls. Many would-be voters were maimed; many were killed. Yet some eighty-three per cent of those eligible to vote voted.

There had been predictions that the entire course of the war would change following the elections and that a negotiated peace would be more ardently pursued. Subtle changes in language used by North Vietnamese representatives in the months following the elections have suggested their possible interest in negotiations. For example, on New Year's Day, 1968, Nguyen Duy Trinh, North Vietnam's foreign minister, said that, under certain conditions, North Vietnam "will" hold talks with the United States. One year earlier the phrase used was "there could be talks." But even if such negotiations should come about, and terms of peace should be established, keeping the peace will always require honest recognition of historic fact in relation to the war. It simply will not do to let "bygones be bygones," if this means pretending that everyone involved has been equally guilty and that even distinctions of degree are totally unimportant. Nor will it do to imply that it doesn't really matter who started hostilities.

Arthur Schlesinger, Jr., maintains that "why we are in Vietnam today is a question of only historical interest." The French newspaper *La Croix*, in an editorial of April 7, 1965, says in effect that it ill behooves the United States, with shameful integration problems of its own, to play the role of crusader in Vietnam. Both statements assume that the situation is necessarily so confused that the "good guys" can't be distinguished from the "bad guys."

Why should it be assumed that clarification is impossible, and that we must throw up our hands in despair of ever getting at the truth? To do so, or to accept the position that it doesn't matter "who started it," or that everyone is equally guilty, is to agree that every thief can win the right to negotiate over how much he will return of what he has stolen. Every thug becomes a legitimate negotiator over the body he has beaten; every rapist has the privilege of negotiating his rights with the husband of the woman assaulted. The only requirements for negotiation become possession and confusion.

Indeed, the truth does matter if world order is ever to be maintained, if justice is to be effected, and if negotiations are to bear even a semblance of honor. To declare that a war must be concluded at any cost may sound extremely pious. It is, in fact, I think, extremely naive and morally irresponsible.

For such reasons I disagree very much with the positions of those who appeal for withdrawal of American troops from Vietnam on the grounds that our willingness to make the "sacrifices" required for peace would have a tremendous impact on the world. One must ask: "Whom would we be sacrificing?" Having served in Vietnam and having talked with many Vietnamese people, I am completely convinced that those sacrificed would be the good peoples of Vietnam, both South and North.

Many observers, of many faiths and professions—political, ecclesiastical, academic—have inclined toward a "halt the war here and now" policy, with only vague reference to the consequences. For a variety of reasons, ranging from the tenets of pure pacifism, which hold that all war is intrinsically immoral, to the conviction that United States involvement in Vietnam has been illegal from the very outset, many outstanding Americans, as well as "just plain people," have urged "peace at any price," or the equivalent thereof. Texts such as *Vietnam: Crisis of Conscience*, authored by Dr. Robert McAfee Brown, Protestant; Michael Novak, Catholic; and Rabbi Abraham J. Heschel, of the Jewish faith; public declarations such as those made by Bishop Fulton J. Sheen, in his cathedral in Rochester, New York; syndicated articles of such priest-lawyers as Father John Sheerin; publications such as the *Methodist World Outlook* (September 1967), in their expressions of detestation for war and outrage over its horrors in general, and in their convictions about the immorality of the war in Vietnam in particular, illustrate the sense of urgency felt by many religious leaders and the tendencies of some to sue for peace without victory, negotiation without condition.

As a priest-chaplain, currently serving with United States Marines, I, too, am vehemently opposed to war. I have yet to talk with a Marine at any echelon of responsibility, from the Commandant of the Corps to a private in the ranks, who does not oppose war with equal vehemence. With Pope Paul VI, we pray fervently for the day of no war. Indeed, one's prayers increase in fervor in direct proportion to the amount of time one has spent in combat—in the unglamorous, dirty business of survival, in digging a hole in a sun-baked hill in the boiling dust of a 120-degree heat, in slogging along through knee-high mud, in fighting insects, tripping over jungle growth, sleeping night after night with one eye open, alert to the whisper of every breeze, the snapping of every twig.

No priest can watch the blood pouring from the wounds of the dying—be they American or Vietnamese of North or South—without anguish and a sense of desperate frustration and futility. The clergy back home, the academicians in their universities, the protesters on their marches are not the only ones who cry out, "Why?"

No one in his right mind likes war or wants war. But wishing won't make it go away; neither will impassioned tirades against its many evils, nor, least of all, will the plea for peace at any price.

Sometimes, I think, those who plead a policy of peace at virtually any price forget, or are unaware, that every responsible individual in government service, in or out of the military, wants peace, too, and that the difference is in one's hierarchy of values. If peace is to be bought at the price of what many of us believe would ultimately be some form of slavery, we think the price far too high—even higher than paying with our lives.

I must confess a feeling of revulsion for those who chant, "LBJ, LBJ, how many babies have you killed today?" Such a charge is an assumption that the Administration actually wants war. Nothing in my experience warrants such an assumption. On the contrary, I am convinced that the Administration has opted to accept the tragedy of war as the only available road to meaningful peace. History would seem to argue on the one hand against such a course, in that no war to date has ever secured a permanent peace.

On the other hand, history also suggests that peaceful interludes have always followed wars.

It seems to me that the Administration has chosen what it is convinced is the only realistic road to peace. I believe that such a conviction results from the logic of historic facts relating to the current situation in Vietnam. I also believe that many opposed to the official United States position would modify their opposition if they viewed these facts as facts, not as fancies that will float away if we either pay them no heed or treat them with sufficient good will.

Naturally, my own main personal and professional concern is about the morality of United States involvement in Vietnam. But moral judgments are only as valid as the facts on which they are based. Stabs in the dark, vague guesses, third-hand references are hardly the stuff of which accurate judgments can be made. Emotional diatribes can not be substituted for truth.

The first question we have to ask when dealing with the morality of war is: "What war?" This is not a specious question. Are we talking about war in general, or a specific war? The failure to make this distinction has led to serious confusion.

An increasing number of Americans have become troubled in recent years by the question: "Can any war possibly be a just war in today's world?" This is a question of tremendous importance, this question of the morality of war in itself. I do not treat this question in detail in this text, not because I feel it should be ignored or its importance downgraded. On the contrary, it is a complex enough issue to require far more time and space than can be given it here. For our present purposes, let me say I believe a just war is possible. The classic principles of a just war, with particular emphasis on the rights of nations to engage in defensive wars, underlie my entire argument in this text.

We must be very clear about this point. If one considers all wars immoral in themselves, one can hardly pursue questions about the morality of a specific conflict, such as the conflict in Vietnam, with an open mind. In fact, there would be no point in trying to evaluate the Vietnam conflict at all. We must, therefore, distinguish carefully between the arguments of those concerned about the conflict in Vietnam in particular and those convinced that all wars are immoral in themselves, or, to use the classic phrase, "intrinsically evil." There is a definite tendency, I think, to confuse these positions.

I believe that certain individuals and organizations opposing United States involvement in the conflict in Vietnam speak from a framework of opposition to all war in itself. These spokesmen generate a climate of opinion that influences the position of others who, while basically not opposed to all war in itself, apply the same arguments to the war in Vietnam.

This climate of opinion includes much more than a set of attitudes about war. It is a climate of uneasiness, of restlessness, of dissatisfaction with the "establishment" and with the status quo. One needn't go to Haight-Ashbury to find it. There is a kind of pervading feeling that we have missed our calling as individuals, our destiny as a nation. We feel we have far too much poverty, too many critical problems with civil rights, too far to go in the matter of fair employment practices. Paradoxically, amid our luxuries and affluence, we seem to have developed an almost paranoid sense of guilt.

The Reverend Philip Berrigan, S.J., questioned at a lecture at the College of St. Elizabeth, is quoted in *The*

New Yorker of April 9, 1966, as stating that he thinks Communism, as an issue in the Vietnam war, is a myth. This war is a sin, he claims, because we are turning in the direction of hatred.

A variety of moral problems are posed in an article in *Sign Magazine*, August 1966, under the title, "Pacifism and America." These range from the absolutely opposed positions (all war is intrinsically evil) to the relatively opposed (wars are evil because of their attendant circumstances, and this is true of the war in Vietnam). The article bears reading in full for several reasons, one of which is that it provides representative opinions of Catholics in various positions. These include Mr. Tom Cornell, of the Catholic Worker Movement. which has been traditionally pacifist in tone; Miss Eileen Egan, of Catholic Relief Services, whose agency is the largest of those volunteer groups aiding refugees in Vietnam; Mr. James Forest, National Secretary of the Catholic Peace Fellowship; the Reverend Philip Berrigan, S.J., previously cited, an activist in areas of interracial justice; and a number of others.

Miss Egan points up the serious dilemma facing the modern Christian by virtue of the "condemnation of total war" on the part of the Second Vatican Council of the Roman Catholic Church. The Council's "Pastoral Constitution on the Church in the Modern World" states: "Any act of war aimed indiscriminately at the destruction of entire cities or extensive areas along with their population is a crime against God and man himself. It merits unequivocal and unhesitating condemnation." But it is for such wars, claims Miss Egan, that modern industrial nations like Britain, France, and the United States are preparing. She refers to the recent loss of the atomic bomb in Spain as an illustration of potential destruction of frightful magnitude, and reminds us that the Vatican Council condemned blind obedience to immoral commands of national rulers.

War is obviously an evil, and an evil easy to flog in the marketplace. No sensible person would try to argue that war is in itself a desirable way to drain our treasury, exhaust our national resources. War makes a good whipping boy, an excellent scapegoat, around which can be rallied all who decry injustice in any form. Once we get caught up in the emotion that war is the common enemy and must be driven out of human affairs forever, at any cost, we tend to lose, I think, the ability to discriminate. This is what I sincerely believe happens in such instances as in the "Pentagon protests" of October 22, 1967. I think many thousands of those who protested in public were not discriminating; they were not evaluating the Vietnam conflict in particular. They were instead caught up in the sense of outrage about social injustices in general, with war as the focal and flagrant symbol of all injustice.

Once again, we must be precise; we must know what question we are asking. We are *not* asking whether we like or dislike, want or don't want to be engaged in the conflict. We are not asking at this stage of inquiry what means are used to wage the conflict (the weapons, strategy tactics, and the like); the number of civilians killed; or how much property is destroyed. We are not asking at this point how the conflict affects our national resources or economy; what beneficial programs it may or may not block; its effect on racial problems, adequate housing, or flights to the moon.

Each one of these further questions is a quite valid moral question. Each of these questions must be answered if a nation is to determine whether the game is worth the candle; how the valid national self-interest may best be served; whether the people of Vietnam or of the world at large will profit more than they suffer, or suffer more than they profit, by our engagement in the conflict and whether the evils concomitant to our engagement are worse than the evils we hope to correct.

If we have no moral right to engage in the conflict in the first place, then our position would be immoral even if there were *no* concomitant evils. If we have the moral right to engage in the conflict, then we must weigh all these other considerations to determine whether or not we should exercise that right. In other words, we must first establish whether or not we have the right to be fighting in Vietnam. Then it becomes morally imperative to discuss the means used and other issues involved.

It could be, indeed, that such discussion might result in a national decision, reflecting the will of the people, not to exercise the right to engage in conflict. This might be the politically prudent decision, in the highest sense. But a decision not to exercise the right of war simply assumes that one has the right of war in the first place; it does not really answer the basic question.

Similar considerations might be weighed in relation to the third moral question that must be asked: "Have we a moral obligation to engage in the conflict in Vietnam?" Once again, various factors involved might suggest that it would be politically prudent not to become engaged. Then one would have to weigh obligations. If we satisfied ourselves that we do have a moral obligation to engage in the conflict, we would have to explore its gravity in comparison with other obligations—to ourselves, to other nations, to the world. We might find that more serious contrary obligations absolve us of fulfilling this particular obligation of engagement at this particular time but they will not obliterate the obligation itself.

To be specific, we are not clarifying the basic question

of our right and/or obligation to engage in the Vietnam conflict by first considering questions extraneous to this one, no matter how important these other questions are. They have their place. They must be answered. But we must not permit them to cloud the basic issue.

Take, for example, the emotionally loaded question: "What right do we have to burn innocent women and children with napalm?" Obviously, we have no right whatsoever to burn innocent women and children with napalm or with anything else. But the question is irrelevant in the context of trying to determine whether or not we have the moral right to engage in the conflict in Vietnam.

The trouble is, however, that in the heat of argument, someone will throw in this or a similar question. Since the answer must be negative, of course, the questioner will inevitably shriek with triumph. He has proved conclusively, he thinks, that we have no right to be in Vietnam. Actually, he hasn't even addressed the basic question.

A sophisticated debater might make his question more subtle and complex. He might ask, for example: "If burning women and children is an unavoidable side effect of our attacks on enemy soldiers, doesn't the evil outweigh any possible good that might result—hence, argue against our 'right' to engage in the conflict?" Again the basic question is clouded. Even if it were true that we were in the burning business, unavoidably or not, the question involved here is one of means. Have we the right to use such means? This is still not the basic question of our right to engage in the conflict. Moreover, even if the only means of waging the conflict were so horrible as to be morally prohibitive, we could still retain the right of engagement, though morally bound to refrain from exercising the right.

In other words, we must ask many questions about the conflict. But the basic question of the right to be involved is a question actually prior to all these others. I think "classic" moralists would consider all these questions "integral" to, but not "intrinsic" to, the question of our basic right to engage in the conflict. In modern moral terms, the "existential situation" might be such as to indicate that we should not become engaged, or that to exercise our basic right in this given way or in this here-and-now situation might be immoral. But once again, the integrity of the right still stands.

We could say much the same thing about the question of our obligation. For example, it neither adds to nor detracts from the basic question to ask whether we are weakening the defense of West Germany by pouring such resources into the defense of South Vietnam. The inquiry might be well worth-while. It might result in a conviction that we should withdraw forces from South Vietnam and send them to Europe. This might be a wise decision, on the basis that our obligation to Europe outweighs our obligation to Vietnam. But wise or unwise, this decision would not absolve us of our obligation to engage in conflict in Vietnam, were this obligation clearly established. It would at most, suspend the requirement.

How, then, do we answer the basic question: "Does the United States have the moral right or the obligation to engage in the conflict in Vietnam?"

I think the most straightforward and direct approach to the question of moral "right" in this context is to find out what the "law" says. This may seem an oversimplification, but the fact is that in our American tradition the just war (that is, the morally "right" war) is the lawful war; the lawful war is the just war. This is what Robert Tucker calls the "American Doctrine of the Just War" in his book *The Just War*. In this doctrine, various international instruments to which we have subscribed, such as the United

Nations Charter, and various security arrangements or pacts into which we have entered are seen as "legal manifestations of the moral law."

Pope Pius XII stresses the need for including "predictability" among the factors to be considered in trying to evaluate the morality of war. The reference is to nuclear and thermonuclear weapons. It would appear that the Pope envisioned the possibility that the use of such weapons does *not* automatically mean "total" war. If accuracy, blast, yield, heat, and other destructive potentials can be reasonably predicted and controlled, then nuclear and thermonuclear weapons might be used in a "limited" war. If the other requirements for a just war are present, and the evil to be overcome is proportionate in gravity to the destructiveness of the weapon, it would appear that the use of predictable, controllable nuclear and thermonuclear weapons can be morally justified.

We have in the United States a tradition of examining the rightness or wrongness of the use of force in terms of what we consider to be universally valid moral and legal principles, such as those we call self-evident in our Declaration of Independence. Invariably, our national representatives defend our national policies in terms of this traditional doctrine. Examples of this are graphically illustrated by the correspondence between Adams and Jefferson on the subject of whether or not to declare war on the Barbary Coast pirates, Lincoln's Gettysburg Address, President Franklin D. Roosevelt's address to Congress following the attack on Pearl Harbor. They are all cut from the same cloth—the American doctrine that considers the just war the lawful war, and the lawful war the just war. This doctrine assumes the same moral and legal values can be applied universally.

If we are on safe legal grounds in our involvement in Vietnam, we are probably on reasonably safe moral grounds in being involved (remembering again that this has nothing to do with whether we should be involved, from a practical point of view, or with the type of weapons we use, the validity of bombing, or anything of the sort). This approach gives us at least a reasonably concrete area of reference to examine. Precisely by what legal contracts or treaties or pacts or charters or other duly authorized international instruments can we claim the moral right to engage in the conflict in Vietnam?

The question of our moral *obligation*, it seems to me, is somewhat more complex. Here we must determine not merely the legal basis for justifying our engagement, but the basis for maintaining that we are bound to such engagement —that we *must* be involved in Vietnam. What binds us? International laws? Treaties? Pacts? Our word of honor? Private agreements between heads of states? Our real or alleged responsibilities as a world power? Self-interest? Public pledges to "defend freedom" wherever threatened? A "moral" obligation to defend the weak from the strong, the oppressed from the oppressor? A divine mission to contain Communism, or to lead the world?

We have many obligations as a nation. Obviously, certain obligations must assume priority over others. If we do have some sort of moral obligation to engagement in Vietnam, is it outweighed, here and now, by other, more serious obligations?

These are valid questions. These are the questions being asked, in one form or another, by dissenters and critics. They should be asked by everyone. They must be answered.

But again, to question the fact of our obligation, or to ask where it originated, is one thing. The question of its gravity, or the political prudence of fulfilling it, or the means we use is something else.

Were we bombing indiscriminately, for example, we

should be morally obliged to stop doing so. Were we wantonly destroying, we should be morally bound to stop such actions. Were we doing anything evil in itself, corrupt, or savage, there wouldn't even be room for discussion. But no matter what unlawful or immoral actions we might be accused of performing, questioning such actions would not be questioning our moral obligation to engage in the conflict. These actions might well affect our international image, our future relationships, our national life and honor and integrity. But unlawful means do not make the objective unlawful, any more than the objective justifies the use of unlawful means.

The fact is, as I hope the following chapters will demonstrate, we are not deliberately or systematically using unlawful means. We are simply not guilty of the charges of wantonness and wholesale destruction, of napalming the innocent and of indiscriminate bombing, of "gas warfare," torture, alienation of the people, corruption, inhumanity. Such charges have been bandied about so frequently and so recklessly that they have won credence. In turn, then, those sincere people who have become agitated over what they believe to be taking place become convinced that *no* goal is worth such barbarity, and that we, therefore, have no right to be engaged in Vietnam.

Later chapters will discuss the legality of our engagement in Vietnam in its historic context and will attempt to show clear title to our moral right and moral obligations. First, however, it is important to ask how these various charges have arisen. What are the sources of the confusion? What has generated the allegation that we are engaged in all manner of atrocities? Why are so many sincere people so badly confused about Vietnam?

2

SOURCES OF CONFUSION

I HAVE CAREFULLY READ MUCH of the literature about the conflict in Vietnam, including books, journals, news reports, editorials, and political addresses. I have reached my own position through combining such reading with my personal experience as a chaplain in Vietnam and almost daily discussions with military personnel of all echelons who have served in Vietnam, as well as with periodic association with veteran newsmen who have reported the war at first hand.

What has astonished me most has been the frequency of misquotation of essential documents pertaining to the war. Entire arguments have been built on such misquotations. I am not talking about mere chance references by the unsophisticated. Scholars, writers, clergymen, Congressmen, and professional diplomats have argued forcefully and persuasively, but unwittingly, on the basis of "facts" that have been born of misquotations. I honestly believe that a tremendous amount of misunderstanding has resulted from this single problem and that much of the heated debate between equally sincere people has been predicated on such misunderstanding.

This does not mean there is no malice, that no one is seeking self-aggrandizement, or even that no one in a responsible position is speaking irresponsibly. It does not excuse culpable or voluntary ignorance, prejudice, or bigotry. But I am convinced that, as always in America, the vicious and the stupid are a minority, if a vociferous and dangerous minority.

This is a terribly important point. I do not believe in a national conspiracy of the press or in widespread malice on the part of journalists. I do not believe that either all those professional politicians who favor the Administration's position or all those who oppose it are doing so in terms of self-aggrandizement or "party politics," any more than I believe that all peace marchers are draft dodgers or Communists. Indeed, if the debate on Vietnam has one dominant characteristic, it is that of sincerity, a sincerity born of genuine concern, an often anguished sense of urgency and dedication.

But why so many conflicts of opinion among sincere and generally well-educated people? When I give an address on Vietnam, I am often asked: "Why haven't we heard those facts before? Are the reporters deliberately deceiving us? Are they simply playing for headlines? Is there a big conspiracy to hide the truth?" Why, indeed, is there so much confusion? I think there are many reasons, and that it is important to be aware of them.

There is, for example, ironically, the problem of abundance. Journalistic reports, speeches, lectures, television reportage, State Department publications, scholarly textbooks, digest-type articles, records of Congressional proceedings—all these materials abound, and not only provide a wide variety of viewpoints, but often seem to contradict one another. This means that it becomes difficult to separate fact from fancy and to appraise information with the incisiveness required for moral judgment.

Other problems are cited by such writers as Richard N. Goodwin in his book *Triumph or Tragedy* and C. L. Sulzberger of *The New York Times*, such as the use of emotionally charged rhetoric, public debate based on gross oversimplifications, and the advocating of causes at the expense of evaluating facts.

The televised Senate hearings of 1966, intended to acquaint the American public with the "truth" about Vietnam, very possibly added to the confusion. When eminent historians, political scientists, and career diplomats who have spent years studying in their respective fields are asked to give simple, brief explanations of national and international phenomena, it seems almost impossible for them not to generalize or oversimplify, and thus perhaps mislead.

David Schoenbrun puts his finger on another critical source of confusion, in an article in *The Diplomat* in May of 1966—sheer ignorance of facts. He asks, "How much do we really know about Vietnam?" His answer highlights problems similar to those suggested before, but adds a third—what he calls a "stupefying lack of information," coupled with "an even more disturbing evidence of misinformation." He cites a meeting of the World Affairs Council, an organization of some of the most alert and well-informed citizens of the country. He discovered that not one of the 1,000 persons present had actually read the text of the Cease Fire Agreement or the Final Declaration of the Geneva Conference of 1954. The same thing proved to be true of other elite groups across the nation to whom Schoenbrun lectured, groups varying from university men to members of political clubs. Few documents are more critical to an understanding of the Vietnam conflict than the Cease Fire Agreement and the Geneva Conference Declaration.

Joseph Kraft in his introduction to Jean Lacouture's *Vietnam: Between Two Truces* sees as a source of confusion what he considers the refusal of most of the American press to study the politics of the war. If Kraft's charge is true, then the claim made by John Mecklin, who was Press Secretary under Ambassador Frederick Nolting in Saigon from May 1962 through January 1964, becomes particularly disturbing. Mecklin says that "American reporters in Vietnam achieved an influence in the making of U. S. foreign policy that had been equaled in modern times only by the role of the New York newspapers in precipitating the Spanish-American War nearly a half century earlier."

Marguerite Higgins emphatically buttresses Mecklin's claim in her book *Our Vietnam Nightmare*. Discussing the impact on Washington of stories concerning the Buddhist-Catholic situation in Saigon during the Diem regime, Miss Higgins reports that Assistant Secretary of State Roger Hilsman, on August 14, 1963, declared that the Buddhist crisis was beginning to affect the war effort. The Hilsman statement was made in the course of a Voice of America broadcast. Miss Higgins says she took the statement to Ambassador Nolting, who told her that he had made a careful check and was certain that it was no more than rumor. He didn't know what Mr. Hilsman could have based his statement on—it wasn't anything that had gone out of the American Embassy, the military mission, or the C.I.A. Miss Higgins points out that since Hilsman was Nolting's boss, Nolting's aides suggested that a public denial of the Hilsman story would hardly be prudent. Therefore the Hilsman version remained uncorrected. Later, in New York, Miss Higgins states that she called Mr. Hilsman and asked him what information he had used as the basis for his broadcast, since the Embassy had denied the truth of his statement. It had been based partly on *The New York Times*, she was told, and partly on other press dispatches out of Saigon.

"And thus," wrote Miss Higgins, "is history recast. All those Vietnamese-speaking Americans circling the countryside for the purpose of testing Vietnamese opinion; all those American officers gauging the morale of the troops; all those C.I.A. agents tapping their sources (hopefully) everywhere; all those dispatches from Ambassador Nolting—an army of data collectors in reasonable agreement had been downgraded in favor of press dispatches stating opposite conclusions. It was the first time that I began to comprehend, in depth and in some sorrow, what was meant by the power of the press."

The incident described by Miss Higgins points up the so-called "credibility gap." It is often charged that there is a big difference between the truth and what the Administration wants us to believe. Such charges have undoubtedly contributed to what the United States Ambassador to the United Nations, Arthur Goldberg, called a "crisis of confidence."

If Richard Fryklund's statement in his article "Building the Credibility Gap," in the Washington, D.C., *Star* of January 3, 1967, about the credibility gap is true, then much of it can be attributed to the public's accepting as "gospel truth" a newsman's report predicated on his own "guesstimate" of what the government is up to.

If, for instance, a newsman reports a press conference with Mr. McNamara, Mr. McNamara may not mention Cambodia. He *may* say that events in a country near Vietnam are being watched closely. The newsman will very possibly report, "Mr. McNamara was obviously alluding to Cambodia." The Secretary may, in fact, have been alluding to Laos or Thailand, but a later denial that he was alluding to Cambodia will probably be met with suspicion, and the credibility gap will widen. Fryklund cites a specific instance in which he himself was involved, including an incident in which "official" troop figures were attributed to Mr. McNamara. In that case, Mr. McNamara had brought up the figures for one purpose only—to denounce them. The originator of the figures was none other than Mr. Fryklund himself.

One word, one headline, one brief TV story—an inflection, a smile, a gesture, a knowing smirk on the part of an announcer can contribute to the gap.

Misquotations, regardless of the good faith of the reporter, seem inevitable. At the New Year's Day reception given by the Commandant of the Marine Corps on January 1, 1968, I listened carefully to the Commandant's brief remarks to the Marine Band. The Commandant expressed the hope that in 1968 we might see at least the beginning of the end of the war being fought by Marines in Vietnam. In essence his short address was a prayer for peace. The next day I saw the Commandant's remarks "quoted" in a society column in a Washington, D.C., newspaper. The reporter indicated that the General was hoping and praying for the beginning of a "successful" year for the Marines. On the basis of the "quotation," the Commandant might well have been opting, not for peace, but for escalation, more troops, fiercer fighting, or whatever else the popular image of Marine "success" might include.

These vagaries are perhaps trivial, but I am convinced that multiplied, as they are, they contribute substantially toward creating a credibility gap.

The choice of an adjective, the shading of a word can make credibility questionable. An example can be found in the reporting of President Johnson's news conference on October 13, 1966, preceding his departure for the Manila Conference. The text of the conference reads as follows:

Q: Mr, President, a number of authorities
have suggested that another pause in the bombing would bring about a good atmosphere for
your trip. Could you discuss the pros and cons
of another pause?

A: No, Ray, I don't think I would like to
suggest our strategy, the pros and cons. I would
observe this: that we have had two pauses. It is
the same people, the same sources, who suggested
the second pause. They asked us for twelve days,
then twenty, and it went thirty-seven days that
our boys sat there and watched the enemy.

Chalmers Roberts reported in the Washington *Post*:
"With considerable emotion, Mr. Johnson linked any talk
of a bombing pause . . ."

Carl T. Rowan, of the Washington *Evening Star*, reported: ". . . a reporter asked Mr. Johnson if he planned
another bombing pause. 'We have had two pauses,' the
President snapped . . ."

There seems to be a question of the personality of the
reporter himself in interpreting the President's intent. It is
difficult to see how the President could properly have
"snapped" an answer when the actual text seems rather
moderate and tempered: "No, Ray . . . I would *observe*
this . . ."

Such nuances might seem trivial until one comes to
the end of Rowan's report: "What the Russians are saying
to each other is that the Johnson who talks peace is a
decoy, but the one who talks war is real."

There can be no substitute for fact in trying to evaluate our position in Vietnam. Opinions, interpretations, and
educated guesses all have their own validity, within certain confines. Moral judgment, however, always demands

precision and accuracy. What did someone actually say, actually do?

In midsummer of 1966, I came across what seems to me an excellent example of the confusion-generating potential of vagueness in areas where precision is essential. A front-page *New York Times* article of July 23, 1966, datelined Geneva, reported what it called a "resolution" condemning "the massive and growing American military presence in Vietnam," stating that this "resolution" had been adopted in Geneva at a world conference of more than 400 Christian theologians and laymen.

The article went on to say: "The resolution of the Conference on Church and Society of the World Council of Churches said there could be no justification for either the American presence or 'the long and continued bombing of villages in the South and of targets a few miles from cities in the North.' "

Since I assumed this would have tremendous impact on a large number of churchgoers, I wrote to the Office of Public Relations, World Council of Churches, to get a copy of the "resolution." A gracious reply, signed by the Secretary for Program, advised me that "the use of the word 'resolution' is very misleading," and that participants in the conference were not speaking officially for the churches.

I was prepared to accept this interpretation at face value and to assume that *The New York Times* had slipped in using the word "resolution" and in the whole tenor of its article, which certainly conveyed the strong impression that the World Council of Churches in Geneva had officially condemned the presence of our forces in Vietnam, until I noted an article in an important religious journal, *Christianity Today.*

"The official conference statement on Vietnam," the article in the issue of August 19 reads, "came from a section chaired by John C. Bennett of Union Theological Seminary, which also called for the admission of Red China to the U.N. The statement read: 'The massive and growing military presence in Vietnam and the long continued bombing of the villages in the South and of targets a few miles from cities in the North can not be justified.' Efforts to get 'can not be justified' changed to 'should be condemned' were defeated on the plea that the wording represented a very delicate compromise."

I wrote a second letter to the World Council—same addressee, then a third. The reply was the same. "I'm afraid that the word 'resolution' was unwise in reporting on our Conference. It is true that quite often conferences of this kind have resolutions, but since this was a conference in which participants were not official delegates of their churches . . ."

There the question stands. Two important journals suggest official disapproval of our military presence in Vietnam on the part of the World Council of Churches— even though the World Council spokesman indicates that the conference in Geneva was not speaking officially for the World Council. No statement forthcoming from the conference could be construed as official and certainly not as a "resolution."

The trouble is that a reader of *The New York Times* report may never be in a position to read the complete, published reports of the conference for himself. That is why scrupulous precision is needed.

Obviously, discrepancies in news media contribute to confusion. But what of the responsibility of the reader? Donald Mintz, a book reviewer for the Washington *Eve-*

ning Star, writing on October 21, 1966, calls the reading situation in the United States "dreadful," in regard both to what people read and to how little they read.

This judgment may be harsh, but Americans tend to demand only the minimal digested or synopsized information—on even the gravest of matters. This tendency not to read in depth is sustained by the availability of a steady flow of capsulized news summaries and the interpretations or interpolations of news commentators. Individuals who appear each evening on television to analyze the news are imbued with an aura of authoritativeness, even though they may have little formal training or expertise in the areas on which they are commenting.

Today we applaud dissent and those who denounce the Administration's Vietnam policies. We tend to be particularly impressed if the denunciation is made by famous "names," whether they are scientists, writers, or clergymen. But we rarely ask ourselves if these people have carefully ascertained the facts, probed for the entire truth, and researched original sources. A misquotation is as erroneous if delivered by a Nobel prize-winner as if given by a youngster in the fifth grade—and can be a million times more dangerous.

It is often this willingness to settle for partial information, or even misinformation, that leads to the dissemination of the big lie. "Where there's smoke, there's fire" is assumed as an absolute maxim. Anything said often enough is certain to get a hearing and eventual acceptance in everwidening circles. This is human, but unfortunate. It isn't necessary to be either for or against the late Senator Joseph McCarthy to recognize that when the term "McCarthyism" is bandied about, there is little concern for the truth or falsehood of the issues involved. Merely used and repeated frequently enough, whispered in the dark, or hurled from the housetops, it is, by its own mystique, almost incredibly destructive. The big lie is a critical enough problem when generated innocently or just through carelessness. When deliberately planted and disseminated through the efforts of Communist fronts, or other pressure groups, it is particularly vicious. People have frequently asked me: "If lies are being told about Vietnam, why aren't these revealed, and the truth made known?" But the big lie is like the proverbial bag of feathers thrown to the winds. To retrieve them is almost impossible.

The big lie technique, for example, has virtually devastated the effectiveness of the House Committee on Un-American Activities. On March 31, 1967, this Committee issued what I consider a carefully documented, exceptionally reasonable report on the peace marches on "Vietnam Day" in New York and San Francisco. I believe the report established beyond reasonable doubt that the plans for these demonstrations were Communist-dominated from beginning to end and were completely "unspontaneous." I have read the report thoroughly, and feel that it should be read by everyone concerned about Vietnam. But the cold reality is that it will be read by very few, and for at least two reasons: one, few people will bother to read it; two, past committee reports have been so effectively smeared that whatever the committee reports is discredited before it is read.

Certainly the students who are duped are sincere—but duped, nonetheless, by those who use them for their own ends. The tragic question is: How many of these students, sincere enough to march, will ever bother to read the report about the march? The inevitable conclusion is that our own intellectual irresponsibility in allowing the big lie technique to exist has meant that the only organization we have that is duly constituted by the Congress of the United States to get at and expose the facts is effectively discredited and its report on duping is virtually ignored. James J. Kilpatrick in the *Sunday Star* in Washington, April 16, 1967, calls the Committee report on the peace marches "measured, temperate, and heavily documented." I agree.

Another source of confusion in studying the situation in Vietnam is a widespread tendency to do it strictly on a "here and now" basis. We find it temperamentally difficult to believe that what happened thirty years ago has any vital relevance to the present. In a brusque, good-humored American way, we want to "get on with the program." The fact is that we can not intelligently evaluate our present position in Vietnam without evaluating it in its historic context.

A further and rather subtle problem contributing to public confusion is that few of us are trained in the game of diplomacy. Diplomatic language and diplomatic maneuvering can be a sophisticated business. In his book *On Escalation: Metaphors and Scenarios*, Herman Kahn discusses the difference between the "ostensible" crisis, deliberately created as part of the diplomatic game, and the real crisis. He uses the Berlin situation as an example. Frequently, the crisis in Berlin is more ostensible than real and is used to vary pressures, depending on the political necessity at the moment. On the other hand, the Gulf of Tonkin incident of 1964 became a real crisis until the United States had carried out its raids in reprisal, at which point the crisis was reduced to being merely "ostensible," even though the diplomatic language of the ensuing weeks was designed to make it sound real. Kahn further examines diplomatic usages and language that are foreign to most of us—the political, economic, or diplomatic gesture as distinct from the solemn and formal declaration, and the use of deliberately arranged newspaper "leaks" to test foreign reaction without committing ourselves in any way. My point is that we, as readers, can become confused simply because we do not understand or are not familiar with diplomatic techniques.

Something of the same could be said about our naïveté in the political arena, whether the politics are local, national, or international, and about the ordinary citizen's lack of sophistication concerning international markets vis-à-vis domestic economics, the potentials of "power vacuums," and all the complexities that govern our dealings with foreign powers.

Then, there is the confusion-begetting problem of our being influenced by perfectly human inclinations—human likes and dislikes, personalities. In his *Mission in Torment*, Mecklin describes a situation in which there seems to be no question of sincerity or integrity, but a very strong question of personality conflict. A Pentagon general and a senior foreign service officer were asked by President Kennedy, in September of 1963, to fly to Vietnam and make a rapid survey of the situation. They traveled together. Mecklin says that they not only appeared to dislike each other, but they also disagreed about Vietnam. During the course of the entire trip they spoke to each other only when it was unavoidable. Upon returning to Washington, the general and the foreign service officer reported to the National Security Council in the presence of the President. The general read his report first; then the foreign service officer read his. When they had both finished, President Kennedy asked, "Were you two gentlemen in the same country?" People are people regardless of their positions.

Before concluding this partial survey of sources of

confusion, I would like to return to certain problems of
the news media. I think it important that we understand
these problems, perhaps because I saw some fine reporters
in action in Vietnam and feel that the generalizations I
have heard concerning the "irresponsibility" of the press
are unfortunate.

Bringing events sharply into focus, meeting deadlines,
reducing stories to meet space requirements, capturing
reader interest, mean that only certain facets of the events
are reported. There is not necessarily any intent to distort
or deceive. The reporter with a "nose for news" or an
eye for a dramatic picture normally tries to get the clever-
est angle, the most provocative story possible in the short-
est period of time.

The basic problem of the news media—to get there
"fastest with the mostest"—is further complicated by finances, the requirements of editing, producing, advertis-
ing, and often enough, by the background, experience,
or inexperience of the reporter himself. I met in Vietnam
the old-timers who were covering their fourth war and
the brand-new young men who had never before heard a
shot fired in anger. I came to know those who unerringly
followed the action, regardless of their own safety or con-
venience, and who risked their lives as often as any Marine,
and those (the minority) whose primary exposure to the
war seemed to be in a restaurant in Danang.

Jim Lucas, of the Scripps-Howard papers, was one
of the best informed of the old hands, though I could cite
many of his caliber. As I recall, during my time Jim was
on his fourth tour of Vietnam. He not only saw and heard
things for himself, as any good reporter; he knew the
literature, the historical background of the war. His book
Dateline Vietnam has the authenticity of Ernie Pyle's re-

ports on World War II, because Jim knocked around from pillar to post, listening to anyone worth listening to, whether private or general. Jim was a pleasure to talk to— quiet, steady, honest.

Then there was Eddie Adams, a young fellow with a camera, from Associated Press, I remember Eddie's coming up to me one boiling day when I was waiting beside General Walt's jeep. Eddie asked me where we were going, and I told him we were going aboard a chopper to Chu Lai, some fifty miles to the south of Danang. He asked if I would ask the General if he could go along. I did; the General welcomed him. North of Chu Lai we saw flames and smoke billowing off an island in the South China Sea. The General ordered the pilot to circle the area, then to land. We dropped down a hundred yards from a bitter fire fight between U.S. Marines and a company of Viet Cong. The General had a .45; his aide, Captain Doug Davidson, had a light machine gun; I had a rosary. We ducked behind trees that seemed to me about an inch in diameter. All except Eddie Adams, who dashed straight ahead, virtually into the firing, to get his pictures. When we finally climbed back into the chopper to continue to Chu Lai, Eddie stayed where he was—with the action. Seeing people like Lucas and Adams and the many others with similar courage and integrity was always an inspiration.

There were those who constantly demanded their "rights" and virtually threatened military commanders with all sorts of reprisals if they weren't given optimum conditions for getting their stories out. There were their opposites, aware that in combat, lines of communication are often less than ideal. I met those who seemed to have come to Vietnam already convinced that our position was unten-

able, the Vietnamese corrupt, the Vietnamese forces cowardly, and the American forces stupid. Others came with an
open mind, looking for the truth, prepared to report it as
honestly as they knew how.

Some of the complexities of the problem are revealed
rather candidly in *Time*, October 14, 1966, under the
title "Television, the Most Intimate Medium." The article
discusses the tyranny of advertisers. It quotes one Saigon
TV correspondent as saying about all the battle footage
he and his colleagues were sending home: "Let's be truth-
ful . . . Here in Vietnam you can get your face on the
network news three or four times a week. It's risky, but
it's money in the bank. We're all war profiteers." (A
correspondent is paid $50 whenever he personally appears
on TV.) The more dramatic the picture, the better its
chance of being aired. One CBS correspondent describes this as the "boy-oh-boy, look-at-all-the-people-riot
syndrome."

The tyranny of money includes the expense of flying film to the United States from Vietnam, developing
it on the West coast, transmitting it to New York via a
line leased at $3,000 an hour. Even if the pictures don't
measure up to expectations, they have a chance of being
aired because of the expense already incurred.

NBC's Chet Huntley is worried and candid about
the fact that too many TV reporters in Vietnam con-
centrate on "flaming action" shots to insure their appearance on the air. ABC's Howard K. Smith, according to
the *Time* article, feels the same way. He is quoted as
noting that television gave the impression during the Buddhist demonstrations that instead of 2,000 rioters, the
whole country of 17,000,000 were rioting. Finally, CBS's
Walter Cronkite maintains that such a slick job is done on
TV that the public is deluded into thinking that it gets

all it needs to know, whereas the bulk of information that it really does need cannot be gleaned from television. The *Time* article is worth reading.

The discrepancies that occur in the sheer hurry to break the news contribute to the confusion. I heard a Washington, D.C., radio station announce at 7 P.M. on August 17, 1966, that an American bomber had crashed in a village near Danang, South Vietnam, and had killed fifty-one Vietnamese. At 10:30 P.M. the same station announced that the bomber had killed twenty-six Vietnamese. At 7 P.M. on September 11, 1966, the station announced that 83.2 per cent of the registered voters in South Vietnam had voted. At 7 o'clock the next morning the same station announced that 75 per cent of the registered voters had voted. Such discrepancies hardly surprised those who recall the 1948 "election" of Thomas Dewey as President of the United States, with banner headlines in early news editions so announcing. Closer to our own day, a number of newspapers must have been quite embarrassed after publishing headlines that President Johnson had settled the steel strike, when it soon became evident that the strikers didn't agree to the Presidential proposals and particularly when they did not go back to work for quite some time.

The problem of getting sufficient and accurate news through the news media might not be so critical if what James Reston, in his book *The Artillery of the Press*, claims is true. Reston argues that the "people" do not shape foreign policy; this is the function of Congress. Hence, he maintains, the concept that the press has a strong influence on foreign policy by way of its impact on public opinion is an exaggeration, at best. I am not at all sure that I agree with Mr. Reston in these days of the politician's sensitivity to public opinion polls, but if it is true that the people don't shape foreign policy, I think it is definitely not true that Congress is uninfluenced by the press.

None of the foregoing should be construed as an indictment of TV, the press, or other news media. The intent, rather, is to point out the problems of these media. There has been much magnificent reporting of the conflict. Even in those instances noted, for example, where different news broadcasts give different figures, this is, at times, due to revision of the figures by the authorities releasing them. The problems of the media in presenting the news are indeed complex. But the point is that whoever is responsible for errors, and no matter how unintentional these errors are, we, the public, are the ones who get confused by them.

Finally, I think it should be said of the sources of confusion under discussion that all have corollaries; at least two of these deserve brief mention here. One lies in the tendency to become more and more abstract and academic about the realities of combat in proportion to one's distance from the scene of the action. The ideals pondered and discussed in the security of the classroom or the living room simply do not fit the reality of the jungle, the rice paddy, the sands, the mountains, the marketplace of Vietnam, or the mud of a foxhole.

The other related problem arises from the size, complexity, and diversity of Vietnam and of the war there. The most astute reporter is limited to a degree by the relative narrowness of his own experience. For example, I know the Vietnam of one area—the area primarily under stewardship of the Marines—fairly well, after having spent many months there. We call this area the First Corps Area, or, simply I Corps—as though it were "Eye" Corps. It is one of five Corps areas, with the other four generally under stewardship of the Army. Naturally, all services, Army, Navy, Air Force, Marines, can be found inter-meshed throughout different areas. I Corps is the northern-most area in South Vietnam, extending north as far as the demilitarized zone (DMZ). Its headquarters is in Da-nang. The overall Marine Command in I Corps is III MAF (Third Marine Amphibious Force).

My knowledge of Saigon, however, is limited to one visit. I am reasonably familiar with Marine tactics in I Corps, and with the attitudes of many of the Vietnamese people there. I have had only limited personal experience with the Army, Air Force, or Navy activities in various other sectors of Vietnam. I think the same could be said of many reporters. Most news stories reflect the circum-stances of a given time and place and group of people. When such phrases as "the peoples of Vietnam feel," or "the average serviceman in Vietnam thinks," or "the mon-soon season has begun [but where?] in Vietnam," are used, it is important to remember how fragmentary basic information may really be.

The question finally to be asked is: What is causing so much anguish? Why do so many Americans question the validity of American involvement in Vietnam?

Many Americans question the validity of involve-ment in any war under any circumstance. Some feel that the loss of lives along with national resources and the potential inhibitions placed on domestic progress outweigh anything that could be achieved by involvement in Viet-nam. Others conscientiously believe that Vietnam is none of the United States' business, that its importance as a test by Communist power has been grossly exaggerated, and that should Vietnam stand or fall, its fate is irrelevant to the security of the United States.

Still others feel that the United States is merely using

Vietnam as a pretext to attack, or at least to limit the expansion of, Red China, and that we have no true interest in Vietnam itself.

Many believe we have doubly violated the "Geneva Declaration" of 1954 by preventing the promised elections of 1956 and by introducing troops and establishing military bases in South Vietnam. Still others feel we have cynically violated our universally preached demand that all peoples have a right to self-determination.

Some are convinced that the conflict in Vietnam is strictly a civil war in which we cannot pretend to be defending one country against another by request.

Others believe we established a corrupt government in South Vietnam, then entered the country by invitation of the same corrupt government, or that since the government that originally invited us was overthrown by "the people," we are no longer either welcome or present by "right," and that since subsequent governments have all been "dictatorships" and have had no authority in terms of the will of the people, we should not be there.

Many Americans urgently fear escalation leading to the ultimate full-fledged entry into the war of Russia and Red China, and a consequent Armageddon.

Certainly there are those who feel that we base our claim to validity on the alleged "commitment" made by President Eisenhower in 1954, in a letter to Ngo Dinh Diem. In fact, they maintain, President Eisenhower's letter did not commit us and was not intended as a commitment. Along similar lines, there are also those who feel that we have violated the letter and spirit of the United Nations Charter and the SEATO agreement, simply to justify our presence and intervention.

Finally, it must be recognized that there are people who simply are inclined to assume that claims made by "our" leaders are, at best, suspect, at worst, hypocritical lies, while charges made by "their" leaders—North Vietnamese, Red Chinese, Russian—are inevitably true and sincere. This sentiment is found in the constant emphasis on the "credibility gap" in the White House and in the idea that the White House has deliberately thwarted Ho Chi Minh's efforts to negotiate peace. I found it shockingly expressed by a university professor, who, in decrying our actions in Vietnam and lauding the righteousness of the Viet Cong, pleaded that "the voices of the Che Guevaras not be stilled."

It is vital to look at all these concerns sympathetically. I believe in Senator Proxmire's statement of March 10, 1966, in a speech he entitled "Legality of United States Participation in the Defense of Vietnam," in which he summed up the moral sentiments of many Americans.

"I feel," the Senator said, "that because we are a country which believes in the legal process and a world of law, as well as a nation of law, it is important that we be precisely certain as to what justification in law there is for our presence in Vietnam."

Before elaborating on the legal questions, I feel that some personal observations are in order—an accounting based exclusively on my own personal experiences, admittedly limited though they be. In such a recitation I can hardly help revealing my credentials, for better or for worse. The reader will have to weigh them for himself.

3

AMERICANS IN VIETNAM

*T*ODAY IS THE FIRST OF OCTO-
ber, on the Vietnamese side of the international dateline,
in the year of our Lord 1967. I am wet to the bone, cold,
and muddy. I have just climbed out of a chopper, infinitely grateful to touch ground once more, after tumbling
through violent gray rain that forced us out to sea and
made it impossible for us to thread our way through the
mountain passes.

Half an eternity ago we left Camp Carroll, a dozen
miles from Con Thien, a fortress in the mud of the northern sector of I Corps. Camp Carroll is the grim guardian
of the "rock pile," brooding over the Street Without Joy,
pointing craggy fingers of ugly granite toward the DMZ.

Finally, here I am physically back in Danang, headquarters of the Third Marine Amphibious Force, but emotionally still in a rain-soaked bunker talking with a young,
red-headed sergeant from Modesto, California, about the
war. He has been fifteen months on the line. I asked him
if he thought we were making any progress. He thought
so. I asked him if he thought we should be there. He had
no doubt about it.

Yesterday Camp Carroll took a lot of "incoming"—
artillery fire that killed four Marines and wounded another
twenty. It had not been the first assault; no one thought
it would be the last. But neither the red-headed sergeant
I talked to nor anyone else at Camp Carroll would listen

to sympathy. Life was so much tougher, they said, in Con Thien or Dong Ha.

This was my first return to this tragic land since late in 1965. In the few days I was to have there, I wanted to talk with troops, to probe their current feelings about the war in general, about the Vietnamese peoples, about the Viet Cong. But I wanted, also, to talk with as many Vietnamese people as possible, particularly with refugees. There were several areas I was anxious to explore with the refugees, especially those who remembered the "pre-Geneva" days, the days of the Viet Minh, and the events that followed the declaration of 1954. My desires were to be fulfilled.

Since reprisals can be so swift and so horrible, I shall purposely omit names of persons with whom I talked, and the hamlets in which they live today. Each person I asked, however, about the reason for leaving his village gave me the same emphatic answer—the Viet Cong. They were puzzled to the point of astonishment to learn that there were Americans who might think they had fled because of American bombing and shelling. Occasionally, they agreed, this might be true, but always they had been forewarned before such bombing took place. (Remember, I am speaking of one sector of the country only.) But the overwhelming number, they insisted, are refugees from Viet Cong terrorism—refugees resolved to leave their hamlets, not because of shelling by United States forces, but to permit such shelling.

Their astonishment was even greater when told that a number of American voices clamor for the cessation of bombing and shelling of both North and South Vietnam. They were amazed that anyone could be unaware of what would happen if the Americans withdrew altogether.

They said the withdrawal of American forces would

invite disaster ranging from the selective assassination of Vietnamese leaders, and anybody else who had collaborated with Americans, to wholesale slaughter.

When I asked them if they wanted Americans to leave their country, they countered with the question: "If we wanted that, why would we leave our villages and come into American-held positions?" Certainly, they agreed, there are isolated incidents in which Americans arouse hostility, but to believe that anti-American feeling is widespread or significant would be absurd.

I pressed them further on this point. Surely, I insisted, there must be something to what some Americans believe—that ultimately the peoples of South Vietnam will hate us for destroying their country and themselves through our bombing.

Each time, such insistence was met with a shrug of the shoulders. "This is war," they told me. "In war there are tragedies. Our people know that Americans destroy only when necessary to fight the war, to drive out the Viet Cong."

I wanted very much to test this attitude further, particularly in light of a poignant letter I had been given— a letter received by one of our chaplains in an American military compound near a refugee camp. Written on September 5, 1967, it read, in part:

> Dear Sir:
>   I am very sorry to announce you: after three nights of fright . . . my people of —— refugee camp decided to leave their camp. . . . Viet Cong profit our situation to disturb the military camp, but we have not means to stop them. . . . You can believe that we are V.C. or that we receive V.C., who are for us the

number one enemies. . . . Most houses and the church are seriously ruined by the bullets. People don't see one real protection against V.C. especially in night.

In leaving our dear camp we can not stop the tears. We leaved our country to come here with the hope we can live quietly. We are now in despair. We became the target of two parties: V.C. and the bullets of U.S. military. In leaving, we cannot forget your help."

I assumed that if any people would have cause for bitterness against Americans it would be such as these, with homes and hopes shattered, and accused in the bargain of being sympathetic with the very Viet Cong they had fled. Caught in cross-fire between Americans and Viet Cong, they could surely be forgiven if they detested both.

So I visited the new hamlet these same refugees had built. Not a flicker of hostility appeared anywhere—in the eyes of the children who surrounded me, laughing and clowning, as children do anywhere; in the bows and the smiles of their parents and their grandparents. I talked at length with their priest, who had led them so many weary miles, over so many weary years, and had inspired them to rebuild after every loss. His warmth was genuine. Over tea he described what had happened, talking quietly. Not until I raised the question of resentment or hostility of his people against Americans did he become agitated. "No, no," he insisted, "my people never angry with Americans. They know very well why you fired on our village. They understand why you would think we were protecting and helping the V.C. These are the mistakes of war."

Former Master Sergeant Donald Duncan, veteran of U.S. Special Forces in Vietnam, whose article in the February, 1966, issue of *Ramparts* drew a great deal of attention, is cited as authority that the theory of Viet Cong terror is a lie. He states that the truth is just the opposite—namely, that Saigon army troops regularly bring more terror to the rural population than the NLF forces. Edward S. Herman and Richard B. DuBoff support these views in their book *America's Vietnam Policy*. This outlook fits in with a belief commonly held among a number of Americans—that the South Vietnamese people secretly consider the Viet Cong the real heroes of their country, and shelter and support them because they believe in the Viet Cong cause.

I sincerely pursued this concept and simply found no justification for it. The 2nd battalion of the 5th Marine Regiment ran into a good example of how erroneous the idea is. They drove the Viet Cong out of a valley where no American or South Vietnamese forces had been for at least two years and were about to leave themselves. But the elders of the two thousand refugees involved, with tears running down their cheeks, pleaded with the Marine commander: "Take us with you or shoot us. We can no longer live under the Viet Cong." Take us with you or shoot us—rather strong language for a people who allegedly are not terrorized.

One chaplain told me of having come upon a hut where two South Vietnamese women were huddled together. One had a leg diseased to the point of being gangrenous. The chaplain enlisted the aid of a corpsman and started to treat the leg, only to have the woman plead with them not to—on the grounds that when the Viet Cong returned they would kill her for accepting American help.

This chaplain also told me about Father ——, a young Vietnamese priest who had been murdered by the Viet Cong. The V.C. had gone to his home at two in the morning, fired rockets into the house, kicked in the door, shot the priest in the stomach. After that they desecrated his church. Troops arrived in time to prevent the murder of his nuns. This was a man, the chaplain said, beloved by his people and by the South Vietnamese military, not because he fought the Viet Cong (on the contrary, he was never known to utter a single word against them), but because he did everything possible to help the poor. Perhaps the Viet Cong saw in him the threat of leadership. They may have assumed that because he helped *all* poor—even those of South Vietnamese military families— he was automatically their enemy. Possibly it was just another of the acts of sheer terrorism and intimidation which say, in effect: "We have absolute power. We can do anything we want. We need no reason."

Ralph McGill, in the Washington, D.C., *Evening Star* of January 3, 1967, describes such acts of pure terror and intimidation. He says that while he was in Vietnam in September and October of 1966, in one village Viet Cong terrorists threw a grenade into a bar, killing seven Vietnamese civilians and wounding two Americans. In another village Viet Cong terrorists smuggled a claymore mine onto a bus, killing a number of Vietnamese children and some men. The bus carried no Americans. Viewed in any way but as an act of intimidation, it made no sense. Within the same weeks of his visit, the V.C. descended on a village that was showing signs of becoming pacified, brutally killing a number of women and children and burning their huts.

Actually, Bernard Fall supports Ralph McGill's thesis in his book *The Two Viet-Nams.* (It is intriguing to see how often Professor Fall is quoted in opposition to our engagement in Vietnam and to discredit our position, and how infrequently he is referred to when his writings bear out our claims.) Professor Fall describes at some length those systematic operations of violence carried out for psychological rather than for military reasons. He discusses the Communist "enforcement" groups who capture the mayor of a recalcitrant village, cut his body into shreds, and leave his head dangling from a pole in the village, with a note pinned to it as a warning to others. These groups burst into a village, call out the names of boys who have joined the South Vietnamese Government Youth Movement, read their "death sentence," then shoot them. The success of these groups results from the psychological impact on bystanders and members of other villages.

The chaplain mentioned previously also told me that the V.C. in his area had kidnapped, tortured, and, deliberately, in front of the people, killed civic leaders who had opposed Communism and endorsed free elections. This took place in village after village.

One group of priests I know in a large city is forthright in describing what they are convinced will happen if free-world troops leave their city under present circumstances. They say the streets will run red with the blood of those who in any way consorted with free-world troops and that such people have already been warned to this effect in various ways by unidentified V.C.

I talked for an hour or more with a South Vietnamese Catholic bishop in another city—a man I had come to know rather well during my earlier days in the country—and asked him what he thought would happen if American forces withdrew right now. His answer was immediate. "Every Catholic would be killed by the Viet Cong."

It was the recollection of such conversations that made me seethe when I listened to the history professor in the college debate I mention in the introduction to this book, telling students that the Viet Cong are singularly discriminative in their killing. "They kill only representatives of the Saigon government and those sent from Saigon to the villages." This is sheer, unadulterated nonsense. I can not look into any man's conscience, so I can not call such nonsense deliberately vicious. But it is certainly vicious in its results.

At any rate, the picture given me by the Vietnamese people with whom I have spoken differs radically from that given by former Master Sergeant Duncan. Perhaps he saw things I have not seen. At least he was there. But I never cease to be amazed at the number of people I meet in various parts of the United States who talk so glibly about the feelings of the South Vietnamese people and the heroic deeds of the Viet Cong—who have never set foot in Vietnam or talked with a single Vietnamese citizen. To me this seems grossly immoral and critically irresponsible.

Again, one must be careful, and remember the reports of the so-called Buddhist riots, the self-immolations by burning that toppled one government after another in South Vietnam. On those occasions, the activities of some 2,000 people were interpreted to represent the entire country, and in the United States we got the impression that all Vietnam was aflame. Who profited by the overthrow of the governments, except the North Vietnamese, the Viet Cong, and their sympathizers?

On the occasion of my recent visit I looked for what *The New York Times* headlined, on October 10, 1967, as an "Angry Anti-U.S. Mood" appearing in South Vietnam. According to the *Times* report written by Bernard Weinraub in Saigon, Saigon university students were claiming that the United States had rigged the recent elections, that we do not want a strong nationalist force in Vietnam but a puppet government, that we are wrecking their economy, dividing their people, prostituting their women. Perhaps this is the feeling among some Vietnamese in Saigon. I certainly found nothing of the sort in the I Corps area.

There is always a tendency, of course, to oversimplify the question of relations between natives and aliens. Who hasn't had the ugly experience of hearing a "one thousand per cent American" insist that those they call niggers, kikes, wops, hunkies, or what will you, should "go back where they came from"? A single incident is enough, at times, to incite violent expressions of this type.

How much is the subtlety of nationalism, how much the influence of Communism, in the "Yankee, go home" slogans met in various parts of the world? I used to wonder about this whenever I would drive in or out of the gate of Camp Courtney, Headquarters for Marines based on Okinawa. A few hundred yards from the gate lives a little man in a little hut with a big, rough sign, "Stay Off Yankee Land Robbers." And while one-half of the gross national income of Okinawa is the result of the American military presence, periodic demonstrations demand "reversion," or return to exclusive Japanese control.

It would be indeed phenomenal if the presence of *any* massed military forces ever proved totally acceptable to every member of the native populace *anywhere*—even when the military forces are themselves natives. It is not too many years ago that one could find signs posted in Norfolk, Virginia, a city whose income came largely through military sources, "Sailors and dogs, keep off the grass." And I recall, when stationed in the nation's capital, in the mid-fifties, a directive by the Secretary of Defense that military personnel in Washington wear civilian clothing, lest the appearance of too many military uniforms might in some way unsettle civilians.

There were other areas of confusion and concern that I wanted to explore in Vietnam on this visit. When I returned to the United States late in 1965, I found it particularly disturbing to be told that American Marines wantonly burned down huts in a village, igniting them with cigarette lighters, as though delighted with sheer and senseless destruction. I knew why huts were burned —to destroy Viet Cong ammunition caches and to make it unprofitable for the Viet Cong to maraud.

The truth as I had seen it was that the Marines were frequently puzzled and distressed about being so severely restricted in the use of force—to the point of critical danger to themselves. Squads of men would be directed to patrol given areas carrying unloaded weapons, lest innocent civilians be fired upon accidentally. Orders were extremely explicit—men were not to load their weapons until fired upon. Artillery was used with extreme care; even when positive identification of an enemy was made, there were still long delays before the men were allowed to fire because our rules insisted that the area must be clear of the innocent. The fact that this policy persists was made clear to me by some 165 young officers and men I talked with on Okinawa on September 28, 1967, Marines who had just left Vietnam en route to the United States. Having to delay fire, while the enemy pounded them—and then escaped—was one of their greatest frustrations.

Mistakes were made, of course, mistakes often fatal to our own troops. But it is difficult to conceive of greater efforts to prevent wanton killing. I saw a battalion commander relieved of his command because of accidental firings—even though no one was killed.

I remember a day in June of 1965 when the then Major General Lewis W. Walt asked me to present a problem to a group of knowledgeable Vietnamese. It was necessary to destroy certain villages for reasons previously cited. We wanted to do everything in our power to avoid hurting the innocent. We planned to send interpreters to drop leaflets, to assure the people that if they would leave their villages we would build them new ones, and clothe and feed them.

I proposed our plan to several key Vietnamese, who knew the territory well. I will not forget their answer.

"You Americans are too moral," they told me sympathetically. "The Viet Cong won't let the people leave the villages no matter what you tell them. You had better understand there's a war going on here. In a war, a certain number of innocent people are killed. This is a tragedy. But you must take that chance if you're going to drive out the Viet Cong. And the Viet Cong must be driven out if we're going to have peace."

It was a strange feeling, to be told by a people we were allegedly terrorizing on a wholesale basis that we were too moral.

It would be absurd to deny that American servicemen have committed atrocities. Under the personal direction of the Commandant of the Marine Corps, five specific examples of atrocities committed by Marines in South Vietnam are dramatically described to officer-students by instructors in the Marine Corps Development and Education Command. More than five cases exist, but these five are typical of atrocity as such, its genesis, its tragic consequences. Young officers are emphatically warned of the hideous cost of each such barbarity. I am in a position to know this. I am one of the instructors.

Walter Cronkite's television news program on October 9, 1967, showed young soldiers cutting off the ears of Viet Cong dead. The commentary carefully pointed out that such incidents were relatively few; that the soldiers were invariably ashamed of themselves later. No one can deny that they committed the act. As horrible as the reality of the act is, we have come a long way from our attitude as a nation during World War II. Then accepted practice in training American troops seemed to be to stir up as much personal hatred toward the Japanese as possible. Japanese were pictured as grinning, idiotic, but diabolically clever and viciously brutal beasts. The stories of atrocities committed on Viet Cong are few—in a day when virtually every American combat move is made in front of television cameras. Our conscience can not be free until there are *no* atrocities; but we do seem to have made progress. Important training materials have been developed for teaching American Marines not to hate, but to understand—to treat everyone as an individual human being. I believe in the sincerity and potential of this movement known in the Corps as the Personal Response Movement, and I anticipate ever-improving behavior on the part of our troops as a result.

No organized program can take the place of personal, inspirational leadership, however. It was largely the personal, inspirational leadership of one man, in my opinion, that set the tone for what I think are our amazingly good relations with the Vietnamese people as well as our unusually intelligent attitude toward the war in general. In conscience I feel compelled to talk about this man's approach as I personally witnessed it. I do so particularly in the light of misunderstandings and downright prejudices about the military "brass." If I sound either dramatic or emotional, it is because I believe so intensely in the approach this man used, and so fervently wish that millions of Americans could have seen and heard him in action.

Steaming rice paddies make for poor acoustics, and hot, dusty hills make apathetic sounding boards. A commanding general is not necessarily spared the inconveniences suffered by the troops. Troops need to be reminded of America's mission, of its justice, integrity, and urgency. They need their commanding general, and they *must* believe in him.

Major General Walt never talked about himself. But I watched him as he climbed in and out of jeeps, in and out of helicopters, a tough, ruggedly bulky figure. I watched him cram into an eighteen- or twenty-hour working day systematized visits to every unit in his complex command. At that time—mid-1965—it stretched from Phu Bai to the north of Danang to Chu Lai to the south. The command's combat center is Danang, which lies in the middle of a one-hundred-mile stretch of beach on the South China Sea.

I listened to a soft voice that managed to overpower angry, screaming jets. The voice was gentle, and matter-of-fact, whether talking to two hundred or twenty. The talks reminded me of a classroom lecture, or, more nearly, a university seminar. But they were compelling.

Although the lesson was the same each time, it changed with the mood of the listeners. The mood of the speaker was always the same—a mood of confidence and of honest humility.

What did he say to them, this general with such frightening responsibilities? He told them about Communism and its intent in South Vietnam. He said that the fight must be fought here, that to withdraw would be disastrous and could mean a victory for Communism in all of Southeast Asia. He described desperate years of struggle by the South Vietnamese peoples, and he discredited the myth that they were cowardly and unwilling to defend themselves. His figures of the thousands who have been killed, captured, or tortured in their struggle grimly supported his claim. Finally, he came to those Americans who think our position in Vietnam is immoral. He told them about sophisticated Americans who attack our position simply because it is our position! Then his voice was less than gentle.

As if every Marine, regardless of rank, had a sacred right to every detail of his battle plan, the General explained his intended strategy. A line of resistance here, an entrenched outpost there, artillery fire ready, air support poised. Fifty first-class privates might well be the Joint Chiefs of Staff being briefed by the Chairman. It sounded sincere because it was.

That is why, when the General asked for their help, the men listened. When he told them how much he appreciated their sacrifices, they believed him. When he talked about the importance of the individual, the individual stood a little bit taller. He reminded them of villages that had lived in fear of the Viet Cong before the Marines landed, and were now living in relative freedom. He pointed out the unfortunate mistakes of the few. Then he mentioned the importance of the Marines—their generosity to the people. The people had been warned by the Viet Cong that Marines were barbarians who would pillage their towns and villages.

On the contrary, the General pointed out, the Americans can't resist engaging in charities. And making jokes in sign language about exchanging money, looking thirstily for beer and Cokes, photographing everything that moves is all a part of being American.

The General urged his Marines never to underestimate the importance of their behavior and never to underestimate the dignity of the human person, white or yellow, North or South Vietnamese, friend or Viet Cong.

I chatted with the men after the General talked to them. One man would tell me, "He makes you feel like you really got something to fight for." "He makes me proud to be out here," another would say. "Proud to be a Marine," would come from a third.

I talked with the General himself after each talk. He was never satisfied that he had said enough. Our responsibilities toward the Vietnamese people as human beings was foremost in his mind. He sought criticism, asked for suggestions, and beamed like a high-school boy when I told him I thought he had clicked. His chagrin was pathetic to witness if I told him he had missed the mark.

To me, what this man did and the way in which his efforts were received speaks volumes about the dedication and intelligent understanding of our servicemen, and of officials at all echelons. General Walt was responsible for the lives and the welfare of thousands of men. He considered none of his multiple duties more important than discussing the human dimensions of the war with his men, and he dramatically demonstrated that sense of responsibility by his personal talks to group after group.

This blunt-looking, chunky man, standing hat in hand, in a semicircle of helmeted Marine troopers, rifles in hand, talked to his men as though they were his entire world. The men watched and listened, fascinated, almost enthralled.

It was this response, I think, that more than anything

made me realize how much the truth meant to our fighting men. In the mid-fifties I had carefully studied the reports compiled on our prisoners of war in Korea. I had talked at length with people who had personally observed and worked with former prisoners, and had been particularly disturbed by the reports of Dr. William Meyer, an Army psychiatrist. Dr. Meyer emphasized repeatedly the critical problems of those prisoners who had had little or no understanding of why they were in Korea.

I became part of a movement in the Navy and Marine Corps to assure that our fighting men of the future would be adequately oriented in the moral dynamics of war. In peace time, it is difficult to explain why we fight when we must. When training schedules are reduced a de-emphasis of what is purely academic is only natural. Unfortunately, questions involving the moral ramifications of war are often placed in this latter category, because they have no immediate, pragmatic import.

It was, therefore, profoundly rewarding to me to watch and listen to General Walt, a man who is a professional warrior, dramatically demonstrating what he considered a top priority—striving to give the men an understanding of why we are fighting.

I can honestly say that I have never met a Marine serving in Vietnam who is insensitive to our relationship with the Vietnamese people or to the problem of atrocities. The American atrocities that may have been perpetrated by Marines, have been both isolated and spontaneous. When they are discovered they are condemned. The men responsible are punished severely by higher authority.

This is simply not true of Viet Cong atrocities. These are deliberately planned as a strategy of terror. The systematic assassination of local village leaders throughout the years has demonstrated this clearly. Viet Cong tactics in North Vietnam are comparable to the purges carried out under Ho Chi Minh—assassinations that amounted to massacres. At that time the peasants revolted, and it was necessary to institute a "Correction of Errors" program. No single one of our atrocities is ever justified by those of the Viet Cong. I merely want to point out that any comparison of American atrocities with those of the Viet Cong is grossly unfair.

The best judges of the differences between Viet Cong and American forces are, after all, the people of South Vietnam. They can't help seeing the differences. This reality struck me forcibly as I revisited Hill 327 in October of 1967. Two years previously I had spent my first night there—in a hole in the ground. I could not help recalling one of the most poignant of my personal memories of our amazing efforts to prevent, rather than encourage, wanton destruction. Headquarters Company of a tank battalion was at the top of the hill, and a friendly Vietnamese hamlet lay at the base. At two o'clock one morning, the world exploded. Twenty-one Marines were carried to the nearest field hospital, dead or wounded from the mortar fire from the friendly Vietnamese hamlet. Within seconds we could have obliterated that hamlet in retaliation. But we didn't fire so much as a single round of ammunition from a single rifle. We could guess accurately what had happened—that the Viet Cong, under cover of the night, had slipped into the hamlet, set up equipment, fired the mortars, slipped back into the night. The V.C. use of the hamlet is in sharp contrast to the American refusal to retaliate. Our respect for the lives of the citizens speaks volumes, since the V.C. has none. This has become more and more obvious to the South Vietnamese people. I welcome their judgment on Americans.

4

CIVIC ACTION, ORPHANAGES,

ADOPTIONS, "OPERATION HARELIP"

*I*T WAS A PLEASANT SURPRISE
to answer the knock on my door, in my quarters at Quantico, Virginia, on an October day in 1966, and find Second Lieutenant Jim Badey on the doorstep—with his wife and two Vietnamese children. I would not have recognized the two little girls if they been with someone else. Healthy and happy, they looked nothing like the scrawny, melancholy twins I had last seen in an orphanage in East Danang.

In April 1965, Badey had asked me to accompany him to the Vietnamese orphanage across the river from our Danang headquarters. He was a sergeant then, married five years and childless. He hoped to adopt a Vietnamese child. At the orphanage, he found himself with a problem—one of selection. When we saw the twins, who were just beginning to recover from a state of severe malnutrition, his problem was solved immediately.

The Badeys are legion among American servicemen. More servicemen want to adopt children and bring them back to the United States than current procedures can begin to accommodate.

Early in October of 1967 I revisited an orphanage I had come to know well in 1965. Two years of American help were dramatically evident. I was not surprised. Rarely had a day passed when I served in Vietnam that at least one Marine hadn't come to my tent, looking for a "project"—an orphanage to help, a school to rebuild, a village to feed. By now—October 1967—the troops had had two years of opportunity.

There had been Operation Harelip, for example. Chaplain Paul Running, Lutheran, of the Second Battalion, Third Marine Regiment, came to my tent one day to ask help in getting military air transportation for a little girl with a harelip. He had been wandering through a hamlet one day when he saw her, talked with her mother and grandmother, told them he wanted to do something about the child. This particular affliction, by the way, seems to be widespread in Vietnam. Children grow into adulthood looking terribly grotesque, virtually unable to talk intelligibly or to get decent employment.

We arranged a flight to an Army hospital a hundred miles away. Neither grandmother, mother, nor child had ever left their hamlet before, and had never been in an airplane. The entire community gathered to bid them farewell on the appointed day, and off went the trembling but courageous threesome.

In a handful of days they returned—to the same excited crowd. Everyone had to look. Despite the signs of the operation, it was obvious to all that something like a miracle had taken place. This was a totally different little girl, a little girl with a new life ahead.

"Operation Harelip," unglamorous as its name is, became a *cause célèbre* instantly. The entire Marine battalion began clamoring for equal time for youngsters they had discovered with similar afflictions. Soon they were competing with other battalions for the restricted facilities of the Army hospital.

We shouldn't underestimate the pervading effect of this kind of thing. Word gets around. Bit by bit, people are won over. I have often questioned the desirability of the phrase "to win the minds and hearts of the people." I am never quite sure of its meaning, and always have the uncomfortable feeling that it has political implications. What I think we are doing, however, is to win the trust of the people. They are coming more and more to believe in us. The longer we stay, the more they believe.

If there were enough American servicemen to fight the battles and engage simultaneously in full-time civic action work, I suspect they could rehabilitate the entire country. They are amazing, these American forces, and one often sees the Vietnamese shake their heads in wonder over the Americans' generosity and know-how.

This brings up the general question of civic action and related efforts in South Vietnam. I have encountered a considerable confusion in the United States about these activities. Precisely what have we been doing, and what is this "other war" so often referred to?

There is no doubt that many have written off our efforts as a failure. When I returned to Vietnam in 1967, I wanted to take as close a look as I could at the pacification movement.

It seems to me that pacification should be thought of as an overall objective, rather than as a technique. On the other hand, the revolutionary development program may be thought of as a technique. The same is true of the civic action program. In military language, pacification is sometimes defined in terms of the numbers of military forces required to maintain security in a given area. The fewer the forces required, the higher the degree or percentage of pacification. I personally don't think the selection of the term was a happy one. Indeed, it may even have been a dangerous choice of words. In common usage we think of a pacified area as one under complete control and totally tranquil. Hence, when the huge Danang airbase is subjected to a mortar attack, Americans understandably question how this can happen in a pacified area—and the credibility gap widens.

Revolutionary development is a method of achieving a high degree of pacification. Basically, it is an integrated military and civilian effort. Its purpose is to expand government functions to continue building up the nation. It is controlled by the government of South Vietnam.

Civic action is the name given chiefly to the efforts of the United States forces to assist—not to interfere with or supplant—the efforts of the Vietnamese peoples. Marines, for example, collect and give away everything from soap to sandwiches, help build schools, teach on their off-hours, arrange for free hospital and clinical services, provide corpsmen and hygiene instructors—in short, do what they can to help. In each case the program is under the direction of a local Vietnamese.

Obviously the three movements intertwine. While pacification is an objective, it clearly must be a prerequisite, as well, for revolutionary development. It is impossible to maintain any kind of orderly development without security from the Viet Cong. At the same time, many of the facets of both revolutionary development and civic action help achieve security.

Within the context of revolutionary development, strong emphasis has been placed on improving educational conditions. This has demanded building many more schools. In 1955, 400,000 Vietnamese children were in the first five grades of school; by 1966, the number had increased to 1,700,000. Between 1963 and 1967, 8,600 new teachers were trained, with some 3,000 of them assigned to elementary schools in hamlets. Within the past two years, more than 9,000,000 elementary-school textbooks have been supplied by the U. S. Aid Program and distributed by the Government of South Vietnam.

Revolutionary development teams currently consist of thirty-nine men, both Vietnamese Popular Forces and American servicemen. The ratio of South Vietnamese to Americans varies, but usually a team is made up of about fourteen American riflemen, an American hospital corpsman, and about twenty-five South Vietnamese. We have some 1,300 Marines on these teams throughout the I Corps area, with approximately 1,900 Vietnamese forces. Marines are eligible for these teams only after they have spent several months in Vietnam and have demonstrated their interest in the Vietnamese people and their ability to relate well to them. During the Viet Cong and North Vietnamese Tet offensive of February 1968, not one hamlet in the I Corps area protected by one of these teams fell to the enemy.

Ideally these teams are intensively trained to help with a wide variety of humanitarian needs, such as the administration of hamlets, construction, self-help projects, dispensaries, classrooms, animal-husbandry programs, and agricultural programs. As almost always, teams fall short of the ideal, in training and in numbers. But the two teams I visited, in two different hamlets, made up in enthusiasm and dedication for their deficiencies. If they are typical of teams throughout the country, the potential is tremendous.

I talked with an American Marine Negro sergeant, a strong-bodied and highly articulate man, who was as proud of the team and of the people in the hamlet as any one could be. Mutual respect and liking that had been developed between him and the people of the community was accomplishing wonders. He had the highest praise for his Vietnamese Popular Forces teammates.

A basic factor in the work of a team is the security of the hamlet. This particular team had been repeatedly successful in repelling Viet Cong attacks. I asked the sergeant if the Popular Forces were strong enough yet to defend the village if the Americans left. Not yet, he said, but that was the goal. In fact, the goal is always to help the people reach a point where no strength other than their own would be required.

I had a lengthy session with Ambassador "Barney" Koren, an American civilian who serves as deputy to the top Marine commander, for the revolutionary development movement in the I Corps area. He was as convinced as the men of the teams themselves that the revolutionary development cadres had vital potential for the future of South Vietnam. He was blunt about over-reliance on statistics. He was equally frank in facing the hugeness of the task ahead—the problem of providing enough teams for the thousands of hamlets throughout the country. But there was no question in his mind about the intrinsic value of the program. When I left him I felt sad that the demands of the war have restricted the expansion of the program, but by no means pessimistic about the future, or unimpressed by what has already been accomplished. The Ambassador has counterparts doing the same job in every other "Corps" area of South Vietnam.

Ambassador Koren divides I Corps into five areas. His estimates, in terms of pacification, are that Area 1 is approximately 80 per cent pacified, Area 2, about 60 per cent pacified, Area 3, about 40 per cent pacified, Area 4, about 20 per cent pacified, and Area 5, less than 20 per cent pacified. Some fourteen of the twenty-eight South Vietnamese Army battalions in I Corps are assigned to revolutionary development. Certain specific activities can reasonably be said to reflect the progress toward stability made possible through revolutionary development and under "pacified conditions." As of August, 1967, 134 village censuses were underway, 123 village defense plans

were being developed, and 123 local defence forces were in
training.

Certainly, developments in the DMZ in late 1967
pulled forces from the pacification program into full-
fledged combat. But certainly also, this has not meant, by
any means, a complete abandoning of pacification or revolutionary development efforts.

Security in South Vietnam was then still a relative
matter, but progress was being made. In October of 1967
in Vietnam it was possible to travel much farther with
relative security along highways than it had been two years
before. A great deal was being done to teach better farming
methods, insect control, multiple seeding, and reforestation
techniques.

It is difficult to feel pessimistic about either Vietnam
or the United States when one sees our men involved in
civic action work. Work means strictly off-duty activity
for many of our men, off-duty activity on a completely
voluntary basis.

Whenever he could get a spare hour, Sergeant Mc-
Grath taught English in a local school. Captain Cillici had
a crew of engineers who seemed to want to do nothing
else on free Saturdays but replace broken windows in
orphanages, paint walls, and play with the children. Father
Bohula, Second Battalion, Third Marine Regiment, must
have an entire village praying for his battalion, after the
way in which he and his volunteers rebuilt the village's
ruined church.

I recall going to Saigon with a young major on a
mission to arrange for surplus food shipments to be sent
directly to our Danang headquarters. We wanted to dis-
tribute the food immediately to hamlets in critical need—
without delay, without red tape. Catholic Relief Services
promised us 2,000 tons of food each week, *if* we could

transport it some four hundred miles to Danang. Once we got it there, of course, we would have to unload it, store it temporarily, then start transporting it all over again, in smaller units, to the hamlets in need. The problems in logistics might well scare off the most experienced long-shoremen, truckers, or chain store managers. The young Marine major, a lawyer in civilian life, actually seemed to brighten as each new phase of the problem revealed it-self. To complete a happy story, a great many people were fed because a young American Marine was determined to feed them.

I have seen American medical corpsmen risk their lives every day by going into villages to give first-aid treat-ment and to conduct do-it-yourself nursing and hygiene courses, not for the wounded, but for those whose illnesses are the results of a way of life born of ignorance. The corpsmen could have been ambushed at any time by Viet Cong. Incidentally, these same corpsmen repeatedly aided wounded Viet Cong.

In I Corps alone, the following figures are, I feel, reasonably gratifying. The figures extend to August, 1967. By that date, some 2,145,320 Vietnamese had received medical treatment through the American civic action pro-gram; 2,017 were given medical training; 6,903,287 were fed; 60,277 students were supported. There were 3,396 English-language classes conducted; 2,036 construction projects; 261,179 pounds of clothing and 4,098,744 pounds of food had been distributed.

I know that these accomplishments are not dramatic in terms of what has yet to be done. No one honest about the situation could feel that we have done much more than scratch the surface. The refugee problem, for example, is gigantic and needs a tremendous amount of attention. But I think it grossly unfair to brush off as insignificant what has been done. What we are trying to do takes years; look at some of our ghetto problems in the United States.

We have not been able to secure hamlets and cities as we would like to, because of the demand to reposition troops to meet the exigencies of combat. Vietnamese military and popular forces still need training and organization before they will be adequate for a fully effective revolutionary development program. Most importantly, no permanent development of any kind can occur without security against the Viet Cong. To insure 100 per cent security against such attacks would require totally unacceptable procedures, ranging from the most rigid restrictions on the movements of Vietnamese citizens to shooting every suspect on sight. But I do not believe we are justified in writing off the pacification program because it has not achieved its goals as rapidly as desired. What we have accomplished is highly significant.

It will always be difficult to assess the effectiveness of these programs. Factors intervene periodically to disrupt our efforts—military operations, concentration on elections, enemy assaults. Finally, how does one measure the effectiveness of building a school for Vietnamese children in terms of the ultimate stability of the country?

The ultimate judgment of the programs, it seems to me, lies in the fact that if the V.C. were given the favor of the people at large, they could move much more rapidly, transport equipment much more openly, and effect much more damage on American positions. Citing current V.C. successes as an indication of our failure to win popular support is a distortion. No major city in the United States has yet coped with its crime problem with total success.

5

HISTORY REVISITED

*A*T BEST, MOST OF US HAVE only a nebulous understanding of even pivotal points of Vietnamese history. Earlier, I pointed out that unfamiliarity with the facts has made it possible to perpetuate some outrageous distortions of historic fact. I feel that all too often "authorities" tend first to create other "authorities," and then to support one another, in circular fashion. It's difficult to tell who starts the circle, or who is truly an authority in his own right. For example, in one part of the United States I have listened to a speech in which Professor John Doe cites as his authority Professor John Brown. Later, in another area, I have heard Professor John Brown call upon the eminent authority Professor John Doe as *his* star witness. That is the way error can be perpetuated, if not immortalized.

I fear that this has happened to certain key phases of Vietnamese history. I am not a professional historian, and, as so many others do, I have to rely on authorities. Hence, I have tried to consult original sources where possible. I have compared a number of authors with one another, and I have talked with individuals who were in Vietnam when certain events took place. What has struck me most forcibly in the course of this research is the discovery that so many writers have completely ignored what a small handful of writers consider critically important.

What am I talking about? I'm talking about the popular assumption that Ho Chi Minh is a benevolent elderly statesman who wants nothing more than the security of his beloved people—an almost pathetically noble David pitted against a monstrous American Goliath; I'm talking about the belief that a band of pure-hearted, gallant knights, called the Viet Minh, were inspired only by the purest nationalism in overthrowing their French oppressors; the curious belief that North Vietnam has an unblemished escutcheon in terms of autonomy as a state and as a lawful self-government, while at the same time fostering the belief that South Vietnam has been a creation of the United States, ruled by puppets of Washington imposed on the Vietnamese people. These and a number of other beliefs seem to me to be no more than intriguing fantasies.

Since selectivity seems to be a popular practice in relation to Vietnam, perhaps I shall be forgiven a certain amount of selectivity in discussing some of the assumptions and beliefs referred to above. Seeing them in a different light can provide opportunity for totally new insights into today's conflict. Some of my sources have been B. S. N. Murti, Indian member of the International Control Commission; Anthony Eden, Co-Chairman of the Geneva Conference; and Theodore Blakely, Canadian member of the International Control Commission. Others, all authors, include J. S. Sebes, P. J. Honey, Bernard Fall, Victor Bator, Marguerite Higgins, Chester Bain, Dwight D. Eisenhower, Susan Labine, Philippe Devillers, Truong Chinh, Vo Nguyen Giap, Stephen Pan, and Daniel Lyons.

Several standard history texts provide adequate information on the Indochinese foundations of Vietnam and the many years of initial French occupation and control. While they are certainly important in terms of today's conflict and especially important in terms of understanding Vietnamese-Chinese relations, space limitations preclude a discussion of those phases of Vietnam's history here. However, it is essential to review, if only briefly, the events that led more immediately to Dien Bien Phu and the Geneva Conference, as well as subsequent events.

The road that led to Dien Bien Phu is strewn with complexities, not the least of which is the life of one Lee Shui, alias Yuong Son Nhi, alias Huong Son, alias Wong Son Yi, alias Nguyen (his true family name) Ai Quoc, and finally alias Ho Chi Minh. After studying Marxism in Moscow, Ho helped found the Indochinese Communist Party and, in the mid-twenties, in Canton, China, he formed the Annam (Vietnamese) Revolutionary Association, working closely with the Soviet's Michael Borodin, in charge of Soviet activities in South China. Illustrative of Ho's developing Communist morality during this period is a report by Hoang Van Chi, found in his *From Colonialism to Communism*. An early Annam, or Vietnamese, nationalist, Phan Boi Chau, was a founder of the Annam Modernization Association, and an advocate of a constitutional monarchy independent of the French. Chau's activities, fashioned after those of Sun Yat-sen, were too conservative in pursuing revolutionary objectives for Ho Chi Minh, and so in 1925 Ho betrayed him to the French because he felt that Chau was no longer useful to the revolution. Ho felt that Chau's trial by the French would further inspire a feeling of nationalism, while at the same time the money the French paid him for betraying Chau could be used for revolutionary purposes.

Such an act by Ho was typical. Another example can be found in his actions in Canton. Through one of his organizations, the Revolutionary Association, Ho attempted to convert the young Annamite (Vietnamese) Nationalists, studying at the Whampoa Military Academy in

China, to Communism. Any who rejected Communism were betrayed by Ho to the French police, so that when they returned home they were arrested for revolutionary activity. These were the same tactics Ho was to use years later, in 1945, in seizing power in Hanoi. The tactics are described in the September 1966 issue of *Hoc Tap*, the North Vietnamese Communist organ, where the 1945 take-over is discussed:

> Our party cleverly applied its tactics. On the one hand it cleverly took advantage of the regional and temporary contradictions of the enemy to sow division among them. On the other hand it united with anyone who could be neutralized, completely isolated the imperialists and their most dangerous lackeys and concentrated the spearhead of the attacks to overthrow them.

During the pre-World War II days, Ho, under various of his aliases, appears, disappears, and reappears on the Vietnamese scene, spending time in Paris and elsewhere, now conducting a group called the "Association for the Study of Marxism," again secretly leading the Indochinese Communist Party in Vietnam, at one time a shadowy, little-known figure, at another an openly declared leader. In 1940 he was called to Moscow, and in 1941, under new orders from Moscow, he returned to South China and formed the "League for Vietnamese Independence," or the *Viet Minh*, a front for the Indochinese Communist Party of Vietnam. Playing a double role, he was able to win economic and military aid from both the Nationalist Chinese and the Communist Chinese, to fight the Japanese aggressors in Indochina. Using the Indochinese Communist Party network, Ho developed a widespread underground in Vietnam. It was during this period, incidentally, that Nguyen Ai Quoc became Ho Chi Minh, or Ho the Enlightened, apparently for the benefit of the Nationalist Chinese. Having become "enlightened," Ho ostensibly no longer believed in Communism. He then returned to Vietnam to direct the Viet Minh in person.

Meanwhile, Vo Nguyen Giap had trained a 10,000-man army, with some 200,000 supporting guerrilla and propaganda units. His success in recruiting these numbers, however, should not be attributed to pure nationalism or to mere Vietnamese antagonism toward the French, as is so often claimed. In fact, Giap was extremely clever in exploiting traditional ethnic hostilities, playing tribe against tribe, and creating new enmities so that one group could be played off against another. It was Giap who developed Mao Tse-tung's doctrine of protracted conflict, which had probably been introduced in Vietnam by Truong Chinh, Secretary-General of the Indochinese Communist Party.

June 1940 marked the fall of France in World War II, and on the 25th of that month French Governor Catroux was dismissed from office and was succeeded by a Vichy appointee, Admiral Jean Decoux. On September 22, Vichy, under German pressure, agreed to the entry of a limited number of Japanese troops into French Indochina. The Japanese established a military occupation, leaving only internal administration in the hands of the French, and on March 9, 1945, the Japanese threw the French out altogether and recognized the independence of Vietnam, supporting Bao Dai as its ruler with Tran Trong Kim as his Prime Minister. At that time Bao Dai had tried to get Ngo Dinh Diem to take the job, but Diem refused.

The situation had indeed changed, not only in Vietnam but in Laos and Cambodia. The Japanese granted Cambodia independence from France, and despite the fact that

France had always protected Cambodia from Thai and Vietnamese oppression, now that France was weak, Cambodia accepted this independence. In Laos, however, the Japanese tried to force a similar declaration of independence from France and a pledge of allegiance to Japan, but Laos resisted and gathered a force of Laotians and French to fight. The Japanese were too strong for them, and the resistance was quickly broken. It is important to note, however, that on August 30, 1945, immediately after VJ Day, the Laotian king addressed an appeal to General de Gaulle, reaffirming loyalty to France, and the French apparently never forgot this pledge. When, some years later, French General Navarre decided to pour resources into Dien Bien Phu—a less than desirable position—he was largely influenced by loyalty to the Laotians, feeling as he did that to protect Laos from the Viet Minh was an obligation of honor. The assumption that General Navarre was simply stupid, or was merely making a military blunder by selecting Dien Bien Phu, is hardly justifiable. He could have selected a much more easily defensible spot, but he would have left Laos completely vulnerable had he done so.

With the Japanese recognition of Bao Dai as chief of state of an independent Vietnam, Ho Chi Minh made his move and declared a "liberalized zone" in the north. His intent was to seize power from the Japanese and create his own government before the Allied takeover which was obviously imminent.

Truman, Stalin, and Churchill met at Potsdam from July 17 to August 2, 1945, and through the Communist network Ho learned of their decision: to work through the Chinese in the north and the British in the south for the liberation of Asia. Lord Mountbatten was to move into Indochina, while the Japanese would be forced into unconditional surrender. Mountbatten would accept the surrender north of the 16th parallel. Automatically the French would be out—discredited and displaced.

On August 6, 1945, the first atomic bomb was dropped on Japan. Almost immediately the Viet Minh went into action, declaring the existence of a "liberated army" in Vietnam. On August 13, Ho Chi Minh called for general insurrection and insisted that the Japanese surrender Vietnam to the Viet Minh. On August 14 the Viet Minh seized control in Hanoi, and thereby succeeded in generating great enthusiasm throughout the land—an enthusiasm carefully nurtured and guided by Viet Minh Communist cells. In a Communist-controlled meeting called suddenly on August 16, Ho formed a "People's Liberation Committee," with himself as chairman. All mention of Communist objectives was carefully avoided.

In the ensuing confusion, Communist assassin squads went to work, killing not merely Japanese but Vietnamese nationalists opposed to Communism. Nationalist groups, wholly unprepared for this surge of power by the tight Communist organization of the Viet Minh, were forced to capitulate, and Bao Dai was forced to abdicate in favor of Ho Chi Minh. Ho was proclaimed President of the newly declared Democratic Republic of Vietnam, coincident with the surrender of the Japanese on board the USS *Missouri* on September 3, 1945. Actually, it is questionable that Bao Dai had the authority to transfer his title to Ho Chi Minh. Under terms of the protectorate agreement with France, he had no authority either to abdicate or to transfer his authority.

The events that followed are related by B. S. N. Murti in his book *Vietnam Divided: The Unfinished Struggle*.

As Murti points out, the British troops, with General Gracey representing Lord Mountbatten, did not arrive in

Saigon until September 12, 1945, which was *after* Ho Chi Minh had achieved his objective of seizing power and had given a façade of legality and national unity to his seizure by the creation of the People's Liberation Committee. However, General Gracey, according to Murti, refused to recognize Ho Chi Minh or the Viet Minh as a valid government. "I was welcomed on arrival by the Viet Minh," says Gracey, "who said 'welcome' and all that sort of thing. It was a very unpleasant situation and I promptly kicked them out." Gracey apparently took it upon himself to restore French power, despite instructions to the contrary. Murti maintains that it is very difficult to discern "at what level" the decision was made to restore France to full sovereignty, and yet, on October 9, 1945, the British Labor Government signed an agreement with the French recognizing the French civil administration. When the British withdrew their troops early in 1946, the French resumed complete administrative and military control in Saigon, and turned to fighting the Viet Minh in the countryside.

North of the 16th parallel, Chiang Kai-shek's Chinese were very hesitant to restore French authority in Vietnam, but they still had confidence in Ho Chi Minh, "The Enlightened One." Ho went to Paris to confer with De Gaulle, and finally, on February 28, 1946, the Franco-Chinese Treaty was signed; under its terms the Chinese agreed to withdraw from Tonkin and to allow the presence of French troops, with the understanding that the French would make an agreement with Ho Chi Minh. France had good reason to fear for the lives of the many thousands of French citizens who had remained in Vietnam during World War II and had been imprisoned by the Japanese in March 1945. Hence, with Chinese pressure adding to these fears, the French felt they had to conclude an agreement with Ho Chi Minh and his Democratic Republic of Vietnam, which was in actuality the Communist-controlled Viet Minh. That agreement was reached on March 6, 1946, and it provisionally recognized the DRV as a "free state with its own government, parliament, army and finances, forming part of the Indo-Chinese Federation and the French Union." This was in line with General de Gaulle's announcement, during the time he was the leader of the Free French, that Vietnam, Laos, and Cambodia would become members of the French Union after the war, implying a quasi-independent status. In spite of this French recognition in 1946, no other state gave recognition to the DRV until the 1950's, and then only Red China, followed by Russia.

At the very time that Ho, with help from Nationalist China, persuaded France to grant provisional recognition to the DRV, he was secretly leading the Communist Party in Vietnam. Praised as a nationalist, Ho soon began attacks on the French military bases, accusing the French of violating their pledges, and at about that time the French began to realize that they were not merely battling national reformers but Communism itself, strongly and consistently supported by Soviet Russia and Communist China.

The issues involved then were based on the fact that the March 6, 1946, agreement between De Gaulle and Ho Chi Minh left unsettled the key question of the administration of Cochin-China. (North Vietnam and South Vietnam, as we know them today, were made up, reading from north to south, of Tonkin, Annam, and Cochin-China, the last being roughly equivalent to the Mekong Delta and having Saigon as its capital.) The French had promised a referendum to determine whether or not Tonkin, Annam, and Cochin-China should be united, and in turn the Viet Minh had agreed to accept the presence of French troops for a period of five years. Relations between the French and the Viet Minh deteriorated quickly, and soon open hostilities were resumed.

Another attempt at negotiations between France and Ho's Democratic Republic of Vietnam failed, and a war that was to continue until the fall of Dien Bien Phu broke out on December 19, 1946. For the next three years relatively little progress was made by either side, but on October 1, 1949, an event occurred that was of tremendous importance in terms of the war in Vietnam and the balance of power in the world at large: the "People's Republic of China" was established, signalling the loss of China to Communism. This was perhaps *the* fatal blow to the French in Vietnam. From that point on, Mao Tse-tung was able to supply vastly increased political and military aid to Ho Chi Minh.

In the fall of 1949, the French persuaded Bao Dai to return as chief of state, in Saigon, and to sign a treaty with France, the Treaty of Ha Long Bay. As nominal leader of the nationalist parties (as opposed to the Viet Minh), Bao Dai now ruled an "independent" state within the French Union, though the independence was, at best, relative. Ho Chi Minh promptly directed his energies against Bao Dai, calling him a tool of the French, and breaking down resistance to Communism by preaching nationalism. Despite a popular belief that China was able to give comparatively little help during this period because of the Korean war, there was, in fact, a great deal of help given, by way of Chinese soldiers, as well as advisers and weapons —both Soviet and Chinese. The armistice in Korea did, indeed, make it possible to increase that help very substantially, but much was given prior to the armistice.

From this point on, by continuing efforts to undermine Bao Dai as a French puppet, by continued use of

General Giap's on-again, off-again type warfare, or "protracted conflict," and, not the least important, by continued
propaganda barrages on the part of Communist countries
all over the world, the Viet Minh attacked the French
incessantly. When the French signed an agreement to
bring Laos into the French Union late in 1953, General
Giap attempted what was apparently only a diversionary
action; he tried to send troops into Laos. Whatever his
intent—to deceive the French or not—he was successful in
prompting General Navarre to occupy Dien Bien Phu to
defend Laos against the Viet Minh, though the decision
had been made by the French to take an all-out stand
somewhere, to draw the Viet Minh into the open.

This was the beginning of the end. When the Viet
Minh and the Chinese Communists learned, in January of
1954, that the French and the British were prepared to go
to Geneva, to negotiate over Indochina, Giap made his
move. In his *People's War, People's Army*, Giap tells the
story of the preparations for Dien Bien Phu. It had to be
attacked and taken, at all costs, if the Viet Minh were to
be in an optimum bargaining position. Red China posi-
tioned a large army near the Vietnamese border, as a psychological threat. For reasons explained later in this account, American help was late in coming, and inadequate
for the job.

The Geneva Conference got underway with the
French virtually doomed. The Conference was stalled by
the Communist participants just long enough to permit
French disaster. Dien Bien Phu fell, and with it, French
prestige and, far more importantly, the French will to win.
On May 8, 1954, the French surrendered to the Viet Minh,
and the Geneva Conference became an exercise in the free
world's attmpt to save whatever pieces it could. It was
virtually an exercise in futility.

6

THE GENEVA CONFERENCE

AT MIDNIGHT IN GENEVA, ON July 20, 1954, Ta-Quang Buu and French Brigadier-General Delteil signed the *Agreement on the Cessation of Hostilities in Viet-Nam.* The Agreement theoretically ended the war between French Union Forces and the Viet Minh in Vietnam. Ta-Quang Buu, Vice-Minister of National Defense of the Democratic Republic of Vietnam (North Vietnam), signed for the commander-in-chief of the People's Army of Vietnam. Brigadier-General Delteil signed for the commander-in-chief of the French Union forces in Indochina. Similar agreements were signed in relation to Laos and Cambodia.

One day later in Geneva the *Final Declaration of the Geneva Conference* was issued. This document was signed by *no one.*

Perhaps most arguments about Vietnam and United States involvement center upon these two documents and the actions that followed their issuance.

Just as it is essential to know something of Ho Chi Minh to understand events predating Geneva, so it is necessary to know something of Ngo Dinh Diem, in order to understand events during and subsequent to the Geneva Conference. Once again, standard texts give adequate biographical data. The concern here is largely with issues immediately pertinent to the Geneva and post-Geneva periods.

Among the many fables about Diem, two seem to be repeated most frequently and most emphatically. One of these is that, prior to the Geneva Conference and his subsequent assumption of power in South Vietnam, Diem was an unknown, an "absentee aristocrat" who had spent years in self-imposed exile while all true Vietnamese patriotic nationalists (the Viet Minh) were gloriously fighting the French. It is further said that he was created as a leader by his political friends in America (ranging from Cardinal Spellman to Senator John F. Kennedy), who allegedly constituted the so-called "Vietnam Lobby," and was then imposed on the peoples of South Vietnam. The other fable is that, once in power, after a short period of accomplishment because of American aid and power, he soon showed himself a "ruthless tyrant," alien to the Vietnamese people, insensitive to their needs and aspirations, insulated by his Catholicism and his family. He is supposed to have developed a highly repressive police state, persecuting Buddhists, suspected Communists, and personal political enemies alike, so that his assassination—desperately hoped for and wildly praised by the people at large—was an inevitable necessity.

The frequently critical Bernard Fall, quoted by practically every writer as *the* American authority on Vietnam, says this of Diem in his *Viet-Nam Witness:*

> The Buu-Loc government resigned on June 15, 1953, after having held a cabinet session at Saigon, stating in its message to Bao Dai that it had "completed its tasks," which consisted in "establishing the international status of the State of Viet-Nam." Ngo Dinh Diem, the attentiste *Vietnamese nationalist par excellence, a man with an excellent reputation for integrity,* par-

ticularly well liked in American Catholic circles and also *respected by Ho Chi Minh*, agreed to form a new government on the following day.

That a man of the stature of Ngo Dinh Diem was willing to accept such a heavy responsibility at that particularly crucial moment in Viet-Nam's history, was hailed as a veritable victory for Viet-Nam's "true nationalists" and as an admission of defeat for Bao Dai. [Italics mine.]

This is hardly the picture of an unknown, thrust upon an unwilling Vietnamese people by a Vietnam lobby in the United States. Diem was, in fact, lionized in many ways by the people as one of the very few important men to refuse to compromise with either the French or the Communists. While Bao Dai was cooperating with the Japanese, Diem refused to be his prime minister. (Much later, on June 17, 1954, after the French had been defeated, Diem was appointed premier and by Bao Dai.)

It seems unlikely that Ho Chi Minh would have taken two most extraordinary steps had Diem been either unknown or unimportant to the people. First, having taken Diem captive, Ho then asked him to take a top government job. Ho critically wanted Diem's support as a man of tremendous influence with the people. Second, upon Diem's blunt and cold refusal (and Diem refused with the knowledge that Ho could execute him on the spot as he had executed Diem's brother), Ho turned him loose, apparently aware executing Diem would provoke the wrath of large numbers.

After coming into power, Diem faced truly monstrous problems: corruption, sedition, and Communism. In his continuing struggle against subversion and in his efforts to rebuild his country, Diem left himself open to violent criticism and vitriolic charges. From a study of the documents, I am convinced that in Diem's case the big lie succeeded beyond North Vietnam's wildest dreams.

Marguerite Higgins, in her *Our Vietnam Nightmare*, quotes verbatim such men as Tran Van Huong, the Prime Minister of South Vietnam from October 1964 to January 1965. This man had spent several months in prison for political opposition to Diem, but he states categorically that the top generals who murdered Diem were "scared to death" because, since they had no popular support themselves, they could not have prevented a spectacular comeback of Diem, had he been permitted to live.

Miss Higgins quotes a personal conversation she held with General Big Minh, one of the successive military junta heads, in which Minh stated that Diem "could not be allowed to live because he was too much respected among simple, gullible people . . ." At the same time many Americans were saying Diem had lost touch with the people.

The same author says that at least six of the generals who masterminded the revolt against Diem personally told her that they staged the revolt to please the United States. They felt this was what the U.S. Administration wanted; they wanted to insure U.S. aid for the war effort, and they acted accordingly.

Possibly there are other instances in which a national ruler has asked the United Nations to enter his country to examine charges against him and give a public verdict as Diem did. I know of none. But I am certain that there is no other instance in which a U.N. Commission issued a preliminary finding, in strong, explicit language, of "not guilty," only to have the report appear irrelevant because the vindicated ruler had been assassinated—allegedly for the crimes of which he was declared innocent!

Miss Higgins says that had Ho Chi Minh been writing the script himself, he could hardly have asked for a better denouement: chaos and lawlessness brought about in the political reign of terror following Diem's death. She quotes an Australian journalist, known for his Communist sympathies, who says that Ho Chi Minh greeted word of Diem's assassination with the comment, "I could scarcely believe that the Americans would be so stupid."

This is the moment when escalation plans for the war, North Vietnamese style, went into high gear.

But the vicious circle was completed in 1964 and 1965 when many of the same Americans who had shouted the loudest for Diem's downfall now used the chaotic political situation that followed, and the instability of each "coup" government, as the excuse for crying for complete withdrawal on the part of the United States. As Miss Higgins puts it, this is equal to cutting off a man's hand, then condemning him to death because he is disfigured.

These events took place years after the Geneva Conference. But it must be emphasized that the pre-Geneva events described in the previous chapter, and the characteristics of Diem are most important for an understanding of the Geneva Conference and of the protests on the part of Diem and others. Unwilling to let mere confusion and the obscurity of French-Viet Minh historical developments cloud the issue, Diem sharply protested the right of either the French or the Viet Minh to negotiate over the fate of all of Vietnam, including Cochin-China (South Vietnam). It is difficult to understand how Diem's protests could have been legally refuted. It is easy, however, to see how they could have been *ignored*—again on the basis of alleged despair at discovering the truth—a throwing up of hands in hopelessness over "who's right, who's wrong"— a decision of expediency to "let bygones be bygones" and start from scratch. Thus came the victories of "protracted conflict."

To return to events immediately prior to Dien Bien Phu and the Geneva Conference, July 1953 saw the cease-fire in Korea. This freed more Chinese Communist equipment, advisers, and logistic help for the Viet Minh. It also helped stir further sentiment in Paris for a negotiated settlement along Korean lines, especially since France, weary of the drainage in Indochina, was beset with problems in Algeria. These circumstances strongly contributed to the idea of a quick ending to the war by an all-out effort to attract the Viet Minh into the open in large force, where they could be defeated *en masse*. That was the idea behind Dien Bien Phu (though the choice of so unlikely a place was influenced, as mentioned earlier, by loyalty to Laos).

Meanwhile, at the December 1953 Bermuda Conference, the United States, Great Britain, and France decided to hold a later conference in Berlin, in February 1954. They did so, together with the Soviet Union, and all four powers then decided to call a conference of interested powers at Geneva, in April 1954, to discuss Korea and Indochina.

At this point, General Giap, Commander-in-Chief of the Viet Minh, went to work with great deliberation. He describes in detail in his *People's War, People's Army* his preparations for assaulting Dien Bien Phu and his rationale in terms of the doctrine of protracted conflict. Ho Chi Minh managed to stall off the Geneva Conference just long enough for Giap to intensify his attack against the French. By the time the conference began on April 27, 1954, in Geneva, the fall of Dien Bien Phu was a foregone conclusion. By the time the question of Indochina went into the discussion stage on May 8, 1954, Dien Bien Phu had fallen. This, of course, gave the Viet Minh a position of tremendous strength for negotiating.

To interject a side issue here, many have argued that we should not withdraw completely from Vietnam but rather should simply withdraw into enclaves. Dien Bien Phu should have exploded the enclave myth by the shattering blow of its own fall in May 1954. President Eisenhower in *Mandate for Change* repeats several times the fact that he argued with the French against committing their forces in this fashion, and speaks of the "almost invariable fate of troops invested in an isolated fortress."

In the same book, Mr. Eisenhower, assessing events that led to Geneva, notes that Russia recognized the political pressures on the French government to achieve a settlement. Russia also realized that the existing French government was important to U.S. policies in terms of the European Defense Community. While we were sympathetic to the French, for these reasons, we nonetheless urged them not to be over-anxious to negotiate.

But the French persisted, and began to issue less-than-subtle warnings: one, that the European Defense Community was at stake; two, if the United States blocked a conference, the moral obligation to continue the war in Indochina would be shifted from the French to us.

Secretary of State John Foster Dulles attempted to get Great Britain and other allies to join in a plan proposed by President Eisenhower to Prime Minister Churchill—the plan which, *after* Geneva, was to become SEATO. The Secretary of State and the President wanted to go *into* Geneva with this "ace up their sleeve"—a coalition that would give them a strong bargaining position. Great Britain, however, continued to demur, despite President Eisenhower's plea. It is truly revealing to read that plea now, in light of the criticisms that an appeal to SEATO commitments is brand new and a "ruse" on the part of the present Administration. It is also thought that the idea of containing aggressive Communism was a latter-day concept with Administration policy-makers. Or, as is said, that the present Administration, in "scurrying around" to find reasons for making war, came up suddenly with "SEATO."

Mr. Eisenhower's letter to Mr. Churchill is dated April 4, 1954—*before* the Geneva Conference. Asking Mr. Churchill's support for the coalition that later became SEATO, he called for "nations which have a vital concern in the checking of Communist expansion in the area [Southeast Asia]." And again, "the imposition on Southeast Asia of the political system of Communist Russia and its Chinese Communist ally, by whatever means, would be a grave threat to the whole free community . . . this possibility should be met by united action. . . ."

But Britain refused, and when Mendes-France came to power in Paris, on the strength of a pledge to reach a settlement of Indochina within one month, all hope of entering Geneva in a position of strength vanished. In brief, what we had hoped for was that the French would continue fighting, while we brought into being a coalition against Communism in Southeast Asia. The French gave up. The British feared the risk of alienating Russia and Red China by getting involved in anything like a SEATO pact prior to the Geneva Conference, since this would provoke the idea of possible intervention by the United States and others in Indochina.

According to Anthony Eden's *Full Circle*, it was Russia's Molotov who demanded that a Viet Minh delegation participate in the Geneva talks. Eden says it was impossible to resist this demand, but in exchange he bargained privately with Molotov and Chou En-lai for Communist cooperation in removing the wounded from Dien Bien Phu.

Meanwhile, President Eisenhower had withdrawn our senior diplomatic representatives from Geneva, downgrading our position to that of "observer." We were not going to risk association with a settlement with which we might be in sharp disagreement. Mr. Eden tried to persuade Mr. Dulles to return, but the plea was rejected on the grounds that American public opinion would never tolerate "the guaranteeing of the subjection of millions of Vietnamese to Communist rule." Finally, a compromise was reached: Walter Bedell Smith, a lower-ranking official than Dulles, would be present at the talks. Smith ultimately issued a unilateral declaration for the United States.

An agreement to establish a Supervisory and Control Commission for Vietnam had been made. On July 18, 1954, Eden says, Chou En-lai proposed that the Commission consist of India, Canada, and Poland. Against the strong protests of the Diem cabinet, Great Britain, France, and the United States accepted Chou En-lai's proposal. On July 20, the French and the Viet Minh announced agreement on a demarcation line—a river immediately south of the 17th parallel. (This river has been giving us a great deal of trouble. The artillery fire in the DMZ area has been coming from North Vietnamese forces firing from north of this river—a river exceedingly difficult to cross in bad weather, hence a fine natural barrier for the North Vietnamese.) The Viet Minh had pushed for almost immediate elections. Mendes-France got them to agree to delay the elections until July 1956.

Finally, at 3:00 P.M. on July 21, the time had come for formal settlement. Mr. Eden says that Bedell Smith had already warned him that the United States could not associate itself with the final declaration. The most the

United States would do would be to issue a declaration "taking note" of what had been decided, and agreeing "not to disturb the settlement." Mr. Eden feared this move, since the Chinese had indicated they would demand that all delegations sign the final declaration. Eden, therefore, negotiated privately with Molotov, and they agreed to eliminate all signatures. The expedient they used was to head the declaration with a list of all participating countries. Thus, with the agreement to end hostilities, signed by the French and Viet Minh military representatives, and the final declaration—unsigned—the war came, theoretically, to an end. Ironically, at the end of August, the European Defense Council was defeated in the French Assembly.

What of the State of Vietnam through all this, the state known today as the Republic of Vietnam, or South Vietnam?

It has frequently been forgotten, I think, that while the French were fighting the Viet Minh, the actual State of Vietnam was within the French Union, by signed agreement with France, dated March 8, 1949. It was diplomatically recognized by the United States on February 7, 1950. It was with this State of Vietnam that the United States signed the Mutual Defense Assistance Agreement on December 23, 1950. In July 1952, the U.S. Ambassador presented his credentials to Bao Dai, the head of state, and a Vietnamese embassy, representing *this* state, not the Viet Minh, was established in Washington. The same Bao Dai, as head of state, appointed Ngo Dinh Diem Premier of Vietnam on July 7, 1954.

France, the Viet Minh, (through courtesy of Russia, as we have seen), Great Britain, Russia, the State of Vietnam (the Bao Dai government), the States of Laos and Cambodia, and Red China were all present at the Geneva Conference. The conference convened on April 27, 1954, and issued its final declaration on July 21, 1954. The State of Vietnam's representative was Dr. Tran Van Do, the Diem cabinet Foreign Minister.

But what voice was given to the State of Vietnam representative? The only heed paid by Mendes-France, Premier of France, noted in President Eisenhower's text, is the Premier's request that the United States use its influence with Diem—the Vietnamese Premier—to prevent his "needlessly obstructing any honorable truce which the French might reach with the Vietminh."

Throughout the Geneva talks Dr. Do fought desperately to save Vietnam from partition, but was ignored. His sense of futility was expressed poignantly in a cable he sent Diem: "Absolutely impossible to surmount the hostility of our enemies and perfidy of false friends. Unusual procedures paralyzed the action of our delegation . . . All arrangements were signed in privacy. We express our deepest sorrow on this failure of our mission."

The State of Vietnam was virtually excluded from all discussion of the cease-fire agreement. This exclusion was officially protested by Dr. Do on July 17 and denied by the French. On July 18, Dr. Do put forth his own proposals for a cease-fire—proposals that, among other things, called for disarmament, for a cease-fire throughout Vietnam with no demarcation line, and elections throughout Vietnam, when, in the opinion of the United Nations, security and order had been established.

Here, it seems to me, was one of the real tragedies of Geneva—that the truly meaningful proposals of the Diem cabinet were ignored.

All of this makes me ask, "What do we *want* of South Vietnam?"

We talk about unification. The Diem cabinet fought against division; the Western powers vetoed the plea. We talk today about United Nations intervention. The Diem representative pleaded for United Nations supervision and a determination by the U.N. of the appropriate time for elections. Instead, France and Great Britain accepted Red China's bid, establishing a Control Commission consisting of India, Poland, and Canada.

Diem issued an ominous warning on July 22, 1954, denouncing the cease-fire agreement as an "inequity" solemnly protested by his government. This warning followed the "solemn protests" registered by the Vietnamese delegation at Geneva against "the rejection of their proposals without examination." These protests included four points: the haste of the agreement between France and the Viet Minh, and the clauses in the agreement that compromised the political future of the Vietnamese people; the fact that the agreement abandoned certain territories to the Viet Minh essential for defending Vietnam against further Communist expansion; the fact that the French military command had fixed the date of future elections, without consulting the State of Vietnam; the manner and conditions of the armistice, which virtually ignored Vietnamese aspirations.

Added to these protests was the declaration that the Vietnamese government reserved "full liberty of action to safeguard the sacred rights of the people of Vietnam to territorial unity, national independence and liberty."

These expressed attitudes and official protests of the State of Vietnam are documented and described by B. S. N. Murti, in his *Vietnam Divided*.

As we have noted previously, Dr. Murti's comments are particularly significant in the light of his position as the Deputy Secretary-General of the Control Commission. His statements are also especially interesting vis-à-vis the

United Nations. He points out that the United States had tried to get the French to take their case to the United Nations, but the French, supported by the British, refused. Red China scored a *coup* simply by being present as a participant at Geneva, since she was not in the U.N.

Murti calls the Indochina settlement merely an "adjustment of power relations, concealing a full Western retreat and a simultaneous Sino-Soviet advance." He points out that Russia and Red China pressed to have the signatory powers jointly assume obligations to guarantee the terms of the Geneva settlement, and to bring Burma, Ceylon, India, Indonesia, and Pakistan into such a pact. The United States refused to associate with such arrangements, or with a British recommendation for joint guarantees.

President Eisenhower made it quite clear that he was unhappy with the Geneva settlement. Despite all the propaganda to the effect that the cease-fire agreement, with its demarcation of zones, would not mean that Vietnam would be politically divided, Mr. Eisenhower was pessimistic—and it turned out realistic—about the future. ". . . The grouping of the regular military units of both parties in delimited zones implied nothing but partition. We knew, from experience in Korea, that this would probably lead to Communist enslavement of millions in the northern partitioned area."

It seems to me truly remarkable that those critics who assail our "establishing the Diem government as a separate state, in contradiction to the Geneva settlement" never refer to this background—that Diem was Premier of Vietnam, *already a state*, and the *only* state, at the time of Geneva, with unquestionable credentials; that he fought against division by military zones, knowing what it would mean; that the President of the United States disapproved of military zones for the same reason, and openly stated his belief that it meant nothing but partition, with consequent Communist enslavement.

These were among the reasons that both the United States and the State of Vietnam refused to go along with the agreements of the final declaration, and refused to sign it, making it very clear that they would refrain from using force to disturb the Geneva settlement only under specific conditions. Great Britain and Russia negotiated an agreement with Red China to dispense with signatures on the final declaration, knowing the United States would refuse to sign. Hence, the ultimate form of the final declaration. It simply began by "noting" which powers had been present at Geneva. To say, then, that we were "morally" committed to uphold the terms of the settlement, and that the matter of signatures was a mere technicality, is a wanton disregard of the facts. It is naive to ignore the background of the Geneva Conference, the "closed-door" maneuvering and diplomatic negotiations that took place. There was nothing accidental, incidental, or merely "technical" about the final format, or our position, or our refusal to sign.

Yet, despite the cease-fire agreement that made subversion so easy and virtually inevitable, the State of Vietnam went along with the United States in respecting the settlements.

Then came the task that practically the entire world considered hopeless—the rebuilding of war-torn South Vietnam. Diem tackled it, against fantastic odds. Diem had to fight internal corruption, powerful organized banditry, frightful conflicts between politico-religious sects, political subversion on the part of the Viet Minh cadres left behind, eventually V.C. terrorism, and, finally, outright infiltration.

The impossible happened. Instead of a collapse in

South Vietnam, Diem clearly established his authority. Emerging as a much stronger leader than Bao Dai, who had appointed him, Diem asked for a popular referendum. He defeated Bao Dai by an overwhelming vote, was elected president, and proclaimed Vietnam a republic on October 26, 1955. On March 4, 1956, general elections were held for a National Constituent Assembly. The Assembly convened on March 15, and adopted and promulgated a Constitution on October 26, 1956. A near-miracle had been performed, in terms of restoration of order and structure in the body politic.

What did the critics say? Foul! The referendum was rigged, they insisted. Meanwhile, not one word was said about the fact that in North Vietnam, not even a semblance of elections took place.

In 1956 North Vietnam realized that a Communist takeover would not be automatic. Its hope for that had been shattered by the fact that South Vietnam had not collapsed. The North was also plagued by its own problems: crop failures, land-reform debacles, the revolt of the peasants, and the blood bath and its "Correction of Errors" campaign.

7

MORAL AND LEGAL OBJECTIONS

TO THE WAR: THE ISSUES

*P*RESUMING THAT A JUST WAR is possible, what of *this* conflict? Have we the right to engage in it? Have we the obligation to engage in it? What about the means being used?

The most commonly voiced objections are these:

Our engagement in the Vietnam conflict violates the provisions of the Geneva Conference on the ground that:

. . . We established and supported an independent government in South Vietnam with neither the legal nor moral right to do so;

. . . We encouraged and supported South Vietnam in rejecting elections in 1956, as promised;

. . . We have taken sides in what is a civil war, attempting to justify our position by calling it a war of aggression;

. . . We have distorted the intent and transcended the restrictions of the SEATO agreements;

. . . We have ignored the provisions of the United Nations for arbitration and have violated its charter;

. . . We have established a puppet government in South Vietnam, a military dictatorship not reflective of the will of the people.

Moreover, this view runs, we have violated every principle of decency, critically damaged our international prestige, and endangered our national integrity. Specifically, it is alleged:

. . . We have engaged in massive, indiscriminate bombing, napalming, and general destructiveness;

. . . We have alienated the peoples of the world, and particularly the "yellow" nations of Asia, including the peoples of South Vietnam;

. . . We have risked provoking World War III and a nuclear holocaust;

. . . We have simply and cynically *used* Vietnam to fight against Red China;

. . . We have sacrificed American lives and resources on behalf of a people uninterested in their own political life, and too corrupt or cowardly to defend themselves;

. . . We have drained our national resources to the point of impeding or endangering economic and social reform at home.

Finally, it is alleged, and this is germane to all other objections, that we have assumed obligations without having any legal or moral right to do so. We have therefore been forced to dig up false evidence to defend our position.

These, I believe, are the main objections to the war on what are termed moral and legal grounds. It is important to understand the basis for these objections, and I have tried to give them here as fairly as possible, substantially in the form in which their proponents present them.

Paragraph 20 of *The Special Report to the Co-Chairmen of the Geneva Conference on Indochina* by the International Commission for Supervision and Control in Vietnam cites violations of Articles 16, 17, and 19 of the Geneva Agreement on the part of the Republic of Vietnam (South Vietnam). (The Commission was composed of representatives of India, Poland, and Canada.) The charges involve receiving increased military aid from the

United States, establishment of a United States Military Assistance Command in South Vietnam, and the introduction of U.S. military personnel beyond the stated strength of the Military Assistance Advisory Group provided for in the agreement.

This is the basic charge proffered, for instance, by the *Christian Century* in an editorial, "The Issue is China," on March 23, 1966. The editorial added charges that we had intervened on behalf of a "ruthless tyrant," Ngo Dinh Diem, whom we had elevated to power, and that we violated Article 2 of the Charter of the United Nations.

During the Senate hearings in 1966, Senator Wayne Morse took the same position in questioning General Maxwell Taylor, former Ambassador to Vietnam. Senator Morse went further than the Control Commission and charged that the establishment of a political government in South Vietnam was in violation of the terms of the Geneva Agreement, which intended the 17th parallel as a demarcation of military zones only. Senator Morse's implication was that we had no right to interfere politically.

I. F. Stone, in *I. F. Stone's Weekly*, March 8, 1965, sharply criticized a State Department *White Paper*, which he said quoted from the Control Commission's report solely in its own favor, by referring to North Vietnam's violations alone. He added that both South Vietnam and the United States had been criticized by the Control Commission for hamstringing the Commission's efforts to check on arms importation.

Bernard Fall in *Viet-Nam Witness* points out that the State Department widely publicized North Vietnam's violations, but failed to display prominently the fact that the Control Commission indicted *South Vietnam's* violations as well. He adds that the Control Commission teams found it increasingly difficult to move about in South Vietnam.

In his *Vietnam: Between Two Truces*, Jean Lacouture states that the fires of war were kindled by the dictatorship in the South, and provoked by American aid, economic in 1954, military in 1956, in direct contradiction to the 1954 Geneva accords.

There are many others who argue that South Vietnam violated the Geneva Agreement and that United States intervention is illegal. The sources I have listed, I feel, represent a reasonable cross section of opinion.

How can these charges be answered? Paragraphs 2 and 3 of the same report of the Control Commission state that armed and unarmed personnel, arms, munitions, and other supplies had been sent from the zone in the North to the zone in the South for the purpose of supporting, organizing, and carrying out hostile activities, including armed attacks, against the armed forces and administration of the zone in the South, in violation of Articles 10, 19, 24, and 27 of the Agreement. Going further, the Commission states its conclusion that the People's Army of Vietnam (North Vietnam) had allowed the zone in the North to be used for inciting, encouraging, and supporting hostile activities in the zone in the South, aimed at overthrowing the administration there, in violation of Articles 19, 24, and 27 of the Agreement. According to the Control Commission, there were violations on both sides.

Three major issues are at stake here. The first is the *timing* of the violations, the second has to do with the proportionate extent of the violations, the third must deal with the obligation to honor the Geneva Agreement.

First, it is vital to consider the question of timing. Who first violated the Geneva Agreement and why is the question important?

In the Senate hearings on Vietnam, Senator Morse refers to the principle of *reciprocity*, calling it one of the most basic principles of international law. By definition, if one partner does not perform his treaty obligation, the other partner is relieved of any obligation to perform his.

Senator Morse was arguing against our position, but note that his argument is precisely the same one used in the Department of State memorandum of March 8, 1965, which presents the "Legal Basis for United States Action Against North Vietnam." The memorandum states ". . . international law recognizes the principle that a material breach of treaty by one party entitles other parties at least to withhold compliance with an equivalent, corresponding or related provision until the other party is prepared to observe its obligations."

If North Vietnam committed the first violations, then, by the principle of reciprocity, South Vietnam is no longer bound to the Agreement. General Maxwell Taylor pointed out, when questioned by Senator Morse, that there had never been, in fact, a cessation of hostilities. The North Vietnamese left behind them in the south several thousand men and large caches of ammunition, and proceeded almost at once to infiltrate armed men from North Vietnam. "The ink was not dry" on the Agreement, as General Taylor puts it, before North Vietnam was violating it. By the time the United States had introduced forces or established anything that might be called a base, the Agreement had been nullified by North Vietnam.

This is the basic argument of the State Department

and many others. The argument in detail is available in the *Congressional Record*, March 10, 1966, under the title, "The Legality of U.S. Participation in the Defense of Vietnam." The argument is noted with approval by E. B. Deutsch, the chairman of the American Bar Association Committee on Peace and Law Through United Nations, in an article in the *American Bar Association Journal*, May 1966, under the title, "The Legality of the United States Position in Vietnam." The threat of subversion and aggression from the north is the subject of the earliest correspondence between President Eisenhower and the President of the Council of Ministers of Vietnam (October 23, 1954). The Assistant Secretary of State for Far Eastern Affairs, in a policy address given on June 1, 1956, notes that the military potential of South Vietnam had been drastically reduced by the withdrawal of nearly 200,000 French troops and the Vietnamese army (South Vietnam) itself had been reduced by more than 50,000 since the time of the armistice, and by disposing of more than $200,000 in war equipment. On the other hand, steady growth had been taking place in the war-making potential of the North Vietnamese, and voluminous quantities of arms and numbers of military workers had crossed into South Vietnam. The Secretary quotes a highly significant diplomatic note from the British government to the U.S.S.R. This note was sent to Moscow in April 1956 and released to the press. (Great Britain was cochairman, with Russia, of the Geneva Conference). The note read:

> The Viet Minh army has been so greatly strengthened by the embodiment and re-equipment of irregular forces that instead of the 7 Viet Minh divisions in existence in July 1954 there are now no less than 20. This striking

contrast between massive military expansion in
the North and the withdrawal and reduction of
military forces in the South speaks for itself.

In his book *Viet Cong*, an exceptionally detailed
study, Douglas Pike calls Dr. Wesley Fishel's estimate
that some 10,000 persons were left behind as a Communist network at the time of the 1954 partition probable.

In an article, "The Faceless Viet Cong," that appeared
in *Foreign Affairs* in April 1966, George A. Carver, Jr.,
gives a thorough account of the events immediately prior
and subsequent to the Geneva Conference. He leaves no
doubt about the violations described above. Carver adds
that as many as 400,000 persons in North Vietnam who
had the right and the desire to leave the north for the
south were prevented from doing so. Indeed, as early as
April 17, 1955, the South Vietnamese government appealed to the United Nations, stating that the North
Vietnamese Communists were preventing northerners from
migrating to the south.

There is no question, then, that immediately after the
Agreement there were certain violations by the North
Vietnamese. In 1959 and 1960 these violations became
intense. By the early 1960's, violation by aggression and
subversion had become big business. The National Liberation Front, the Hanoi-controlled apparatus, was functioning through the Viet Cong in the South.

But what about the violations initiated by South Vietnam in terms of introducing foreign troops in excess of
the Agreement, and, in effect, establishing bases? How
does the timing relate to that of the violations by North
Vietnam? *It is noteworthy that North Vietnam did not
protest to the chairmen of the Geneva Conference against
a "formidable" increase of personnel in the American*

Military Assistance and Advisory Group in South Vietnam, until April 17, 1960. At that time North Vietnam accused the United States of turning South Vietnam into a "U.S. military base for the preparation of a new war." Interestingly enough it was also in 1960 that the Communist Party of North Vietnam openly stated its purpose. Its spokesmen said they would have to liberate the south from the "rule of U.S. imperialists and their henchmen." Actually, it was not until October 1961 that President Kennedy sent General Maxwell Taylor to Vietnam to examine the desirability of bolstering military strength in South Vietnam. At the time of General Taylor's visit, the United States had only 1,400 military personnel in Vietnam. As a matter of fact, in 1960 we had only 775 such personnel in Vietnam. These numbers were certainly within the spirit of the Geneva Conference. Yet, remember, it was as early as 1956 that North Vietnam went from seven to twenty divisions.

In December 1961 President Diem asked President Kennedy for further military assistance, stating that in October 1961 alone, more than 1,800 incidents of terrorism had occurred.

In 1962 our military assistance program was greatly enlarged, with American advisors and logistics personnel increasing to 10,000 by the end of the year. By the end of 1964 the flow of men from North Vietnam into South Vietnam had gone above 40,000, and by December of that year North Vietnam had begun to introduce regular units of the North Vietnamese army into South Vietnam. It was not until February 1965 that we started bombing the north, and not until March of 1965 that we brought over a brigade of American Marines—some 4,000 troops. From that point on, of course, our build-up has continued (by March of 1968 we hovered around the half million mark), joined by some 59,000 troops from other countries.

There seems to be no reasonable doubt that violations of the Geneva Agreement were first initiated by North Vietnam. In accordance with the principle of reciprocity it appears equally certain that South Vietnam was acting legally in responding to these violations by introducing American forces and establishing bases, and this action was not taken until several years after North Vietnam's initial violations. Before seeking American help, South Vietnam had registered a large number of complaints about alleged violations on the part of the North Vietnamese to the International Control Commission. South Vietnam's approach seems admirably restrained.

This view was supported by Theodore B. Blakely, former acting head of the Canadian Delegation to the International Commission for Supervision and Control in Vietnam, in October 1966 when he wrote to the *Montreal Gazette:*

> In 1957, long before American soldiers were helping the South Vietnamese Army, I reported to the Canadian government that the evidence before the international commission indicated a mounting intensity of attack by North Vietnam against South Vietnam. . . . flagrant violation of the cease-fire agreement . . . The evidence included the failure of North Vietnam to grant exit permits, persecution of political opponents and establishment (in the South) of secret bases (among other violations) in flagrant breach of the (1954 Geneva) Agreement. For me, the late President Kennedy's promise of protection of South Vietnam . . . is sufficiently binding upon

the present Administration—morally binding.
Any abandonment of South Vietnam to the
tender mercies of the North Vietnamese regime
would be an act of the gravest moral turpitude.

The second issue involved in the Control Commission report is the proportionate extent of the violations
of the North and of the South. It certainly seems to me
that the South's response to the type of violations initiated by the North were relatively mild and restrained.
Senator Mike Mansfield has a reputation as a scholar who
has not infrequently questioned or disagreed with Administration policy in Vietnam. Yet Senator Mansfield
reported to the Senate Committee on Foreign Relations
in 1955, after returning from Vietnam and Laos:

> While the last official Vietminh units have
> been withdrawn in accordance with the Geneva
> accord, clandestine elements remain south of
> the 17th parallel. Agents and propagandists are
> active in infiltration and subversion. Secret Viet-
> minh village councils have been set up in many
> areas and function at night in opposition to the
> regular administration. Small armed bands even
> operate openly in the mountainous regions. In
> the event of a breakdown in the present truce,
> the Vietminh have in these units a fifth column
> ready to go into immediate action.

Much later, in January 1966, when he reported to
the chairman of the Senate's Committee on Foreign Relations, Senator Mansfield referred to the National Liberation Front as "a 'terrorist group'—a group which has
gained its position through force and terrorism."
If the claims of President Diem and of our own

State Department are true as set forth in the State Department publication *Aggression from the North: The Record of North Viet-Nam's Campaign to Conquer South Viet-Nam* (and these claims are verified by the Control Commission's Report), then Diem's use of U.S. assistance in establishing bases was strictly a matter of intelligent self-defense. Neither official documents nor the Control Commission's reports indicate that South Vietnam retaliated against infiltration in the same way the North attacked the South. That is, South Vietnam did not attempt to infiltrate the North, subvert its government, or terrorize its people. Surely, the South Vietnamese violations were considerably less than those of the North.

Finally, there seems to be a tendency to shrug off the question of just how far either South Vietnam or the United States could be held to the Geneva Agreement. We noted the cold, hard fact that South Vietnam was given no voice in the settlements, that it publicly protested this treatment, and appealed for United Nations intervention.

Since neither South Vietnam nor the United States signed or approved of the Geneva treaty, it is difficult to see how they can be accused of violating it. At worst, the United States might be charged with violating its promise to refrain from force or threatening to disturb the settlement. But we argue that we used force, when we finally did, not to *disturb*, but to *defend* the terms of the settlement, already disturbed by the North Vietnamese.

A second major charge in terms of legality is that in giving support to South Vietnam, the United States is treating South Vietnam as a separate state, apart from North Vietnam. This act is said to violate Article 6 of the Final Declaration of the Geneva Conference. The article reads: "The Conference recognizes that the essential purpose of the agreement relating to Vietnam is to settle military questions with a view to ending hostilities and that the military demarcation line is provisional and should not in any way be interpreted as constituting a political or territorial boundary."

Senator Fulbright expressed the charge succinctly in his questioning of Secretary Rusk during the Senate hearings. "The 17th parallel was provisional and was not in any way to be interpreted as constituting a political or territorial boundary: On the basis of it the United States is saying both that it stands on the principle that there is no political or territorial boundary separating North and South Vietnam and that we must stand and fight in South Vietnam because that nation has been attacked by its aggressor neighbor of the north."

Peace in Vietnam, by the American Friends Service Committee, makes explicit charges of the same nature. Similar comments are made by Quincy Wright, in his article "Principles of Foreign Policy" in *The Viet-Nam Reader*. Mr. Wright adds that the United States attempts to justify itself under Article 51 of the U.N. Charter to engage in "collective self-defense" at the invitation of the government of South Vietnam. Not only does this assume that South Vietnam is an independent state (in violation of the Geneva Declaration), but, says Wright, we base our stand on having a commitment to the government of South Vietnam. In fact we made no commitments to the government except to the Diem administration, which ceased to exist in 1963.

Senator Morse makes basically the same point—that it was the United States and Diem who proceeded to set up the government of South Vietnam, "in clear violation of the agreement."

One of the most detailed reports of the American effort to establish and support Diem as leader of a sovereign state is in an article, "The Vietnam Lobby," by Robert Scheer and Warren Hinckle, in the July 1965 issue of *Ramparts*. They maintain that various important figures in the United States sold Diem to the American public and pressured the Eisenhower administration into accepting him.

On February 11, 1961, the Program of the National Front for the Liberation of South Vietnam was issued. This charges that American imperialists have plotted to partition Vietnam, to enslave the southern part, and are preparing for an aggressive war in Southeast Asia. In order to accomplish this, the United States brought the Ngo Dinh Diem clique to power, under the signboard of a faked independent state.

What response can be made to the accusation that we violated the article of the Geneva agreement that established only a military demarcation line, not two distinct political entities?

One reply to the charge of this specific violation is offered by E. P. Deutsch in his article in the *American Bar Association Journal*. Mr. Deutsch says the essential purpose of the agreement was to settle military questions, and to provide a provisional military demarcation line. This does not exclude the possibility of later political partition of Vietnam. He notes that the next article of the final declaration, Article 7, clearly states that the settlement of political problems is to be solved on the basis of respect for principles of independence. The article reads:

> The Conference declares that, so far as Viet-
> Nam is concerned, the settlement of political
> problems, effected on the basis of respect for the

principles of independence, unity and territorial integrity, shall permit the Viet-Namese people to enjoy the fundamental freedoms, guaranteed by democratic institutions established as a result of free general elections by secret ballot. In order to ensure that sufficient progress in the restoration of peace has been made, and that all the necessary conditions obtain for free expression of the national will, general elections shall be held in July 1956, under the supervision of an international Supervisory Commission, referred to in the agreement on the cessation of hostilities. Consultations will be held on this subject between the competent representative authorities of the two zones from 20 July 1955 onwards.

The Vietnamese people must be allowed to enjoy the fundamental freedoms. These freedoms should come about as a result of free general elections. The ballots should be secret. It is hardly accurate, therefore, Mr. Deutsch indicates, to suggest that the military demarcation line was not a political line or that the Geneva Declaration explicitly prohibited the establishment of separate political states.

B. S. N. Murti, in *Vietnam Divided*, states categorically that whatever interpretations are given, "with the simple application of the *de facto* doctrine, one can say that there are two sovereign States at present in Vietnam." He makes the point that these are two completely independent and full-fledged governments, owing no allegiance to each other. He emphasizes the significance of a message from the co-chairmen of the Geneva Conference, May 8, 1956, concerning a meeting in London of representatives of the co-chairmen. This message was addressed to the "Government of the Democratic Republic of Vietnam" (North Vietnam) and to the "Republic of Vietnam" (South Vietnam). *The message was not addressed to the signatories of the Geneva Agreement.* By this message, both Great Britain and the Soviet Union recognized the existence of two sovereign governments in Vietnam.

In *Viet-Nam: An Enigma*, J. S. Sebes observes that while the Geneva Conference did not intend to establish *de jure* and permanently two separate countries, *de facto* separation came into existence and has existed ever since. Neither Russia nor Red China has ever strongly contested this fact. On the contrary, *in early 1957 the U.S.S.R. proposed the admission of both Vietnams to the United Nations*, certainly expressing a recognition of two Vietnams *de facto*.

On *February 7, 1950*, our State Department recognized diplomatically the "formal establishment" of the State of Vietnam, the Kingdom of Laos, and the Kingdom of Cambodia as independent states within the French Union. The French-Vietnamese agreements of March 8, 1949, had provided the "basis for evolution of Vietnamese independence within the French Union." The status of the American consulate general in Saigon was raised to that of a legation.

In 1950 and 1951 our State Department issued communiqués about the economic and military aid program for the "Associated States" (Vietnam, Cambodia, Laos). On *June 18, 1952,* a communiqué about discussions between representatives of the United States, France, Vietnam, and Cambodia on the defense of Indochina was issued. The French representative carefully stressed the independence of Vietnam, pointing out that the governments of the Associated States were now on their own, unless limited by the exigencies of the war, which was in

French hands. Then presumably the French would inter-fere. The Associated States were free to negotiate trade treaties and agreements. *It was noted that these states had been recognized by thirty-three foreign governments.*

On *December 17, 1952, NATO* resolved that the campaign waged by French Union forces in Indochina deserved continuing support from the NATO govern-ments. The resolution expressed whole-hearted admiration for the valiant struggle of the French forces and the armies of the *Associated States* against Communist ag-gression (the Viet Minh).

The terms "Viet Minh" and "Communists" are used interchangeably in the communiqués. The conflict, in other words, was not merely between the Viet Minh and France; it was also between the Viet Minh and the State of Vietnam. Ignoring the State of Vietnam, then, at the Geneva Conference seems flagrantly unjust. Pre-tending that the Geneva Declaration could authoritatively have disestablished the State of Vietnam (South Viet-nam) seems incredible. Sympathy with Ho Chi Minh and his followers, using the argument that those who fought the battle against the French certainly deserve representa-tion, is one thing. But arguing sympathetically about the legality of South Vietnam's statehood is another matter entirely. It is very clever to divert attention from the question of North Vietnam's right to exist as a state by questioning South Vietnam's right. But the ruse is pre-cisely that.

8

SEATO, THE UNITED NATIONS,

AND COMMITMENTS

A THIRD AND VERY STRONG objection to U.S. involvement in Vietnam is that the United States has trumped up arguments based on the SEATO Treaty, the U.N. Charter, and on alleged "commitments" made by President Eisenhower. The critics say these arguments are fraudulent.

The critics are also firm in their belief that we have rejected U.N. efforts to arbitrate the conflict. The United States is accused of being insincere and reluctant to negotiate.

Richard N. Goodwin, in his *Triumph or Tragedy*; the American Friends Service Committee, in *Peace in Vietnam*; Senator Morse, in the *Senate Hearings on Vietnam*; and James Finn, writing in *The Catholic World*, May 1966, are among those who feel that no "commitment" was made by President Eisenhower in his 1954 letter to Premier Diem. Senator Morse stated that the former President denied that commitments to Diem involved U.S. military intervention when he said on August 17, 1965: "We said we would help that country. We were not talking about military programs, but foreign aid."

Precisely what did that letter say? The full text is found in *Background Information Relating to Southeast Asia and Vietnam*, July 1967, a publication of the Committee on Foreign Relations, United States Senate. After a brief introduction, it reads as follows:

> We have been exploring ways and means to permit our aid to Vietnam to be more effective and to make a greater contribution to the welfare and stability of the Government of Vietnam. I am, accordingly, instructing the American Ambassador to Vietnam to examine with you in your capacity as Chief of Government, how an intelligent program of American aid given directly to your Government, can serve to assist Vietnam in its present hour of trial, provided that your Government is prepared to give assurances as to the standards of performance it would be able to maintain in the event such aid were supplied.
>
> The purpose of this offer is to assist the Government of Vietnam in developing and maintaining a strong, viable state, capable of resisting attempted subversion or aggression through military means. The Government of the United States expects that this aid will be met by performance on the part of the Government of Vietnam in undertaking needed reforms. It hopes that such aid, combined with your own continuing efforts, will contribute effectively toward an independent Vietnam, endowed with a strong government. Such a government would, I hope, be so responsive to the nationalist aspirations of its people, so enlightened in purpose and effective in performance, that it will be respected both at home and

abroad and discourage anyone who might wish to impose a foreign ideology on your free people.

Two major points are made by those who say this letter is not as a document of "commitment." They point out that President Eisenhower merely made a highly conditioned offer to examine the feasibility of economic aid. They maintain that the conditions President Eisenhower set were never met by the Diem regime, arguing that that regime never became capable of resisting subversion or aggression or was even responsive to the nationalist aspirations of its people and the needed reforms. Therefore, runs this argument, the letter was not binding, since its conditions were not met.

Is the case that simple? Suppose the letter merely offered to examine the possibilities of economic aid, and imposed specific conditions before the offer could become a reality. If no other letter, public statement, or action followed, then the matter might rest at that. But if the original letter was followed by other letters actually promising aid and indicating satisfaction with developments in Vietnam, then together they presumably constitute an actual commitment to provide that aid.

Less than three months after President Eisenhower's October 23rd letter, on December 31, 1954, direct aid to Vietnam, Cambodia, and Laos was promised in a statement by the Department of State:

> Arrangements have been completed so that on January 1, 1955, the United States can begin supplying financial aid directly to the Governments of Viet-Nam, Cambodia and Laos for the purpose of strengthening their defense against the threat of Communist subversion and aggres-

sion. This direct aid reaffirms the independent status these Governments now possess. . . .

In May 1956 Secretary of State Dulles stated:

. . . our policy is to continue to help strengthen Vietnam under Prime Minister Diem. He has . . . done better than could have been expected in establishing his authority. Whereas, it seemed there would be no real strong point to stop the flow of the Chinese Communists southward after the French defeat at Dien Bien Phu, now it seems there is a strong position in Vietnam and we are assisting them in that respect.

On April 4, 1959, President Eisenhower in an address at Gettysburg College stated:

Vietnam must have a reasonable degree of safety now—both for her people and for her property. Because of these facts, military as well as economic help is currently needed in Vietnam. We reach the inescapable conclusion that our own national interests demand some help from us in sustaining in Vietnam the morale, the economic progress, and the military strength necessary to its continued existence in freedom.

On November 17, 1961, Secretary Rusk made note in a news conference of additional aid given:

. . . As President Kennedy *assured* President Diem last October 24th, the United States is determined to help Viet-Nam preserve its independence, protect its people against .the Communist assassins, and build a better growth. In that same letter the President noted that we would be consulting with the Vietnamese Government about what additional measures we might take to assist the Republic of Viet-Nam in its struggle against the Communist aggressors . . . In the meantime there has been an acceleration of deliveries under our mutual defense assistance program. It can be expected that . . . some changes in the type of equipment delivered and in the nature of our training under the military advisory and training program will be required. . . .

On May 11, 1957, a joint statement was issued in Washington by the President of the United States and the President of Vietnam:

President Eisenhower complimented President Ngo Dinh Diem on the remarkable achievements of the Republic of Viet-Nam under the leadership of President Ngo Dinh Diem since he took office in July 1954. It was noted that in less than three years a chaotic situation resulting from years of war had been changed into one of progress and stability . . . internal security had been effectively established . . . A constitution had been promulgated and a national assembly elected . . . President Eisenhower assured President Ngo Dinh Diem of the willingness of the United States *to continue to offer effective assistance* within the constitutional processes of the United States . . . *It was noted with pleasure that the General Assembly of the United Nations by a large majority had found the Republic of Vietnam qualified for membership in the United Nations*, which has been prevented by Soviet opposition. . . . Noting that the Republic of Vietnam is covered by Article IV of the *Southeast Asia Collective Defense Treaty*, President Eisenhower and President Ngo Dinh Diem agreed that aggression or subversion threatening the political independence of the Republic of Vietnam would be considered as endangering peace and stability. . . . [Italics mine.]

Again, Secretary Rusk, in his news conference of May 4, 1961, commented on:

. . . the remarkable success which the Govment of the Republic of Viet-Nam under President Ngo Dinh Diem had achieved in consolidating its political position and in attaining significant economic recovery in the 5 years between 1954 and 1959 . . . the President has authorized an increase in the amount of military assistance, and a number of other measures have been determined upon. Furthermore, the United States has undertaken training and advisory measures which are designed to strengthen both materially and militarily the ability of Viet-Nam armed forces to overcome this increased Communist threat. . . .

On August 2, 1965, Assistant Secretary of State MacArthur gave Senator Fulbright a paper, *The U. S. Commitment to Assist South Vietnam*—which is quoted in *Background Information Relating to Southeast Asia and Vietnam*, June 16, 1966. Senator Fulbright had asked the Department to supply a statement for the record. Beyond referring to material already mentioned here, the paper includes other statements and messages of President Johnson that reaffirm the United States' intention to continue military and economic support of South Vietnam, stating that no one "should doubt that we are in this battle as long as South Vietnam wants our support and needs our assistance to protect its freedom."

It is hard, in light of all this, to argue that President Eisenhower and his successors made no "commitment" to South Vietnam. It seems to me that we are without a doubt committed morally. In his Johns Hopkins address on April 17, 1965, President Johnson put it very well: "We are there because we have a promise to keep." If any nation ever made a promise, we did.

It is quite popular, in this connection, to quote President Kennedy's famous statement that we can only help the people of South Vietnam, and that it is "their war," which they must win. But the concluding remarks made by the same President Kennedy in the same CBS interview, September 2, 1963, in which he made the statement cited, place this statement in a somewhat different perspective. ". . . I don't agree with those who say we should withdraw," said Mr. Kennedy. "That would be a great mistake. That would be a great mistake. I know people don't like Americans to be engaged in this kind of effort. Forty-seven Americans have been killed in combat with the enemy, but this is a very important struggle even though it is far away."

If we did, in fact, by our public utterances, various Presidential messages and communiqués, speeches, and similar media create the *impression* that we felt ourselves morally committed to the peoples of South Vietnam, have we now, or have we had in the recent past, the moral right to rescind, or "welsh" on such a "commitment"? Here we are in an area of diplomatic activity where pious platitudes and righteous breastbeating contribute little but confusion. To build a family a house, move them into it, guarantee them security, then burn the house down in a burst of moral scrupulosity over having made a mistake in building it in the first place—is this morally justified?

The recent tragedy in Hungary serves as a grim reminder of what can happen if the United States even permits the *inference* that it will support rebellion against tyranny. There are more than a few observers convinced that Voice of America broadcasts beamed to Eastern Europe before the fall of Budapest incited Hungarians to revolt because we were strongly implying material, not merely moral, American support. Crushed by Soviet tanks, the Hungarians looked in vain for what they interpreted as promised help. In the same vein, a great many observers are strongly convinced that the VOA broadcasts in Vietnam preceding Diem's assassination were saying that the United States agreed to the "liquidation of the Diem regime," and that United States support would continue "only if such were accomplished." Certainly the reports circulated in the United States of Buddhist self-immolations and the persecution of Buddhists contributed strongly to the American prejudice against the Diem regime and to that regime's ultimate downfall. It is tragically ironic that Diem's assassination occurred almost simultaneously with the submission of the interim report of the United Nations mission that declared him innocent. The United Nations did not seem to think it immediately necessary to publicize the report, even posthumously, though it was published by a Senate committee for the information of the United States Senate.

The question is, have we grown up as a nation sufficiently to live with our mistakes, or do we "withdraw" on the grounds that we didn't really mean what we said, when we see the result of our "commitments"? Is this the great power, the righteous, decent, mighty nation that now wants to say: "We didn't understand the situation. We didn't know what we were getting into. We were only equivocating, trying to bolster up the courage of a desperate people. You should not have taken us at our word"?

Is it any wonder that our possible withdrawal from the conflict is an obvious fear of the Vietnamese people with whom I talked recently? I recall going into Saigon in 1965 and talking with people appalled even then by what they thought the United States role had been in regard to President Diem and his assassination. Just what *is* a commitment?

A French priest who had been in Saigon for years and who was occupied in running a kind of hostelry for students of the University of Saigon was pretty well able to keep his finger on the pulse of feelings. He was particularly intense on this subject. Unlike some of his fellow countrymen, he felt that the American presence in Vietnam today is not only necessary—it is required in justice as compensation for our alleged contributions to Diem's downfall. He maintained, as did others, that only because of profound trust in the present Administration in the United States would the people continue to associate with American officials whom they believed to be responsible for Diem's death.

Many feel U.N. intervention can not be legally justified in terms of the SEATO treaty. Richard Barnet argues the case in his article "The American Responsibility," as reprinted in *The Viet-Nam Reader*, as does I. F. Stone, in *I. F. Stone's Weekly*, August 24, 1964, under the title

"International Law and the Tonkin Bay Incidents." The Lawyers Committee on American Policy Towards Vietnam (whose report appears in the *Congressional Record*, February 25, 1966) and the representatives of the Friends Committee on National Legislation who testified in the hearing on the War in Vietnam, conducted by Congressman Robert Kastenmeier in Wisconsin, share this view. I have read all this material carefully. I recommend it for its thoroughness; it should be read.

A detailed article accusing the United States of intervening illegally in terms of SEATO and of failing to use the United Nations appropriately in relation to the Vietnam conflict is one written by William L. Standard, of the New York bar, in the *American Bar Association Journal*, May 1966. Mr. Standard refers to a statement by thirty-one professors of law that appeared in the *Congressional Record* of January 27, 1966, disagreeing with the American Bar Association findings that our position in Vietnam is legal.

Without reprinting the articles mentioned, it is impossible not to sin by oversimplification. But perhaps I can be forgiven, in the interests of brevity, for listing the major charges as these: that SEATO does not approve of intervention into a situation where "aggression" from without is not definitely proven; and that we have not sincerely used the machinery of the United Nations to settle the dispute. There are various other charges, and corollaries of the two I have given, but these, I think, are the major points.

I believe, however, after careful study of the documents, that we do have the legal right to intervene, in terms of SEATO and the United Nations, and that we have consistently attempted to use the machinery of the United Nations appropriately to try to settle the war.

On April 25, 1964, Secretary Rusk referred to a meeting held in Manila the week before of the eight SEATO members, who considered all aspects of the attack on South Vietnam. "None suggested that the free nations should turn their back and walk—run away from this aggression." Seven of the eight members of SEATO "agreed that it is an 'aggression' and that it is 'directed, supplied and supported by the Communist regime in North Vietnam, in flagrant violation of the Geneva accords of 1954 and 1962.'" "They also agreed," Mr. Rusk continued, "that 'the members of SEATO should remain prepared, if necessary, to take further concrete steps within their respective capabilities of fulfillment of their obligations under the treaty.'"

After President Johnson's message to Congress in August 1964, the Senate and House resolved to take all necessary measures to repel any armed attack against the forces of the United States protecting security in Southeast Asia, and to prevent further aggression in that area.

At least Sections 2 and 3 of this resolution bear reprinting here:

Section 2. The United States regards as vital to its national interest and to world peace the maintenance of international peace and security in southeast Asia. Consonant with the Constitution of the United States and the Charter of the United Nations and in accordance with its obligations under the Southeast Asia Collective Defense Treaty, the United States is, therefore, prepared, as the President determines, to take all necessary steps, including the use of armed force, to assist any member or protocol state of the Southeast Asia Collective

Defense Treaty requesting assistance in defense of its freedom.

South Vietnam is, of course, a protocol state of SEATO.

> Section 3. This resolution shall expire when the President shall determine that the peace and security of the area is reasonably secure, assured by international conditions created by action of the United Nations or otherwise, except that it may be terminated earlier by concurrent resolution of the Congress.

To observe the obvious: Despite the criticism of the legality of our position, as of this writing in March 1968, Congress has yet to terminate its initial resolution.

On August 3, 1965, Secretary Rusk noted in a statement before the House Foreign Affairs Committee that beginning in 1955 Congress has each year approved overall economic and military assistance programs. The continuation of major aid to South Vietnam has been specifically considered.

As far as our efforts at the United Nations go, it is important to note that Hanoi has repeatedly insisted that the Vietnam situation is "none of the United Nations' business."

On August 5, 1964, Adlai Stevenson, U.S. Representative in the U.N. Security Council, presented charges of North Vietnamese attacks to the Security Council. He referred to the Tonkin Gulf incidents (roundly scored by I. F. Stone as trumped-up distortions) and to various acts of sabotage and terrorism perpetrated by the North Vietnamese in South Vietnam. He made it clear that the Tonkin Gulf incidents were only part of a pattern.

A complaint about the coordinated attacks of the Viet Cong on South Vietnamese airbases in Pleiku and Tuy Hoa was issued to the United Nations in a State Department letter of February 7, 1965. The letter informed the President of the United Nations that the governments of South Vietnam and the United States had agreed that it was necessary to take defensive action. The defensive action was then described. The violations of the Geneva Accords of 1954 by North Vietnam were mentioned. The letter then noted with regret that the Hanoi regime, in its statement of August 8, 1964, "explicitly denied the right of the Security Council to examine this problem."

Ambassador Stevenson reported to the U.N. Security Council again on February 27, 1965. Mr. Stevenson cited incidents of aggression by the North. He noted that the National Liberation Front in South Vietnam is an integral part of the governmental machinery of Hanoi. He asked that copies of the report be circulated to the delegations of all member states as a Security Council document.

The State Department issued a statement on March 4, 1965, asserting that there was no doubt that the actions we had taken in Vietnam fall within the constitutional powers of the President of the United States and that these actions were backed up by the Congressional resolution of August 1964. The statement pointed out, as did a second memorandum, of March 8, that the inherent right of individual and collective self-defense as practiced in South Vietnam is clearly recognized in Article 51 of the U.N. Charter.

On March 8, 1965, the State Department issued a memorandum entitled *Legal Basis for United States Action Against North Viet-Nam.*

The specific question this memorandum considers is whether the United States–South Vietnamese actions against military targets in North Vietnam are justified in international law, particularly in light of the U.N. Charter and the 1954 Geneva Accords. It concludes that these actions are fully justified. In regard to the U.N. Charter, the argument is based on Articles 2 and 51.

Article 51 guarantees the right of individual or collective self-defense. In accordance with international law, the individual is free to act *until* the Security Council has taken the measures necessary to maintain international peace and security. Measures taken in self-defense, the article says, must be reported immediately to the Security Council. The United States' position is that North Vietnam's conduct adds up to armed attack, meaning that South Vietnam had the right, under international law, to call upon assistance from the United States, and that the United States had the right to provide the same. No violation of Article 51 occurred, and actions taken were reported immediately to the Security Council. It is important to note that the Security Council took no measures to maintain international peace and security. The United States, therefore, has the right to go on providing assistance.

Article 2 of the Charter prohibits the use of threat or force in any other manner inconsistent with the purposes of the U.N. This is not an absolute prohibition on the use of force. It permits the use of force in a manner consistent with the purposes and principles of the Charter. The actions of the United States and of South Vietnam are defensive in character, and designed to resist armed aggression, hence they are consistent with the purposes and principles of the Charter and specifically with Article 2. Further, as required by Article 51, the United States has reported action taken to the Security Council, as, for example, in the Tonkin Gulf incident. The Security Council did not see fit to take any action to maintain or restore international peace and security in the area. Indeed, North Vietnam refused to participate in the deliberations of the Security Council and explicitly denied the right of the Council to examine this question.

The State Department memorandum on legality points out the frequently forgotten fact that the Geneva Conference of 1954 concerned itself with Laos and Cambodia, as well as with Vietnam. Various provisions relating to Vietnam are applied to these other two states. The use of Laos by North Vietnamese forces for infiltration into South Vietnam is in violation of both the 1954 and the 1962 (Laotian) agreements at Geneva. The memorandum then cites the principle of reciprocity.

At a press conference on July 28, 1965, President Johnson was asked if he would like to see the United Nations move to achieve a settlement in Vietnam. The President replied that he had made it very clear in his San Francisco speech that he hoped the Secretary General would explore every possibility that would lead to a solution of this matter. He referred to a letter he had sent that same day to U Thant. It reiterated the President's hopes that the members of the United Nations, individually and collectively, would use their influence to bring all the governments involved to the negotiating table. He asked the Secretary General to continue his own efforts and repeated that the United States is prepared to enter into negotiations for peaceful settlement without conditions.

On July 30, 1965, Ambassador Goldberg wrote to the President of the Security Council, listing some of the efforts the United States had made to open a path to a peaceful solution. His letter stressed that the United States "stands ready, as in the past, to collaborate unconditionally with members of the Security Council in the search for an acceptable formula to restore peace and security. . . ." Mr.

Goldberg concluded with the hope of the United States Government that the Security Council members would somehow find the means to respond effectively to the challenge raised by the state of affairs in Southeast Asia.

Two additional letters were presented to U Thant by Ambassador Goldberg, expressing hope that U.N. members would do all they could to bring about unconditional discussions and promote peace.

On January 31, 1966, Ambassador Goldberg requested an urgent meeting of the Council to consider the situation in Vietnam. This followed *a thirty-seven day pause* in the bombing of North Vietnam. His request read, in part:

> . . . my Government has concluded that it should now bring this problem with all its implications for peace formally before the Security Council. We are mindful of the discussions over the past months among the members of the Council as to whether a formal meeting could usefully be held in the context of other efforts then in train. We are also aware that it may not be easy for the Council itself, in view of all the obstacles, to take constructive action on this question. We are firmly convinced, however, that in light of its obligations under the Charter to maintain international peace and security and the failure so far of all efforts outside the United Nations to restore peace, the Council should address itself urgently and positively to this situation and exert its most vigorous endeavors and immense prestige to finding a prompt solution to it. . . . In this connection we are mindful of the renewed appeal of His Holiness the Pope only two days ago in which he suggested that "an arbitration of the

United Nations confided to neutral nations might
tomorrow—we would like to hope even today
—resolve this terrible question."

Once again, on September 22, 1966, Ambassador
Goldberg addressed the General Assembly of the U.N.
(see *The New York Times*, September 23, 1966, for the
full text). He said that North Vietnam's actions violated
not only the U.N. Charter, but also General Assembly
resolution 2131, entitled "Declaration on the Inadmissibility
of Intervention in the Domestic Affairs of States and the
Protection of Their Independence and Sovereignty." He
reiterated the United States' willingness to negotiate anywhere at any time, to cease bombing, withdraw troops,
disestablish bases—whatever could be reasonably required
for peace—and stated:

> In this spirit we welcome discussion of this
> question either in the Security Council, where
> the United States itself has raised the matter, or
> here in the General Assembly, and we are fully
> prepared to take part in any such discussion. We
> earnestly solicit the further initiative of any or-
> gan, including the Secretary General, or any
> member of the United Nations whose influence
> can help in this cause.

Early in November of 1967 Ambassador Goldberg
backed Senator Mansfield's proposal to provide the President with a "sense of the Senate" vote urging him to
exert all possible pressure to obtain U.N. action on Vietnam. The Ambassador confessed at that time that his
repeated failures to obtain U.N. action to date were the
source of bitter personal disappointment.

In addition to the arguments of governmental officials, the American Bar Association resolved, in February 1966, that the position of the United States in Vietnam is legal under international law and is in accordance with the Charter of the United Nations and the South-East Asia Treaty. The Bar Association sent its resolution to the chairman of the Foreign Relations Committee of the United States Senate. In May 1966 E. B. Deutsch, of the American Bar Association, presented his closely woven argument in support of this resolution—in an article, "The Legality of the United States Position in Vietnam."

Mr. Deutsch notes that the Lawyers' Committee on American Policy Towards Viet Nam quotes a news release that had been read into the *Congressional Record*. The release said, "there is no evidence that Congress thought or understood that it was declaring war." Mr. Deutsch points out that the debate on Vietnam was so thorough, the questions asked and answered were so clear, the specific statements of Chairman Fulbright combined with the warnings issued by Senator Morse (who dissented to the resolution) were so explicit, that it is extraordinarily difficult to imagine that the Congress did not realize what it was doing. As a matter of fact, Senator Russell later states: "Personally, I would be ashamed to say that I did not realize what I was voting for when I voted for that joint resolution. It is only one page in length. It is clear. It is explicit. It contains a very great grant of power."

Almost two years later, on March 1, 1966, Senator Morse offered an amendment to the proposed military appropriations bill. This gave the Senate an opportunity to repeal the 1964 joint resolution, with its extensive Presidential powers. Furthermore, Senator Morse was extremely lucid about the purpose of his amendment.

Nonetheless, the Senate voted to table it, 92 to 5, and the unamended appropriations bill was carried by a vote of 93 to 2. The vote in the House on the same bill was 392 to 4.

In September 1967, when disagreement about our Vietnam policies had reached a new high, unofficial "polls" were made in Congress to test the feasibility of a new vote on the same subject—the "Tonkin Gulf" resolution. No vote materialized.

Despite Congress' stand, the plea for "instant negotiations" keeps coming up. *The New York Times* (August 17, 1967) announced, "4 Catholic Bishops Urge Negotiations on Vietnam." The article went on to say that these four bishops had announced their endorsement of the national "Negotiations Now" campaign and its program for attempting to end the war in Vietnam. With due respect, one is impelled to ask: What is constructive in their plea? The President, the Secretary of State, the Ambassador to the United Nations have offered repeatedly to negotiate at any time, in any place, with representatives of all parties concerned. The "Negotiations Now" group, according to the *Times* article, adds such imperatives as: stop the bombing of North Vietnam; name a time and place at which our negotiators will appear; reaffirm our offer of a billion-dollar economic program through the United Nations; give vigorous support to internationally supervised free elections.

Those advocating an end to the bombing have to admit, at least, that the President has heard extremely strong arguments presented by proponents of both courses of action—stop, decrease, continue, increase. He has had to make decisions based on a variety of complex variables—military, political, economic, diplomatic. Any human judg-

ment can be wrong. No one has yet proved that an opposite judgment would be right. Some newsmen who have
visited Hanoi have described grave devastation caused by
our bombing; others have described a business-as-usual climate of activity. All high-ranking military men actually engaged in fighting the war have urged a continuance of the
bombing. As Secretary Rusk pointed out on October 16,
1967, in a widely publicized news conference, no one, no
individual, no nation, has yet been able to give any as-
surances whatever that a pause in the bombing or a complete halt would lead to negotiations. On the contrary,
we have had several bitter experiences in the past, with
bombing suspensions leading to immediate North Vietnamese military build-ups and heightened military activity.

The President and the Secretary of State have expressed repeatedly, forcibly, publicly, and through diplomatic channels that one word, one gesture on the part of
Hanoi to indicate that a pause in bombing would lead to
negotiation would be enough to stop the bombing. In those
instances in which Poland and India have notified us that
Hanoi might be ready to listen, we have immediately explored these semiofficial leads. It is said that on one occasion, rather than stopping the bombing while exploring a
lead, we increased it, and "infuriated" Ho Chi Minh. On
this basis, we have been accused of being insincere in our
desire to negotiate. This is absurd. It is naive to think that
even the President of the United States, with all his power
and authority, can "push a button," or pick up a telephone,
and instantaneously stop every bullet from being fired. To
argue that one such incident renders insincere the endless
efforts that have been made to bring about negotiations is
nonsense.

On September 29, 1967, speaking in San Antonio,

Texas, before the National Legislative Conference, the President of the United States addressed this question of "negotiations now."

> I know there are other questions on your minds, and on the minds of many sincere, troubled Americans: "Why not negotiate now?" so many ask me. The answer is that we and our South Vietnamese allies are wholly prepared to negotiate tonight. I am ready to talk with Ho Chi Minh, and other chiefs of state concerned, tomorrow. I am ready to have Secretary Rusk meet with their foreign minister tomorrow. I am ready to send a trusted representative of America to any spot on this earth to talk in public or private with a spokesman of Hanoi.
>
> We have tried twice to have the issue of Vietnam dealt with by the United Nations—and twice Hanoi has refused. Our desire to negotiate peace—through the United Nations or not—has been made very, very clear to Hanoi—directly and many times through third parties. The heart of the matter is this: The United States is willing to stop all aerial and naval bombardment of North Vietnam when we are assured that this will lead promptly to productive discussions. We must assume that, while discussions proceed, North Vietnam would not take advantage of the bombing cessation or limitation. But Hanoi has not accepted any of these proposals.

What am I saying except that the decision to continue bombing has been made and repeated with exceeding care and on the basis of what the President has considered the best advice available? I certainly support the right to disagree with his decision. I do not support the thesis that mere *desire*, however pious and virtuous, to save lives, is a responsible argument to countermand those given the President in favor of continued bombing. The proponents of the "stop the bombing" argument, it seems to me, have offered no basis other than this. Their conjecture that the bombing stiffens the will of the North Vietnamese and prevents negotiations is precisely that—a conjecture. I have heard nothing to "validate" it except the argument that the British resolve to fight back was strengthened by the German bombings of England. The comparison is very dangerous. Can a comparison be validly made at all?

Some say that the United States position is that of the blackmailer. "Talk or we bomb" are the terms of blackmail. I disagree. I think what we are saying is: "You (Hanoi) are aggressors in the South and you have incited insurrection, which you continue to support with men, weapons, supplies, political direction. This is basically why we are bombing you. However, we will stop bombing if you will agree to sit down and talk about some sort of peace. If you don't agree at least to this, why should we stop bombing, since the reasons for our bombing continue?" I can't consider this blackmail. It would be blackmail if the North were doing nothing by way of aggression, and we simply decided we wanted to talk with them. To make them agree to talk, we threaten them with bombing, or actually bomb them. That would be blackmail.

While on the subject, it seems to me that the entire question, to bomb or not to bomb, has become morally cloudy. Many critics of the bombing seem to be saying: "It's morally outrageous, obscene, evil all the way through —and anyway, it's proved ineffective!"

The two are not necessarily related at all. If it is thoroughly evil, then its effectiveness would not make it

morally good. The question of effectiveness, in terms of
military and political or diplomatic strategy would appear
to be one for military, political, diplomatic professionals
to evaluate. Once again, of course, they may be correct or
incorrect. But this has nothing to do with whether or not
the bombing is "intrinsically" immoral. Would the moralists who have been objecting to the bombing as "morally
intolerable" object as strenuously if it had proved dramatically decisive in ending the war?

There is nothing mystical about the United Nations.
It is composed only of member nations. If they agree in
sufficient numbers to a certain action, that action can be
carried out. If a sufficient number disagree in the General
Assembly, or a major power disagrees in the Security
Council, the action cannot be carried out. Even a U.N.
declaration, indictment, or condemnation by itself does not
stop a war.

Requests have been made by the United States, Great
Britain, Hungary, Austria, Norway, Zambia, Iceland, and
Ethopia to have the U.N. act, directly or indirectly, to
end the Vietnam war. Why has the United Nations failed
to act? U Thant is praised highly for insisting that there
can be no negotiations until the bombing is ended. Plaudits
to Mr. Thant—yet it was he who declared in 1965 that he
would not consider it practical to bring the matter of
Vietnam before the Security Council himself. His statement of his reasons, as quoted in *The Viet-Nam Reader*,
is extremely explicit:

> The government of North Viet-Nam has
> all along maintained that the United Nations is
> not competent to deal with the question of Viet-
> Nam, since, in its view, there is already in ex-
> istence an international machinery established in

1954 in Geneva. They have all along maintained that position, and, as you all know, it is a position that is also maintained by the People's Republic of China. As far as the United Nations is concerned, I think the greatest impediment to the discussion of the question of Viet-Nam in one of the principle organs of the United Nations is the fact that more than two parties directly concerned in the question are not members of this organization. I therefore do not see any immediate prospect of a useful discussion in the Security Council. . . .

It is surprising that this statement by U Thant is not widely disseminated. Former Ambassador Kennan's statement made during the Senate hearings, "I personally do not think that the United Nations itself could be useful in writing the terms of any compromise solution to the Vietnam conflict," is not much talked about either.

According to Ambassador Goldberg, the Soviet Union presents the great obstacle to the negotiation of a treaty by the United Nations. On October 7, 1967, Ambassador Goldberg said that the Soviets effectively blocked the Security Council's efforts to deal with the Vietnam question when the United States brought it up in 1966. The Soviets have made it very clear, in response to our own diplomatic probing, that they oppose U.N. action on Vietnam.

On March 27, 1967, a North Vietnamese Foreign Ministry spokesman reiterated North Vietnam's views toward U.N. action. Speaking over Radio Hanoi, he stated, ". . . it is necessary to underline once again the views of the Government of the DRV, which has pointed out that the Viet-Nam problem has no concern with the United

Nations and the·United Nations has absolutely no right to interfere in any way in the Viet-Nam question." This was North Vietnam's reply to U Thant's message to the parties involved in the Vietnam conflict.

During the Senate hearings of 1966, Secretary Rusk was questioned at length by Senator Sparkman on the question of negotiations. Secretary Rusk cited the Soviet Union's veto of a Thailand resolution requesting the Peace Observation Commission to investigate the threat to the governments of Laos and Cambodia caused by the presence of Viet Minh troops in those countries. The question came up again before the Security Council in September 1959. The Security Council dispatched an investigating mission but took no further action. In August 1964, after a United States request, for once the Soviet representative moved that representatives of both Hanoi and Saigon be invited to come to the table. *Hanoi refused to come.*

Mr. Rusk noted that Hanoi sent a delegation to Moscow in late 1965. There was a possibility of a conference on Cambodia and Laos, but "something happened" to the idea after the Moscow meeting disbanded. The conferences were not held, Mr. Rusk says, perhaps because of Peking.

Vietnam Crisis, by Stephen Pan and Daniel Lyons, points out that even if the United Nations determined who the aggressor is in Vietnam, neither the General Assembly nor the Security Council has yet furnished a definition of the term "aggression." Nor has there been a definition of war or of civil war. We maintain that North Vietnam has been an aggressor in South Vietnam. North Vietnam claims that the war in South Vietnam is a war of liberation. Others maintain that it is a civil war. Pan and Lyons give an interesting example of U.N. problems along these lines.

In 1949 the Chinese delegation accused the Soviet

Union of treaty violations in aiding the Chinese Communists to overthrow the Nationalist Government. This
accusation became Item 68, General Assembly agenda,
1949. According to Pan and Lyons, the American delegate
at the Political Committee of the General Assembly considered the war between the Chinese Nationalist Government and the Communists a "civil war," and not a war
of aggression on the part of the Soviet Union. It was not
until three years after China fell to the Communists that
the U.N. General Assembly decided that the Nationalists
were right in accusing the Soviet Union of treaty violations. On February 1, 1952, the General Assembly adopted
a resolution indicting the Soviet Union on this charge.
By 1952, however, with the mainland in Communist hands,
the resolution was purely academic.

The same authors note that on February 26, 1966, the
then President of the Security Council, Akira Matsui, reported that among its fifteen members, the Soviet Union,
France, Mali, and Bulgaria declined to discuss the Vietnam
issue. Although nine members favored a peace effort by
the United Nations, and two expressed no opinion, there
was no immediate hope for a resolution. The representatives of the Soviet Union had even refused acceptance of
a notice sent to them by the President of the Security
Council.

It is ironic to remind ourselves that the first appeal
to the United Nations relative to the Geneva Conference
was made by South Vietnam. It requested that the United
Nations, not the International Control Commission, super-
vise elections!

Vietnam Crisis also discusses Eric Sevareid's famous
story about Secretary of Defense McNamara, who is supposed to have obstructed peace talks with North Vietnam.
Mr. Sevareid reported in August 1965 that Mr. McNamara

opposed a potential meeting between Hanoi and American representatives because such a meeting would demoralize the Saigon Government. The book then looks into Mr. Sevareid's claim, made in *Look* Magazine, November 30, 1965, that, in disagreement with the President's Vietnam policy, Adlai Stevenson planned to resign as Ambassador to the UN.

The charges against Mr. McNamara are denied outright in Department of Defense Press Release No. 809–65, November 15, 1965, in Mr. McNamara's specific words: "There is not one word of truth in the remarks made about me or the position attributed to me in the [Sevareid] article."

As for Mr. Stevenson's position, the Ambassador's Special Assistant, Clayton Fritchey, strongly denied Mr. Sevareid's claim. Mr. Fritchey quotes from a letter written by Mr. Stevenson on December 14, 1965, and now a part of the Stevenson Papers at Princeton University. The letter was a specific response to a group suggesting that Mr. Stevenson resign. Rejecting their suggestion, the Ambassador stated: "I do not believe the policy of retreat in Asia or anywhere else would make any contribution whatsoever to the idea that violence cannot be the formal arbitrator in world affairs."

In further denial of any idea that his father intended to resign, Adlai Stevenson, III, stated in Chicago on December 14, 1965, that his father "on the contrary, intended to restate publicly and firmly his support of our Viet Nam policy in a letter to Paul Goodman of North Stratford, New Jersey." The letter to Mr. Goodman describes Peking aggression against Tibet, India, and the Malays, and infiltration in North Thailand. It goes on to say: "I do not think the idea of Chinese expansionism is so fanciful that the effort to check it is irrational."

I suppose that what I am trying most to say is that behind the repeated references to a "credibility gap" created by the Administration too often lies the implication that the Administration is deliberately deceiving the American people and the world—is, in short, lying about its position.

Secretary Rusk in a press conference on October 12, 1967, made what I consider a particularly valid point about critics of the war—a man may be highly skilled in his own field, but totally unqualified to speak intelligently about matters in Vietnam. He added that some of the problems are far too delicate and serious to be explored appropriately under klieg lights, with the whole world looking on. Finally, the Secretary denied categorically that we were informed by the Soviet government, on the authorization of Hanoi, that if the bombing were stopped there would be a conference between the United States and North Vietnam within three or four weeks. What we need, said the Secretary, is someone able to tell us what would happen if we stopped the bombing. We needn't guess about it, he said, because we have checked it out with Hanoi—and they won't tell us.

The New York Times, in an editorial of October 15, 1967, noted that General Giap, North Vietnam's Defense Minister, called the antiwar movement in the United States today "a valuable mark of sympathy." This is what Secretary Rusk was warning the nation about—the danger of giving other nations the belief that our word about our international commitments is not credible, and that we were willing, as a people, to withdraw from Vietnam.

On top of all this, of course, is the fact that the Viet Cong's National Liberation Front still insists that it is the sole and genuine representative of the South Vietnamese people. Does the "Negotiations Now" group want U.S. officials to appear at a previously designated spot, to await the will of the Viet Cong?

Speaking from the deck of the USS *Enterprise* on November 11, 1967, President Johnson asked that North Vietnam and the United States meet on any neutral ship, in any neutral sea, to discuss peace. He said: "You force us to fight, but you need say but the word for our quarrel to be buried beneath the waves." The President's plea was again rebuffed by Hanoi.

The painfully careful efforts the Administration has made, day by day over the course of month after month, are brushed off as insincere "propaganda." This is not intelligent dissent; this is sheer naïveté—or downright malice, in my opinion.

Early in January 1968, Hanoi announced, in highly ambiguous terms, that talks with the United States "will" take place, under certain conditions. The news media stressed the change in terms—from "could" of one year ago, to "will." A careful analysis revealed ambiguity, as well as an apparent repetition of a condition obviously unacceptable to South Vietnam or the United States—that the NLF alone represents the people of South Vietnam. (It is exceedingly difficult to discern precisely what Hanoi's terms for negotiations are.)

Secretary of State Rusk responded publicly to the Hanoi statements, indicating that cautious but exhaustive consideration would be given them. We would determine precisely what they meant and what the next steps should be. Immediately, however, the critics cried for more positive exploration of the "peace feeler" from Hanoi, suggesting, *a priori*, that the administration was either indifferent to the possibilities or had already determined to reject them.

Finally, in addition to the entire question of halting

the bombing, and negotiating immediately, it would be helpful if the North Vietnamese and the Viet Cong would observe at least the truce periods declared from time to time. For example, their own New Year's "truce" had scarcely begun (January 27, 1968), when they were firing rockets into our Marines in Khe Sanh.

9

THE ELECTION ISSUE AND

THE QUESTION OF CIVIL WAR

*M*ANY CRITICS INSIST THAT WE were completely out of line in supporting and encouraging Diem not to hold the elections in 1956 as promised at the 1954 Geneva Conference.

Paragraph 7 of the Final Declaration of the Geneva Conference, July 21, 1954, reads as follows:

> The Conference declares that, so far as Viet-Nam is concerned, the settlement of political problems, effected on the basis of respect for the principles of independence, unity and territorial integrity, shall permit the Viet-Namese people to enjoy the fundamental freedoms, guaranteed by democratic institutions established as a result of free general elections by secret ballot. In order to ensure that sufficient progress in the restoration of peace has been made, and that all the necessary conditions obtain for free expression of the national will, general elections shall be held in July 1956, under the supervision of an international commission composed of representatives of the Member States of the International Supervisory Commission, referred to in the agreement on the cessation of hostilities. Consultation will be held on this subject between the competent representative authorities of the two zones from 20 July 1955 onwards.

By the nature of our own history as a nation and our specific commitment at Geneva, we are pledged to honor the right of all peoples to self-determination. At Geneva we agreed to "seek to achieve unity through free elections in Vietnam." Yet, when President Diem refused, in 1956, to hold the elections, we encouraged his refusal and supported it. Hence the argument that we intervened illegally in internal affairs and went back on our word.

The Christian Century took this position in an editorial on March 23, 1966. The editorial said that "our man in Saigon," Diem, fully supported by the United States, announced in 1955 that the promised elections would not be held and rejected Hanoi's efforts to hold them. His reason, says *The Christian Century*, was that he knew he was hated by the people he ruled and that Ho Chi Minh would win elections overwhelmingly. The United States knew this, too, says the article.

Peace in Vietnam, by the American Friends Service Committee, puts it this way: Diem made civil war inevitable by refusing to permit the elections Hanoi wanted. His refusal was consistently backed by the United States.

In a "teach-in" on Vietnam policy, as reported in *The Viet-Nam Reader*, George McT. Kahin says that Diem's regime enjoyed several years of grace after Geneva. During this period Ho Chi Minh's followers left it alone. Ho withdrew armies from the South and suspended revolutionary activities there for a considerable period. According to Kahin, these actions were based on the premise that the Geneva Agreements had promised nationwide elections in 1956. Civil war became inevitable when Diem, encouraged by America, refused to permit the elections. By encouraging Diem, we allegedly reneged on the position we had taken in our unilateral declaration.

David Schoenbrun, in his article in *Diplomat*, May

1966, does not accept the theory that free elections were not held because, as Diem insisted, conditions for free elections did not exist. Schoenbrun says perhaps they didn't, but the United States did nothing to bring them about.

But the popular way in which this argument is buttressed is to call upon President Eisenhower as an authority. Richard N. Goodwin is one of many who do this. President Eisenhower, Goodwin says, in his *Triumph or Tragedy*, estimated that "possibly eighty per cent of the population [of all Vietnam] would have voted for the Communist Ho Chi Minh."

George F. Kennan, former Ambassador to Russia, questioned by Senator Morse in the Senate hearings, gives the Eisenhower quotation a bit more loosely. "I don't claim to know a great deal about these realities there, and I go largely on the statement in the book of a respected ex-President, who said that everything he could learn indicated that the election would have gone 90 per cent in favor of the Communist side had it been held at that time."

Senator Morse pursued the same argument, writing in *The Viet-Nam Reader*, by saying, "Undoubtedly, the Viet-Minh under Ho Chi Minh would have won such a free election. President Eisenhower declares in his *Mandate for Change* that all the experts he talked to in that period believed Ho would get at least 80 per cent of the vote."

I would like to examine this "quotation" first, because it is so widely and definitively used as "proof" of why Diem refused to permit the elections, and because it is a classic case of misquoting. The simple fact is that President Eisenhower did *not* say what so many observers quote him as saying.

The precise text is found in Chapter XIV of President Eisenhower's *Mandate for Change:* "I have never talked or corresponded with a person knowledgeable in Indochinese affairs who did not agree that had elections been held\ *as of the time of the fighting,* possibly 80 per cent of the population would have voted for the Communist Ho Chi Minh as their leader *rather than Chief of State Bao Dai.*" (Italics mine.)

In other words, the President specifically referred to the period of the fighting—1953—one year *before* Geneva, when the French and the Viet Minh were still at war, when Bao Dai was in power, well before Diem came to power, and *three years* before 1956, the date of the promised elections.

If it were merely a matter of referring to President Eisenhower's statement vaguely in a parlor debate, little harm would be done. But when a U.S. Senate Committee, politicians, scholars, and journalists who are presumed to be authorities in the field, and who have such an impact on public opinion, refer to the statement as though it provided virtually irrefutable proof that we were guilty of blatant violation of our word as a nation, then such vagueness of reference loses its innocuousness.

Precisely what was Ho Chi Minh's situation in 1956, as time drew near for the proposed elections? There seems to be a widespread impression that a gentle, patient, tolerant Ho was trying to negotiate reasonably with Diem, only to be arbitrarily rejected at every turn.

To take it for granted that Ho would have won a free election hands down is to ignore what was happening in North Vietnam. The thoroughly documented fact is that Ho was facing exceedingly critical problems.

A text called *Primer for Revolt,* written by Truong Chinh, the former Secretary General of the Vietnamese Communist party and Vice-President of North Vietnam, is described by Bernard Fall as "a perfect blueprint for a Communist *coup d'état*."

Professor Fall says that Truong Chinh was the ideal scapegoat when the terroristic "collective-farm" program of North Vietnam backfired in 1956. Late in October of that year, Truong Chinh confessed that he had committed grave errors. He was dismissed as Secretary General of the Party, and Ho took the job himself. General Giap, at the time, felt it was necessary to apologize publicly. Giap declared the need for the "rectification of errors" that followed just in time to subdue, but not prevent, the revolt of the peasants on November 4, 1956. It is estimated that one hundred thousand or more were put to death by the Communists in North Vietnam. Tragically, in terms of world understanding, these events culminated precisely on the date that events in Budapest and the Suez took the spotlight. Even the peasants of Ho's own native province rebelled and had to be subdued by regular troops.

Professor Honey describes Truong Chinh's activities in *Communism in North Vietnam*. Chinh forced the agrarian reform campaign with a brutality and gross disregard for justice that shocked the peasants more than they had been shocked by the war. Hundreds of thousands of obviously guiltless people were put to death with great cruelty, until the infuriated peasants, armed only with farm tools, rebelled. Even the loyalty of the army became questionable, and the entire Communist regime was gravely threatened. Ho rapidly initiated the correction-of-errors campaign, but the people still demanded the punishment of the guilty, so Chinh and several of his colleagues became the scapegoats.

With this in mind, it could be called at least presumptuous to insist that if an election had been held during the latter part of 1955 or early in 1956 the "beloved" Ho would have won.

As a matter of fact, Diem *did* risk an election by plebiscite in South Vietnam in 1955. Three months before, he had announced publicly that he would refuse to cooperate with the North Vietnamese in holding election talks because the Communist tyranny at work in North Vietnam made free elections impossible. In seeking a plebiscite and asking the people to choose between him and Bao Dai, Diem was, in effect, asking the South Vietnamese to approve or disapprove his attitude toward the proposed 1956 elections. By overwhelming majority (98.2 per cent) Diem was chosen by plebiscite. Hence the people specifically indicated that they did not want the 1956 elections. Diem critics consistently maintain that the elections were shamelessly rigged. However, at least elections were held. None was held in North Vietnam. Why not?

Neither Russia nor Red China pressed hard on the election issue in 1956. On the contrary, they registered exceptionally mild protests. The British position was expressed on April 10, 1956, only a few months before the proposed elections. "Her Majesty's Government did not agree that the Government of the Republic of Vietnam were legally obliged to follow this course [open consultation with the Viet Minh for the organization of elections in 1956]."

Ho had been pressured by Russia and Red China during the Geneva Conference to allow free elections, and at that time he undoubtedly took it for granted that South Vietnam would fall into his hands and would be unable to survive on its own. Ironically, when the actual time for the elections came it was North Vietnam that faced the bitter struggle for survival. Even Ho, therefore, seemed to have been less than enthusiastic in pressing for elections.

The accusation that Diem refused to cooperate with pre-election discussions with Ho Chi Minh becomes somewhat ludicrous in the light of North Vietnam's violations of the Geneva Conference. In addition to violations already cited, Chester A. Bain, in *Vietnam: The Roots of Conflict*, points out that while Diem's government permitted free movement to the north on the part of those who wished to return after Geneva, many thousands were prevented from migrating to the south. Some 32,000 petitions were presented to the International Control Commission protesting the Viet Minh's abduction of youths to the north, but the Commission was unable to take effective action. A 1955 agreement to exchange postal cards was sabotaged by the North Vietnamese in typical Communistic fashion. When the cards were delivered to addressees in the north, the recipients suffered various threats and punishments. Those sent to the south carried calls for rebellion and, ironically, Hanoi complained when the latter were not delivered.

The document entitled *The Legality of U.S. Participation in the Defense of Vietnam*, prepared by the office of the legal advisor of the Department of State, states categorically that "South Vietnam was justified in refusing to implement the election provision of the Geneva Accords."

Even if one argues that South Vietnam was bound to the Geneva settlement, it would have been impossible to obtain a free expression of the national will in North Vietnam as required by the settlement. General Giap, in addressing the 10th Congress of the North Communist Party in October 1956, publicly acknowledged that the Communist leaders had been running a police state where executions, terror, and torture were commonplace. An election in such circumstances would have meant turning the country over to the Communists, without consulting the will of the people.

Those who claim that North Vietnam was justified in resuming force when South Vietnam refused to participate in the election program are contradicted by the legal position paper referred to above. It points out that under international law, North Vietnam's recourse lay, not in violence, but in an appeal to the co-chairmen of the Geneva Conference.

J. S. Sebes, in *Viet-Nam: An Enigma*, reminds us that at Geneva Diem had asked that elections be supervised by the United Nations. Sebes also mentions the British diplomatic note of April 1956 pointing out that North Vietnamese regulars had increased from seven to twenty divisions, in violation of the Geneva Agreements. On the basis of those violations, Diem considered the Geneva Agreements, which he had protested vehemently in the first place, null and void.

Senator John F. Kennedy, of Massachusetts, made some interesting remarks in "A Symposium of America's Stake in Vietnam," sponsored by the American Friends of Vietnam, when he presented "a plea that the United States never give its approval to the early nationwide elections called for by the Geneva Agreement of 1954. Neither the United States nor free Vietnam is ever going to be a party to an election obviously stacked and subverted in advance, urged upon us by those who have already broken their own pledges under the agreement they now seek to enforce."

Phillippe Devillers is often cited as one of the foremost French authorities on Vietnam. In *North Vietnam Today*, he notes that China's reply to Diem's refusal to hold the elections was simply to ask that a new conference be held at Geneva. Great Britain and Russia merely agreed to extend the Control Commission's term beyond the period originally fixed (July 20, 1956). North and South Vietnam were asked to advise the co-chairmen of the

Control Commission when they had agreed on a date for consultations and elections.

Every time North Vietnam raised the question during the next few years, both Soviet and Chinese support was very strictly limited. Nor was a single effective move made by any nation of the Bandung group—India, Burma, or Indonesia.

In January 1957 Hanoi must have recognized that its cards had been trumped. The careful propaganda campaign blaming the United States for Diem's refusal to seek "unification" began then, and anti-Americanism became a national binding force.

Is the conflict in Vietnam essentially a civil war, in which we have no right of intervention? Have we branded it a "war of aggression" by North Vietnam, to justify our acts, and have we recently decided that the conflict in Vietnam is merely a phase of Communist aggression, which we must thwart at any cost? These intermeshed accusations indicate that we have distorted the truth and denied a people the right to self-determination through civil war.

In an article, "A Reply to the White Paper," in *I. F. Stone's Weekly*, March 8, 1965, I. F. Stone rejects State Department figures on infiltration and declares that the war in the south is a civil war, not a war of aggression. He says the war is due to Diem's dictatorship, the economic weaknesses under the Diem regime, and intervention on the part of the United States.

Hans J. Morgenthau, writing in the *New York Times Magazine* on April 18, 1965, attacks the same *White Paper* (entitled "Aggression from the North: The Record of North Vietnam's Campaign to Conquer South Vietnam"). Mr. Morgenthau maintains that until the end of

February 1965, the United States considered the conflict in South Vietnam a civil war, aided, but not created, from abroad. Desperate over our losses, however, at that point we allegedly changed the nature of the war, and charged the North with aggression. Our purpose in so doing, he says, was to develop a policy which would enable us to "negotiate from strength." Saying that the overwhelming majority of Viet Cong are South Vietnamese, Mr. Morgenthau claims that Diem polarized the political situation with himself and his family on the one side and the people of South Vietnam, supported by the Viet Cong, on the other—hence laid the ground work for civil war. He considers our holding Hanoi responsible for the Viet Cong absurd.

Senator Morse argues that as far as SEATO members are concerned, there is no proof that armed aggression has taken place. He adds that this must be the reason we have had no substantial help from other nations—the United States is alone in thinking peace and security are threatened by armed aggression. He feels the world has to be skeptical of us when it sees that we have pitted such a massive number of troops against the much smaller number of North Vietnamese we claim have infiltrated to support the Viet Cong.

Both Senators Church and Pell, during the Senate hearings, maintained that the war in the south is basically a civil war. Comparing it to a degree to our own Civil War, they suggest that our intervention could be interpreted by North Vietnam as we would have interpreted intervention by England, had she entered our Civil War on the part of the South.

Father James Sheerin, C.S.P., priest-lawyer, writing in the *Homiletic and Pastoral Review*, in July 1966, says the Administration, claiming that it went into Vietnam to help a beleaguered government repel invasion, is now helping a military clique fight its own people. We have sought a military victory rather than a reasonable political settlement, rejected the moral leadership of the Pope, and deliberately escalated the war by bombing Haiphong, he holds. And he adds that we are engaged in the "first war" that has not had the overwhelming support of the people of the United States.

Innumerable other critics make essentially the same charges.

On the other hand, George A. Carver, Jr., in his article, "The Faceless Viet Cong" in *Foreign Affairs*, April 1966, makes the major point that the current struggle in South Vietnam is the "third act" of a drama that began at least as long ago as 1930, and that, if we are entering the "theater" of Vietnam for the first time at this late date, we are bound to be woefully confused. For Mr. Carver, the drama has one prime actor—Ho Chi Minh, hard-core Communist. To give the substance of his argument, a backward glance must be taken here.

Whatever Vietnamese nationalism erupted in the early thirties and in the periods during and immediately after World War II was undermined by Ho and carefully diverted to the Communist party. Ho and his colleagues are the same men who today, Carver says, direct the Communist state in the north and the insurgency in the south.

Carver states that, besides the networks of cadres the Communists left behind them in the south, with instructions to deny Communist affiliation, at the time of the Geneva Agreement, large numbers of personnel designated to return to the south in the future were taken north, many by coercion. These, in turn, were strongly encouraged, and in many cases directly ordered, to contract marriages in the south, for future use.

By 1958 the Viet Cong constituted a serious threat to political stability in the south, but Hanoi was not satisfied with the pace of progress. In 1959 the Lao Dong Central Committee (the Communist Party), headquartered in Hanoi, issued "Resolution 15," to be used by Viet Cong training cadres in the south. This resolution forecast the entire course of southern insurgency, including the establishment of the National Liberation Front, under the control of the Central Committee of the South Vietnamese *branch* of the Lao Dong Party. In May 1959 the Lao Dong Central Committee declared that "the time has come to struggle heroically and perseveringly to smash the G.V.N. [the government of Vietnam—South Vietnam]."

From that point on, Viet Cong activity increased by leaps and bounds. The Communists secured the corridor along the North Vietnamese border in Laos, and infiltrators began moving down the Ho Chi Minh Trail. In August 1958 Hanoi began broadcasting instructions to the Viet Cong armed forces and village cadres in the south. In February 1960, when Hanoi commented on Viet Cong attacks, it called them "our attacks" and praised the "skill of our commander and the good will of our soldiers."

A conference of "Marxist-Leninist delegates" met in South Vietnam in December 1961 to establish the "People's Revolutionary Party." The party began functioning officially in January 1961 and immediately took control of the National Liberation Front. The People's Revolutionary Party is the southern branch of the Lao Dong—the Communist Party controlled by Hanoi. Carver quotes a Party directive that says: "The People's Revolutionary Party has only the appearance of an independent existence; actually, our party is nothing but the Lao Dong Party of Viet Minh Nam [Viet Minh Communist Party] unified from north to south under the direction of the central executive committee of the party, the chief of which is President Ho."

Mr. Carver states that the Viet Cong military establishment, as of 1966, had more than 90,000 paramilitary personnel and part-time guerrillas. These ethnic southerners were drawn from the some 75,000 Viet Minh troops and supporters taken north at the time of the Geneva Conference and trained for return to the south. They are the squad leaders, platoon leaders, political officers, unit commanders, village, district, and provincial and regional chiefs who built the Viet Cong's political apparatus. Earlier arrivals in this group had had at least five years of indoctrination and training in North Vietnam before returning south; later arrivals had as long as a decade of such training. In view of this it is hard to argue that since so many of the Viet Cong are South Vietnamese, the revolt is internal and represents civil war.

The "facelessness" of the Viet Cong is unique—the shadowy nature of the higher-level Viet Cong leadership probably indicates the tightness of control by North Vietnam, where it is important to assure that no strong hero figures arise in the south who might become too independent. This point is noted by Swearingen and Rolf in their *Communism in Vietnam*.

Anthony Eden pointed out in 1966 that while the National Liberation Front may have its own following and momentum, if it tried to be independent of Peking or Hanoi it would not get very far. Local resources and captured weapons would be insufficient for continuing the fight indefinitely.

Rowland Evans and Robert Novak, writing in the *Washington Post* on October 12, 1967, refer to what they call an "extraordinary interview." United States officials interrogated a captured official of the Communist Party of South Vietnam (once the People's Revolutionary Party). According to the captive, no major decision of any type (excluding local military tactics) can be made by the Viet Cong, or National Liberation Front, without permission from Hanoi. In other words, the NLF is totally barred from independent action in any broad sense. All leaders of political cadres at Viet Cong battalion level and above are returnees—southerners who went north in 1954 and returned in the early 1960's. Messrs. Evans and Novak describe the NLF as "a wholly owned subsidiary."

In his *Viet-Nam: An Enigma,* J. S. Sebes gives a scholarly account of the background of current events in Vietnam. He agrees with Mr. Carver in saying that many of the Viet Cong cadres are "returnees" who had originally been taken north; many are southerners who have been terrorized into joining the Viet Cong; many are northerners. He, too, explores the development of the National Liberation Front and the People's Revolutionary Party and has no doubt that this is a war of aggression.

However, is it necessary to look farther than the Report of the International Control Commission for evidence of "aggression"?

The present administration is accused of being unable to prove satisfactorily its allegations of aggression on the part of North Vietnam or that SEATO obligations justify our intervention. The administration is also charged with using Vietnam as a testing-ground for Communist "wars of liberation" on the basis that we must stop Communist aggression and expansionism here and now.

What is, in fact, the history of our national position on this issue?

Former President Eisenhower was in Paris in command of NATO when the Indochina affair came to his attention early in 1951. NATO needed more French support, but French forces were being drained in Indochina. General Eisenhower proposed that the French unequivocally pledge the right of Indochina to independence and self-determination. He asked France to announce publicly to the NATO associated states that the war was not an effort to retain French control over Indochina, but was a clear case of freedom's defense against Communist aggression. General Eisenhower argued that that would make it feasible for France's allies to enter the war. However, France persisted—virtually until Dien Bien Phu, in treating the Indochina situation as a "family affair," thereby precluding the possibility, Mr. Eisenhower says, of help from other free nations. Even when the French finally did ask for military intervention, they did not request it on the basis of defending freedom and international peace. They asked for American military help, to be used under the French commanders. To this, President Eisenhower objected strongly.

Along with other accusations, the present administration is said to have violated American "tradition" in committing ground forces to Asia. The question of intervention in Indochina was raised again in January 1954, when Dien Bien Phu began to become a serious matter. Mr. Eisenhower, by then President, felt that there were enough ground forces in Indochina. He, therefore, stated that "at that moment" he could not see the value of committing U.S. ground forces to Southeast Asia. This can hardly be construed as permanent exclusion of the very idea, on "traditional" grounds. If any argument about our involvement in Vietnam seems contradictory to me, it is the idea that President Eisenhower was indomitably opposed to our ever getting into a land war in Indochina under any circumstances. As his memoirs show, he had several reasons for not doing so, but these were apart from opposition to the idea as such.

In March-April of 1954, a new question arose. Suppose the Chinese Communists attacked French positions with aircraft? What would the United States do? President Eisenhower said that while he would not attempt to answer that question, if we did send land, sea or air forces under our own flag, we would consider success essential.

The possibility of employing our ground forces in Indochina persisted. President Eisenhower feared that if the French were defeated, a great many people would end up under Communist rule. But the French remained convinced that only they could run the military operations. Mr. Eisenhower says he made it clear that he would never let our ground troops go there as "mere reinforcements" for French units, "to be used only as they saw fit."

Various critics give us their interpretations of Mr. Eisenhower's position on intervention and stress that the President was opposed to unilateral intervention as such, and to acting except in union with Congress. But I don't think this is a proper interpretation of Mr. Eisenhower's *total* position, as expressed in his text. The President consistently appears to have opted *for*, not against, U.S. intervention, but wanted combined action with other nations to avoid our being accused of colonialism. He is explicit about this. "While we recognized that the burden of the operation (combined forces intervention) would fall on the United States, the token forces supplied by these other nations, as in Korea, would lend real moral standing to a venture that otherwise could be made to appear as a brutal example of imperialism," he states in *Mandate for Change*.

In regard to Congress, while he frequently alludes to the desirability of Congressional assent, Mr. Eisenhower also made it clear that he would veto a proposed rider to an appropriations bill, limiting Presidential authority to engage troops. The bill was not passed.

While President Eisenhower says he would have wanted Congressional authorization, before intervening militarily, he apparently knew that Congress would be satisfied with a "moral" unity if token forces from other nations supported a coalition move (by free nations of Southeast Asia, the Philippines, and the British Commonwealth). Congressional support, however, would also demand, he points out, French agreement not to withdraw their forces from the war if we intervened.

On April 16, 1954, Vice-President Nixon gave an address to the American Society of Newspaper Editors. Mr. Nixon said that ". . . if to avoid further Communist expansion in Asia and Indochina, we must take the risk now of putting our boys in, I think the Executive has to take the politically unpopular decision and do it." In other words, no matter what coloring may now be put on Mr. Eisenhower's never having bound us to commit large ground forces during his regime, it is obvious that he wrestled with the possibility many times and forebore, not because of a tradition of not landing troops in Asia but for specific reasons in each specific circumstance.

Mr. Eisenhower's preoccupation with the problem of Communist expansion, vis-à-vis the Vietnam war, is reflected time after time in the text of his book. He says that the conflict is of utmost importance to the major powers because the Viet Minh was inspired and led by Communist elements.

And he points out that the loss of all Vietnam, together with Laos and Cambodia, would have resulted in the Communist enslavement of millions and that Thailand would have been exposed to infiltration and attack.

His letter of April 4, 1954, to Prime Minister Churchill, which requests support for a regional grouping of nations, expresses his anxieties explicitly by stating that if Indochina should fall to the Communists, the ultimate effect for Great Britain and the United States, in terms of global strategy, would be disastrous: ". . . the imposition on Southeast Asia of the political system of Communist Russia and its Communist ally by whatever means, would be a grave threat to the whole free community . . . in our view this possibility should now be met by united action and not passively accepted . . ." This is the basis for his proposal of a coalition for "the checking of Communist expansion in the area."

While recognizing the tragedies of the Indochinese conflict, Mr. Eisenhower maintains that much good came of it, including the fact that the free nations of Southeast Asia were alerted to the dangers of international Communism.

Of the Geneva Conference, he says: "It paved the way for a system of true cooperation [between the Western powers and the nations of Southeast Asia] . . . in the never-ending struggle to stem the tide of Communist expansionism."

Who, then, conceived the idea that the present administration has "changed the nature of the war"?

Mr. Eisenhower makes one matter crystal clear. He never suggests that the Viet Minh were pure nationalists or that the war in Indochina was a civil war. He indicates that from at least as early as 1951 the United States was concerned with Communism—Communism as illustrated by the Viet Minh and embodied in the person of Ho Chi Minh and as shown in the aspirations of Soviet Russia and Red China. This is not to say that Mr. Eisenhower advocated "using" the people of Vietnam to check the advance of Communism. On the contrary, Mr. Eisenhower recognized that if Communism went unchecked, it would engulf Vietnam and all of Southeast Asia.

Finally and unmistakably, these words from *Mandate for Change* illustrate his point: "If I may refer again to history; we failed to halt Hirohito, Mussolini and Hitler by not acting in unity and in time. That marked the beginning of many years of stark tragedy and desperate peril. May it not be that our nations have learned something from that lesson?"

10

SOME MORAL COMPLEXITIES:
COMMUNIST EXPANSION,
THE ENCLAVE THEORY

THE QUESTION ABOUT COM-
munist expansionism is frequently complicated by the introduction of further objections. Are we, for instance, obsessed with the "domino" theory? Are we clinging to an
archaic belief in a "monolithic" Communism and using
South Vietnam to get at Red China here and now?
("What right have we," it is asked, "to make Vietnam
suffer in order to avoid our suffering in Seattle?")

I find it difficult to understand any of these arguments and especially difficult to understand how we can
be validly accused of using South Vietnam as a sacrificial
lamb, so this might be a good issue to consider first.

Successive South Vietnamese governments have requested our assistance and our presence. The present government is free, by direct action on its own or by plebiscite, to ask us to leave or to desist in our military activities. They have expressed anxiety over the possibility that
we *might* leave. There is an old Latin maxim of moral
law, "*Scienti et consentienti, non fit iniuria*"—when someone knows what you're doing and consents to it, he is
not being treated unjustly.

Since the Saigon government is so often called the
puppet of the United States, presumably if the "people"

had their way we would be asked to leave and the war would end almost immediately. On October 15, 1965, the Viet Cong called for a general strike to demonstrate their popular support. It was a complete failure—"business as usual" was the order of the day. From the beginning of the "Chieu Hoi" (open arms) program in 1963, more than 60,000 Viet Cong have defected. In a survey conducted in Vietnam by a firm under contract to the Columbia Broadcasting System, 1,500 Vietnamese were asked if they wanted the NLF to participate in the government when the war ends. Six per cent said *yes*, seventy-three per cent said *no*. Five per cent blamed the continuation of the war on the United States and Saigon governments, sixty-two per cent blamed it on the Viet Cong, North Vietnam, and Red China. Those questioned were selected at random in the five largest cities and in fifty-five hamlets in eleven provinces.

None of these events would seem to suggest widespread popular dissatisfaction with the American presence. Refusal to support the Viet Cong in areas where they were once all powerful, combined with the flow of more than 1,000,000 refugees away from Viet-Cong-held areas in the south since 1960, would suggest the opposite. Moreover, I have never been given the impression by Vietnamese people that *they* think we are using them. Really, they should know.

What of the "domino" theory? If this means an automatic, chain reaction, in accordance with which every country must fall to Communism if its next-door neighbor falls, then, of course, the theory is fallacious. But if it means referring to the increased difficulty and pressure—political, military, economic—a nation experiences in holding out against Communist aggression if its neighbor has succumbed, then it has validity. Opportunities for infiltration, economic blockades, amassing troops along borders, ease of air strikes—all these increase rather obviously in proportion to proximity. Aggression unleashed, on the prowl, will devour every nation weak or indifferent enough to be readily devoured.

The strategy of fighting a "war once removed," that is, of using a third nation to "get at" one's actual target nation, is, it seems to me, a long-standing practice of Communists. Both General Giap, Defense Minister of North Vietnam, and Lin Piao, Defense Minister of Red China, have been forthright in declaring the United States as the ultimate target for Communism, with South Vietnam simply a proving ground.

But doesn't our real blindness lie in our obsession with Communism and our naive belief that Communism is still a monolith? And aren't we, in fact, trying to provoke war with Red China before she develops greater nuclear strength?

I, for one, have come very much to fear what I consider excessive optimism in stressing the fact that Communism is no longer monolithic. It has become exceedingly popular to accuse the Administration of being obsessed with the fear of monolithic Communism. But monolithic Communism, we are told, is no more. Witness the split between Soviet Russia and Red China. Observe the diversities in the Communism of Yugoslavia, Albania, Poland, and East Germany. Recognize the spirit of nationalism pervading and dominating the Communism of individual, autonomous nations, like North Vietnam.

It seems to me that such demonstrations miss the point and lead to complacency. I do not find in Administration policy any evidence of obsessive concern with Communism as a monolithic organization. The concern is with Communist aggression. Would it matter, basically, whether Communist East Germany vanquished West Germany and subjected it to Communist rule, acting strictly on its own, or whether it did so by direction of Soviet Russia? The United States has expressed much less anxiety about ideological unity among Communist nations than about a Communist state's inviting and supporting a "war of liberation" in a non-Communist state whose people have no desire to be "liberated" into a condition of subjection to a Communist government. In terms of here-and-now aggression, it makes little difference whether the nation inciting rebellion is Russia, Red China, or Cuba, or whether or not these nations are in ideological sympathy with one another.

Regardless of modifications—nationalistic or other—in the Communism of various nations, it has yet to be proved that Communism in itself is not aggressive and does not rob men of basic freedoms. To argue that, left to itself, Communism eventually loses its Lenin-Stalin characteristics, becomes enchanted by capitalism, and "softens" its international policies, is simply to argue that once Communism is no longer communistic, it need not be feared.

In Southeast Asia, we are confronting the type of force that made the question of "monolithic—nonmonolithic" Communism purely academic when Soviet tanks rumbled into Budapest to crush the revolt of the nationalists who had dared for a day to believe that their country was truly autonomous!

On the other hand, the tragedy in this "autonomous" communistic country called Hungary warns us, perhaps, not to be too smug in brushing off the entire idea of a world-wide Communist conspiracy as a quaint and archaic superstition. It has not been that long since President Eisenhower, the year before he left office, stated:

Strategically, South Vietnam's capture by the Communists would bring their power several hundred miles into a hitherto free region. The remaining countries in Southeast Asia would be menaced by a great flanking movement. The freedom of 12 million people [today it is 17 million people] would be lost immediately, and that of 150 million in adjacent areas [now 200 million] would be seriously endangered. The loss of South Vietnam would set in motion a crumbling process that could, as it progressed, have grave consequences for us and for freedom . . .

In 1965 Lin Piao, the Vice-Chairman of the Chinese Central Communist Party and National Defense Minister, wrote a document that has been justifiably referred to as a Chinese Communist *Mein Kampf*. *Long Live the Victory of the People's War* is the title of this remarkably candid work. Says Lin Piao:

Just as Communism in China succeeded by capturing the countryside and then encircling and defeating the cities, so the global Communist movement will ultimately succeed first by capturing Asia, Africa, and Latin America, thereby encircling North America and Western Europe, and then by finally and decisively defeating the United States and its Western Allies . . . We'll win Asia, Africa, and Latin America through wars of national liberation . . . And the United States and its Western Allies will be surrounded. They will be encircled, and they will be overwhelmed . . . Vietnam is now the focus of the revolutionary movement against the United

States, and no matter what action America may take, in Vietnam, the Communist Chinese determination is unshakeable to drive the United States out."

Tan Sri Ong Yoke-Lin, the Malaysian Ambassador to the United States, takes this document very seriously. United States withdrawal from South Vietnam at present, he says, would put Red China well on the road to accomplishing Phase One of Lin Piao's plan—the domination of Asia. The only country in the world with the will and power to stop Red China's expansionist march, the Ambassador says, is the United States.

Secretary of State Rusk's news conference of October 12, 1967, was widely interpreted as an indication that our policy was shifting emphasis. The defense of South Vietnam, in this view, was becoming secondary to our own self-interest in checking Communist expansion. I, personally, saw no new emphasis in Mr. Rusk's remarks. President Eisenhower had been extremely forthright in his efforts to develop an alliance to prevent Communist expansion. This was behind the creation of SEATO. In 1953 and 1954, on several occasions, Secretary of State Dulles had made himself clear on the subject. Stating that the United States had no desire for war with Communist China (we would have been justified in carrying out a war based on Chinese aggression in Korea, had that been our desire; instead we concluded a Korean armistice with Communist China), he nonetheless made it clear that should Red China pursue a policy of aggression in Indochina or elsewhere, it would be a different matter. Overt military Chinese Communist aggression in relation to the Pacific or Southeast Asia area would threaten island and peninsular positions that are vital to the security of the United States and its allies. We would meet such a threat.

Few statements could have been stronger than that of the then Senator John F. Kennedy, quoted in *New Guard* of February 1966: "Viet Nam represents the cornerstone of the Free World in Southeast Asia, the keystone to the arch, the finger in the dike. Burma, Thailand, India, Japan, the Philippines and obviously Laos and Cambodia are among those whose security would be threatened if the red tide of communism overflowed into Viet Nam."

In a major policy address at Johns Hopkins University, on April 7, 1965, President Johnson reiterated his concern over "the deepening shadow of Communist China." This concern, in one form or another, has been expressed repeatedly in Presidential and State Department communiqués. The repeated promises that we do *not* want war with Communist China; that we do *not* want to destroy Hanoi, or the integrity of any Communist country; but that we *do* want to resist aggression, and will, is always within the context of these communiqués. The President made this forcefully clear once again in the *Declaration of Peace and Progress in Asia and the Pacific* issued in Manila, October 1966. "We must seek reconciliation and peace throughout Asia. We do not threaten the sovereignty of territorial integrity of our neighbors, whatever their ideological alignment. We ask only that this be reciprocated."

Nothing in the effort to check the spread of Communist aggression, it seems to me, in any way subordinates our effort in behalf of South Vietnam. Our motives remain what they have been from the outset: defense of a nation that asked for our help, defense against aggression in Southeast Asia, resistance to Communist aggression throughout the world, our own justifiable self-interest.

President Johnson, addressing the National Legislative Conference in San Antonio in September 1967, quoted remarks made by President Kennedy in November 1961: "We are neither warmongers nor appeasers, neither hard nor soft. We are Americans determined to defend the frontiers of freedom by an honorable peace if peace is possible but by arms if arms are used against us."

I do not believe that we are in Vietnam for any *single* reason, any more than I believe that the morality of the conflict can be defined in any simplistic terms. It is popular for critics to seize upon single issues and to accuse the United States of ambiguities. Today, it is charged, we offer the SEATO treaty as our "alibi" for involvement in Vietnam. Yesterday it was to honor a commitment made by President Eisenhower. At another time it is to contain an aggressive Red China. Next week it will be something else. The fact is, they say, we don't really know why we are there. We blundered and now must justify our blunder with whatever excuses the public will buy. Thus the critics.

I repeat that even a superficial reading of official documents dating back to at least 1950 would adequately answer these charges. The reasons are complex and extraordinarily varied but I think they have been stated with sufficient clarity—which is not the same as simplicity—and have been consistent through the years. People who would hardly expect a one-sentence explanation, in one-syllable words, of the theory of relativity frequently demand a "quick and dirty" explanation of what they consider the "dirty little jungle war" in Vietnam.

Finally, in this entire issue of national objectives vis-à-vis Communist aggression, I think we are too apologetic about the term "self-interest." It has somehow fallen into disrepute. In an address at Amherst College, on December 9, 1964, former Secretary of State Dean Acheson observed that if our effort to oppose those nations who brutally threaten the independence of others serves to make our own independence secure as well, that effort is certainly no less admirable. Amidst moral platitudes, this may sound unidealistic and pragmatic. To me it makes sense. I remember that when His Holiness Pope Paul VI issued his Encyclical on Peace (Rome, September 19, 1966), a number of moralists quoted, and are still quoting, with great enthusiasm, his poignant plea: "We cry . . . in God's name to stop . . ." But they seem to pay little heed to the immediately subsequent statement in the same encyclical: "But this peace must rest on justice and the liberty of mankind, and take into account the rights of individuals and communities, otherwise it will be shifting and unstable."

Critics say that our only real interest in Vietnam is to get at Red China and that we have deliberately blocked potential negotiations and deliberately continued to escalate the war. The implication is that we don't want to end the conflict in Vietnam until we have brought Red China to her knees.

Once again, it is difficult, if not impossible, to discuss any of the issues in isolation; they are too intimately associated with various other moral issues. Hence, I hope I shall be forgiven for touching upon other issues, in passing, and that my doing so will not strain logical sequence too gravely.

Oversimplification accounts for a great deal of confusion of issues, as seen in the frequent use of various catch words couched in high-sounding moral contexts. We have come to use the words "escalate" and "de-escalate," for example, as criteria of the noble and the ignoble. One who "escalates" the war is evil. The good cry for "de-escalation." But who defines the terms? What in the world do they really mean? In all our bombing, for example, we have killed far fewer civilians than in any previous war in which bombing was carried out. Hence, I would say there has been a "de-escalation" in the killing of civilians. But we have dropped more bombs than ever before. Therefore, paradoxically, I would say there has been an "escalation" in bombing. We have been criticized for not demanding that the South Vietnamese do more of the fighting. But one of the reasons given for this is the fear—justifiable or not—that South Vietnamese pilots might not be nearly so discriminating as Americans, if flying over North Vietnam, or close to Red China, with bomb loads. So we don't use them under these circumstances, say some of our authorities, because we must guard against "escalation."

Father John Sheerin illustrates an approach that seems to me a moral oversimplification in his repeated references to the horrors of the war. For example, on August 18, 1967, various Catholic newspapers carried his comments about U Thant's address on the subject of "The United Nations and the Human Factor." U Thant noted that we should think of the Vietnam conflict in terms of the human beings victimized by the war rather than in terms of democracy and Communism. Father Sheerin lauds this approach and then talks about the hundreds of thousands who have been killed in wars in the name of ideologies.

What does this really mean?

Time and again the Administration has talked in terms of people. In South Vietnam today people are being murdered. Our forces in Vietnam are fighting people. But the people who started the war and who are determined to continue it are people impassioned by an ideology.

Father Sheerin says it is foolish to speak about war as a protection against Communism. Of course it is, if we pretend that a "shooting war" protects us against a philosophy. But who says anything like this? Not the Administration; not our field commanders. Why have we offered to pour millions into a Mekong Delta project? Why have we supported the AID program, which through the years has cost billions in Asia? We know that poverty, hatred, corruption, oppression, ignorance, superstition, hunger, disease—provide carrion for Communism to prey upon. So we try to fight another war in the classroom and hospital building and in the fields. No one, I suspect, feels that we are doing enough in this area. But we can't do it under hostile fire. We can't do it until we silence the guns that Mao Tse-tung has so bluntly stated are indispensable to political power throughout the world. To say that war is no protection against Communism is, I feel, a cliché. The weapons of war are being used against those Communists who terrorize those peoples who choose not to live under a Communist regime.

Father Sheerin, in the same context, reminds us of the lesson to be learned from the death of the early Christian marytrs: you cannot kill an idea, or a philosophy, or an ideology. But why did the martyrs die? Because they believed in certain ideas, in an "ideology," if you will, which taught them, "Greater love has no man than this, that he lay down his life for his friends."

If our massive (but still, extremely discriminative) use of force shortens the war and reduces the number killed, is this escalation or de-escalation? Would it assuage moral sensitivities if more people were killed—but quietly, without fuss, and over a long period of time?

Some critics favor withdrawal into "enclaves" as a means of "de-escalating." Did the French escalate or de-escalate when they decided to establish themselves in a fortress at Dien Bien Phu? In a matter of weeks they lost

20,000 men. The Viet Minh losses will probably never be known with accuracy, but by the very nature of the assault their losses, too, must have been frightful.

Let us examine the enclave theory from a moral viewpoint and, at the same time, look at a question that bothers many people: "Why aren't we winning the war faster, since we have superior force? How long will it take?"

I think that inherent in the question and in the entire "enclave" theory is a misunderstanding about the nature of protracted conflict, in general, and the Viet Cong method of conflict, in particular. We tend, it seems to me, to make a great deal of intellectual understanding of the theory of protracted conflict, but I'm not sure we are really convinced that it is the practice of Communist warfare. I'm not even sure we recognize it when we see it in action. As I said before, General Vo Nguyen Giap's *People's War, People's Army* is a perfect blueprint of the war in Vietnam. It is must reading to understand the nature of the fighting today, the ever-shifting Communist tactics and their long-range strategy.

For an understanding of the political phases of protracted conflict, however, an even more important work is that of Truong Chinh, *Primer for Revolt: The Communist Takeover in Viet-Nam.* Chinh's uses of protracted conflict politically to keep the French-Viet Minh struggle from coming before the United Nations are instructive; they can provide considerable insight into Ho Chi Minh's tactics in his insistence that the current conflict is "none of the U.N.'s business." Chinh takes to task those who seek U.N. intervention and calls this "inimical to a long war of resistance."

This is the same Truong Chinh, by the way, who initiated the campaign of terror in the mid-1950's in North Vietnam, which resulted in the condemnation and execution of at least a hundred thousand people. Part of his strategy, as noted by P. J. Honey in *North Vietnam Today*, was to bind the entire population to the Communist regime by making everyone participate in the atrocities of the people's courts. Afterward, everybody shared the guilt and the blame.

James E. Dougherty, in *Morality and Modern Warfare*, describes the strategy of protracted conflict. It is a strategy marked by a constant shifting of tactics, prescribing the gradual defeat of the West over a relatively long period, by piecemeal conquests, mixing diplomatic reverses with violence, economic and social penetrations, and psychological manipulations. It always falls short of provoking the West into using atomic weapons.

A primary characteristic of protracted conflict is the belief in *time* as a "fourth dimension." Giap has observed repeatedly that we Americans are an impatient people, not geared to a long war. Should we withdraw into enclaves and give up the offensive, we would very soon withdraw altogether—as did the French.

In 1958 a top Party leader in Hanoi went south to survey the situation and draw up plans for the future. His plans stress *time*,—recognition of the need for a long, drawn-out struggle.

Suppose we did withdraw into enclaves. What tactics of protracted conflict would go into play? First, in my opinion, there would be the retaliatory slaughter of those who had cooperated with us before our withdrawal into enclaves, including the refugees. These are the people to whom we promised security if they would cooperate, and reveal Viet Cong.

Second, virtually everything we have done to secure rivers and streams—extremely important to Viet Cong transportation—would be lost. Viet Cong could again prey, maraud, and terrorize at will. In *time*, hopefully, stability will be achieved by South Vietnamese forces themselves. But the time is not yet. Moreover, when North Vietnam stops supporting the Viet Cong, the latter will not be able to continue as a major military force. But if we withdraw into enclaves, Viet Cong supplies and logistic support could be readily increased, and North Vietnamese troops could pour into South Vietnam virtually unchecked.

One aspect of the war that is frequently overlooked is the morality of Viet Cong tactics. In line with Communist morality, they use methods that are totally unacceptable to us. This is a major reason why a handful of guerrillas, using terroristic tactics, can be subdued and eventually routed out only by a large number of organized, legitimate forces. Often the term "counter-guerrilla warfare" is misunderstood. We can train forces to become experts in such guerrilla tactics as silent ambushes, secret patrols of rivers and jungles, living for long periods on little food and in a primitive way. We cannot validly train our forces in Viet Cong morality—and it is in his moral evaluations that the Viet Cong compensates for inferiority of numbers. A moral code that approves any tactic found expedient gives a military or paramilitary force the same advantage enjoyed by the thug, the bank robber, the paid murderer, the member of the underground criminal syndicate.

For example, during my time in South Vietnam, on May 5, 1965, in the mountains near the Cambodian border, the Viet Cong road-blocked Route 14 and stopped two buses. Sixteen civilian passengers were led into the forest, where they were forced to lie down and then were shot to death. Senseless? Not in the context of terrorism—as a warning that the Viet Cong intend to rule at all costs and are capable of controlling lives at will.

The story of Viet Cong terror at Dak Son in early December 1967 is even more blood-curdling. In this Montagnard village some seventy miles northeast of Saigon, again near the Cambodian border, almost two hundred villagers were slaughtered, and some sixty huts were burned to the ground. The reason for the slaughter of these simple, primitive people was itself simple and primitive. The Montagnards had already fled from the Viet Cong, and now refused to return to the jungles as beasts of burden—"helpers" in the Viet Cong cause.

The destruction of Dak Son was by no means senseless in Viet Cong terms. It was a warning to every other Montagnard village: "Join with us, or be destroyed."

This has constituted, and hopefully will always constitute, a critical problem for legitimate military forces and particularly for U.S. servicemen. There is unquestionably a "national conscience," which rejects any theory that the end always justifies the means.

There is still much anguish over the bombing of Hiroshima, even though grave deliberation and an agonized weighing of moral values preceded the decision. It would be exceedingly difficult to convince the American public at large that the needs of counter-guerrilla warfare require American servicemen to adopt a moral code of complete expediency: to terrorize, decapitate, pillage, rape, torture, murder. The very sight of an American Marine setting fire to a Vietnamese thatched-roof hut, using a cigarette lighter, was enough to arouse storms of protest on the part of television viewers, even though, in the specific situation, the act was not one of brutality or terrorism at all.

Portions of Robin Moore's book *The Green Berets* chilled many an American reader by creating a feeling that our own Special Forces use tactics similar to those of the Viet Cong when it seems expedient. The American theory of a just war emphasizes that the American "national conscience" scrutinizes not only the question of war itself, but the means used to wage a war. This is a point stressed in *The Just War* by Robert W. Tucker. If our moral judgments have been erroneous from time to time in evaluating a particular means, it does not indicate that we are not concerned with the moral dimensions of the means.

Paradoxically, then, the requirement for substantially larger forces than those of the Viet Cong and the necessity to stay on the move, depriving the guerrillas of easy access to food, shelter and weapons, is at least partially imposed by what we would consider the immorality of the tactics of the Viet Cong themselves. The enclave theory, it seems to me, is morally unrealistic.

The same holds true, I believe, for any approach toward peace that ignores the doctrine and practice of protracted conflict. This includes efforts to negotiate that ignore the maxim that rarely has anything substantial been settled at the negotiating table which has not been settled on the battlefield.

In the Korean war 95,000 Americans were killed or wounded during the period of negotiation alone. In his penetrating text *How Communists Negotiate*, Admiral Turner Joy describes the manner in which the Communists turned the negotiating tents at Kaesong and Panmunjom into highly successful battlefields. In a chapter entitled "From This Thorn, These Wounds, These Warnings," Admiral Joy, who attempted to negotiate for us for so many weary months in Korea, pleads that we never again do what we did there. He strenuously urges that we not accept the first armistice feeler and that we also not relax the pressure on the enemy when he begins exploring for an end to hostilities. Finally, he warns us against letting the Com-

munists determine the time and the place for the negotiations. In brief, Admiral Joy, having witnessed the continuance of American casualties in frightening numbers
during the Korean negotiations, begs that we *not* do, under
any circumstances, what many who urge immediate negotiations want done.

In my opinion, the words of Pope Paul VI in his
Christmas message on peace in 1967 are vitally applicable
to the questions of negotiations:

> A warning must be kept in mind. Peace can-
> not be based on a false rhetoric of words which
> are welcomed because they answer to the deep,
> genuine aspirations of humanity, but which can
> also serve and unfortunately have sometimes
> served, to hide the lack of true spirit and of real
> intentions for peace, if not indeed to mask senti-
> ments and actions of oppression and party inter-
> ests.

> Nor can one rightly speak of peace where
> no recognition or respect is given to its solid
> foundations: namely, sincerity, justice and love
> in the relations between states, and, within the
> limits of each nation, in the relations of citizens
> with each other and with their rulers; freedom of
> individuals and of peoples, in all its expressions,
> civic, cultural, moral, and religious; otherwise,
> it is not peace which will exist—even if, per-
> chance, oppression is able to create the external
> appearance of order and legality—but an unceas-
> ing and insuppressible growth of revolt and war.

11

WHAT DO WE WANT OF

SOUTH VIETNAM?

*H*OW JUSTIFIABLE IS THE PRO-
test concerning the nature of the Saigon government—
allegedly a puppet of the United States, a military dictatorship, a junta that in no way reflects the will of the people?

How realistic is our moral outrage when we consider
the purported cowardice and corruption of Vietnamese
armed forces?

As I was working on this manuscript on Friday
evening, October 27, 1967, a news report said that an important elected American official had called the President
of the United States a "phony." I couldn't help thinking
of the spate of American critics during the Thieu-Ky
election campaign in Vietnam who attacked the fairness
of the forthcoming elections because the candidates were
calling one another names.

It is truly amazing to discover the demands made of
the Vietnamese people by various critics. They are equaled
only by demands made of our own Administration that
are invariably phrased in terms of intense moral righteousness. Not infrequently they contradict each other.

For example, priest-lawyer-writer Father John Sheerin
mourns the failures of the Diem regime, and expresses this
wish: "Would that our leaders had prodded the Diem
regime and its successors into a large-scale program of
social justice." In contradiction, I place his statement side

by side with former Ambassador Kennan's remarks in the Senate hearings: "To commit yourself, in any way, to assure the internal security of another government, means to commit yourself to interference in the most vital process of its own internal political life . . ."

I weigh Father Sheerin's remarks about social justice against the long list of Diem's achievements, as given by Suzanne Labin in her *Vietnam: An Eye Witness Account*. Among other reforms, Diem eliminated the sale of public office, eradicated usury, tripled the numbers of schools and universities, and increased the numbers of Buddhist places of worship. Miss Labin also notes that a 1958 investigation by a U.S. Senate committee cleared Diem of alleged misuse of American aid.

The Diem regime has already been discussed. It seems to me that history may well calculate that we owe our present extensive involvement in Vietnam to Diem's assassination. Marguerite Higgins quoted the British adviser Robert Thompson as saying long before Diem's assassination: ". . . the overthrow of the Diem regime in the middle of a war would set back the war at least twelve months, perhaps forever."

After Diem, successive governments came to power. What did we want of them? We pressed for a "democracy"—for free elections. The critics said the elections would never take place. Despite the predictions, newsmen such as Bob Considine, Jack Steele, Joseph Alsop, and others reported that 75 per cent of the registered voters of South Vietnam went to the polls in September 1966 to deliver a smashing blow to Viet Cong hopes. In the face of Viet Cong threats and terrorism and after twenty-five years of war, huge numbers voted for a constituent assembly, to draft a new constitution.

Jack Steele says he visited thirty-four polling places. He saw election procedures followed to the letter, no coercion by Vietnamese troops, no pressure on voters.

Mr. Considine reports ninety Viet Cong attacks on voters and polling places, both in the cities and in the provinces during the night, and forty-two in the morning, with nineteen persons killed and a hundred and twenty wounded. Sixty-five per cent of the registered voters voted in Quang Nam, 72 per cent in Chau Doc, 79 per cent in Go Cong, 81 per cent in Kien Tuong. But, as Mr. Considine points out, these are places completely unsafe after dark, places where the Viet Cong collect taxes, force conscription, seize rice, and murder civic leaders. The people voted anyway.

The Considine, Steele, and Alsop articles appear in the *Congressional Record* for September 14 and 19, 1966.

Yet, in the September 19th *Congressional Record* Arthur Schlesinger, Jr., pleading for negotiation with the Viet Cong and for their inclusion in a coalition government, tells us, "In our whole time in Vietnam, there has never been a government in Saigon which had the active loyalty of the countryside." He says that Ky had better learn "the facts of life"—in other words, shape up to our image. He also quotes Robert Shaplen's report in the August 20, 1966, issue of *The New Yorker*. Mr. Shaplen reports that the atmosphere in Saigon (under Ky) "is being compared to the miasma that surrounded Diem . . ." and that many Vietnamese consider the United States responsible for the Ky government's "repressive acts."

I can only reflect poignantly on the critics who say that the United States has far transcended its prerogatives by trying to enforce American political concepts on a people of southeast Asian culture. Now, Mr. Schlesinger would have us determine the fate of a gentleman named Ky, as we are accused of determining the fate of Diem.

I find myself asking: Did the September 1966 elections mean nothing in terms of the will of the Vietnamese people? Do cynical American news reports have the right to interpret definitively the mind of the Vietnamese people? They did this in the days of Diem. Is the mind of the same people to be interpreted again in the days of Ky (or now, Thieu)?

What do we expect of South Vietnam? In September 1967 some 83 per cent of the registered voters of South Vietnam—in a land that was purportedly making no progress—went to the polls. They elected a president and a vice-president, Messrs. Thieu and Ky. And they did this in a country at war, plagued by terrorism.

William S. White noted in the *Washington Post*, September 6, 1966, that in the month before the election the Viet Cong killed, wounded, or kidnapped 2,118 civilians in an all-out effort to terrorize possible voters. Yet, in a country with little experience in democracy, 83 per cent of all registered voters turned out.

In the city of Hoi-An, for example, about 500 to 600 people were lined up four abreast at the polls. The Viet Cong attacked with mortar fire. The people scattered. Seven were killed, eighteen wounded. The bodies were removed, the wounded taken to the hospital. Immediately the people lined up again and continued to vote. The same thing happened in six different places in I Corps area alone that same day. Does this sound like a people who want their will represented by the National Liberation Front?

But again the cry of "foul" rang from the American critics, who immediately rallied to the defense of "per-

secuted" candidates—among them one who was later con-
victed of financial fraud. Troops of prophets had warned
that the elections would be a failure and a fraud. The
South Vietnam government invited observers from the
United States and elsewhere. President Johnson sent
twenty. All came back praising the honesty of the elections. The critics now insisted that the observers weren't
really in a position to observe. The observers—who were
there—said they were.

Is there justice in the wry remark attributed by Joseph
Alsop to Mr. Ky, as reported by Pan and Lyons in *Vietnam Crisis,* that "it does not pay to agree entirely with
the Americans because they may change their mind. The
Americans told President Diem not to worry about stability, that democracy is what really counts. But now they
say, don't worry about democracy. Stability is what really
counts"?

Frequently the critics have blithely and cynically assured us that honest elections in South Vietnam are impossible. With what I consider grave irresponsibility, they
have made reckless charges about government censorship
and suppression and persecution of opposition parties and
unwarranted use of troops to assure that people voted
"the right way."

It is extremely ironic, I think, that during the September 1967 elections all American military personnel were
ordered by American authorities (wisely) to stay away
from the polls. For the most part, U.S. forces were con-
fined to their own bases. This was to avoid the accusation
that the mere sight of our troops near the polls would be
construed as pressure on voters. On November 6, 1967,
National Guard troops were ordered to Gary, Indiana, in
the United States, to try to prevent or control anticipated

violence during the elections to be held there the following day.

Immediately after the Vietnam elections, defeated
candidates called the voting fraudulent and lodged protests with the Constituent Assembly. A number of U.S.
critics enthusiastically supported the charges, indicating
it was now obvious that our entire effort in South Vietnam
had been futile. Elections in the United States are frequently challenged on grounds of alleged fraud, and American voters are familiar with these phenomena during every
major election in the United States. Few of them interpret
the accusation of holding a rigged election as indicative
of a catastrophic breakdown of democracy in the United
States. Most Americans are sophisticated enough about
the diatribes candidates hurl against one another to treat
the entire elective process with an almost humorous toler-
ance.

The Christian Science Monitor, on September 1, 1967,
ran an editorial on democracy and the elections in South
Vietnam, under the title "Viet Cong Terrorism." *The
Monitor* has repeatedly expressed dissatisfaction with the
degree of democracy in South Vietnam, but it has also
emphasized what is stressed again in this editorial—that
for all its weaknesses the democracy of South Vietnam
is infinitely preferable to the "absolute, one-party autoc-
racy of utter ruthlessness" in Hanoi. In North Vietnam,
the editorial observes, there is not the "slightest peep" of
free speech. In the South, a constituent assembly was
elected; it has been permissible to attack government fa-
vorites in an election campaign; and protest marches have
been allowed.

The same editorial mentions important data released
by the British Embassy in Saigon, an embassy that "by

no means gives unconditional backing" to the U. S. position in Vietnam. An "embassy spokesman" is quoted as stating that the Viet Cong have been responsible for three times as many civilian casualties in South Vietnam as all the allied forces—and this was before the recent step-up in Viet Cong slaughter of civilians. (The editorial does not identify the spokesman.)

The Philadelphia *Evening Bulletin*, August 29, 1967, observed a striking difference between the attitude of the National Liberation Front toward the elections (increased Viet Cong terrorism to block them) and what appeared "to be a campaign" in the United States to discredit the elections even before a single vote was cast. An example of this was seen in *The New Republic*, September 2, 1967: ". . . a continuation of the puppet military government after the September 3 elections seems virtually assured." I personally wonder how an elected government can be called a "puppet government."

In the article referred to above, William S. White maintained that the integrity of South Vietnam's elections was overwhelmingly established, but that afterward American critics turned to efforts to discredit Nguyen Van Thieu, the winner. Mr. White points out that in getting less than 40 per cent of the vote Thieu was instantly vulnerable to U.S. critics. Had he received more than 50 per cent, the election would have been indicted as rigged—in other words, a perfect example of the "heads-I-win-tails-you-lose" approach. If the Thieu election did not constitute the "mandate from the majority" required by the critics, neither did Mr. Kennedy's in 1960, says Mr. White.

White observes that, in what he calls a "spasm of irresponsibility," not only did the critics condemn the election in advance, but now, unfortunately unable to produce a single responsible witness to support their pre-election claims, they say, "Yes—*but!*" They proceed with astonishingly contradictory statements about the showing of Mr. Dzu, the "peace" candidate. Before the elections they predicted that the military government would never let a peace candidate get anywhere. When Dzu received a large number of votes, they exulted in the "proof" that the South Vietnamese want peace at any price, and want to be rid of a military government. But how could Dzu have received such a large vote if the elections were rigged? As always, says Mr. White, the critics want it both ways.

It has also been argued that the South Vietnamese voters are so politically ignorant, and the list of unknown candidates was so long, that the elections were a travesty. How many voters in the United States vote for "names" only, knowing little or nothing about the candidates? Until recently, how many American citizens were excluded from voting altogether? How many voters have been illiterate to the point of marking an "X" where advised to by "helpful" people at the polls? How many, when voting for a President, simply pull a "one-party" lever, because it's so much easier—and thus cast votes for innumerable lesser officials about whom they know nothing? How many vote for an individual because he is Catholic, or white, or Negro, or Protestant?

Hanoi's "official" attitude toward the elections was expressed in an article in the North Vietnamese Army newspaper, *Quan Doi Nhan Dan*, in August 1967, just before the elections were held:

> The curtain has yet to go up and the outcome of that farce is already known to everyone. Old clowns in new garb play on a rotten stage newly varnished. This farce staged by Johnson is a mere legalization of Thieu and Ky,

the two traitors who bear the most responsibility for crimes against the people of the South. The civilian candidates are only puppets to make the election look free.

The tone of mockery in this article, quoted in *The New York Times*, August 30, 1967, was echoed in South Vietnam by the Viet Cong, who called the elections "buffoonery."

The Communists' true feelings are reflected in captured Viet Cong documents, described by Robert A. Erlandson in the *Baltimore Sun*, August 30, 1967. The documents reveal plans directing the Viet Cong to kill, kidnap, and threaten prospective voters, set up ambushes near polling places, and throw grenades into the polls. The Viet Cong were told to warn people that if they voted they would be sentenced to "thought-reform" camps. Yet, the people voted—in droves.

The current Ambassador to South Vietnam, Ellsworth Bunker, had served as "Chief U.S. poll watcher" during the 1966 presidential election in the Dominican Republic and certainly was not naive about such matters. Mr. Bunker was disturbed by those who demanded that Thieu and Ky resign their governmental posts before the election campaign. The Ambassador notes the obvious—that the President and Vice-President of the United States do not resign to run for re-election. Mr. Bunker also supplied detailed answers to accusations against Thieu and Ky, when they were charged with intimidating their opponents. Thieu and Ky were also accused of arbitrarily denying their opponents the use of appropriate facilities. Ambassador Bunker again explains the obvious: when opposition candidates landed by air in a place inconveniently removed from their destination, without either a reception committee or transportation awaiting them, the circumstances were due to bad weather and, perhaps, poor planning on the part of the candidate. Mr. Bunker's explanations are supported without reservation by *New York Times* reporter R. W. Apple, Jr., who covered the South Vietnam elections on the spot. What absurd standards were the critics demanding for the elections in South Vietnam?

In 1966 the critics charged that the South Vietnamese were too politically ignorant to draft a constitution, but that if they did draft one the generals would reject it. Both accusations were proven false. They drafted a constitution that was accepted and is working today.

To me, the most exasperating criticism involved election observers. Premier Ky invited the United States and a number of other nations to send observers. President Johnson appointed former Ambassador Henry Cabot Lodge to accompany the U.S. group of twenty observers. The Ambassador remarked wryly that South Vietnamese pre-election criticism reminded him of the story of the Tammany Hall boss who recommended, "claim everything, concede nothing, and if defeated, charge fraud." The team of observers was careful to include a panel of electoral specialists. Nonetheless, critics instantly cried that the whole effort was a waste; the observers would, by circumstance, be rendered incapable. Indeed, said some, not only could they do no good, they could do a great deal of harm by giving the appearance of American intervention and domination.

The world waited for action; the verdict was up to the South Vietnamese Constituent Assembly. Charges of fraud had been presented to the Assembly, and approval of the elections by the Assembly was required before the newly elected president and vice-president could be installed. When the Assembly met, on October 2, 1967,

Thich Tri Quang, the militant Buddhist monk, kept vigil outside its doors. He had consistently protested the election results and supported a move to invalidate them. (Tri Quang will be remembered as the "hero" of the Buddhist immolations under Diem.) The Assembly voted. The elections were validated. A president and a vice-president, elected by the people, confirmed by the elected Assembly, took office. What more can we demand of the peoples of South Vietnam?

Charges of fraud and corruption are not limited to elections. It is maintained that profiteering is rampant, with everyone in an authoritative position taking his "cut" from American aid funds. Black-marketing is wide-spread. Bars and brothels flourish.

When I am reminded of corruption in Vietnam, I am forced to remember the "5 percenters" in Washington a handful of years ago. War profiteering reminds me of a woman who stood beside me in a butcher shop in Philadelphia on VJ Day. As church bells rang out and people danced in the streets, she informed all listeners that she was "damn sorry" the war was over. Apparently her husband had been working seven days a week and getting the benefit of time-and-a-half for overtime. They had "never had it so good." This story does not justify corruption anywhere else, but perhaps it shows that weak Vietnamese human nature doesn't differ much from weak American human nature.

Large quantities of American supplies are supposed to disappear into the black market. This supposedly means that the South Vietnamese people are turning the war to their own ends. In any war, black-marketing constitutes a problem. It has constituted a problem for every nation at war throughout history, and no one can deny that a certain number of Americans severely regretted the end of World War II.

It is an additional tragedy that profiteering is involved in the Vietnam conflict. It would be naive to expect anything else, but imperceptive to conclude that the Vietnamese people are insincere about the war effort. I have talked with the ordinary people, paddy farmers, peasants, refugees, and I am sure that accusing them of "living off the fat of the land" by black-marketing would be absurd.

Definitions of corruption undoubtedly differ in different areas of the world. I wonder why such furor centers on corruption or mismanagement in Saigon, particularly when I remember the countries (Russia and Red China) who supply the Viet Cong's deadly weapons. I am aware that corruption in San Francisco does not justify corruption in Saigon, but I do think we tend a bit toward self-righteousness.

It is frequently maintained that the average Vietnamese neither knows nor cares about the kind of government under which he lives—that Communism would be as welcome (or unwelcome) as any other form of rule. The result is seen as cowardice and unwillingness to engage the enemy. Is this true? Are U.S. forces doing all the fighting? Why have there been periods when we have had more American than Vietnamese casualties? Why have the Vietnamese people tolerated—even seemed to welcome and shelter—the Viet Cong for so many years?

I think there are many answers to these questions; some involve attitudes, others involve objective facts.

It seems to me we have to remember that practically every family in South Vietnam has had a son, a brother, a father wounded or killed. The Vietnamese live in a blood-drenched land. War has been their daily bread. The casual observer who sees the populace go about its daily tasks routinely is justified in thinking these people are oblivious or perhaps totally indifferent to the war. This is probably a necessary evil to a generation born to war. One can not live in constant, conscious tension all the days of one's life. One adopts a philosophy, a fatalism, perhaps, in some cases, a form of acceptance of what can apparently not be changed for the time being.

American forces, on the other hand, almost always have a sense of urgency. They know their normal tour of combat duty is twelve or thirteen months, at most. They have traveled many thousands of miles, trained incessantly, and are sharpened to a razor's edge of fighting efficiency. They fight, and, in due time (and barring death or casualty) leave. The Vietnamese forces remain. Vietnamese youngsters grow up and climb into helicopters in the middle of the night. They are dropped into jungle clearings to fight the Viet Cong, as their fathers fought—with or against the Viet Minh.

Desertion within the South Vietnamese army would be called absence without leave in American terms. The deserter, in these cases, usually goes home for a while to work a rice paddy and to feed his family. Perhaps he may desert to join a unit closer to his home. Defectors to the enemy are relatively few in number.

The problems posed by desertion are insignificant when compared to the problem of lack of organization and effective leadership. The Popular Forces are singularly lacking in officers. Regional force troops are led largely by noncommissioned officers or by junior lieutenants retired from the regular army. The regular army—the Army of the Republic of Vietnam (ARVN) has found it impossible to train enough leaders to keep up with the necessary expansion of enlisted troops. (These have doubled within the past five years.)

When I look at Vietnamese military forces I see something akin to our own Revolutionary forces—troops ragged, bedraggled, ill-equipped, grossly underpaid, and above all, untrained and poorly led. A student of American history will remember that our Revolutionary forces, in the early days, broke and ran at the first sight of tough, disciplined British troops. Von Steuben, along with his French counterparts, came along in time to give our revolutionaries thorough drills. Finally they were turned into the fighting force that won our freedom.

I have talked with a number of American Marine officers stationed near the Demilitarized Zone. They were profoundly impressed by the ARVN units with which they were fighting. They did not hesitate to call them courageous. They said, in fact, they were as courageous as any men they had ever seen. They added that their professional skills were comparable to our own.* Vietnamese refugees I have talked with felt that Vietnamese military forces do the best they can under many handicaps. Only one Vietnamese priest told me he wished the ARVN forces would fight harder. His evaluation may have been influenced by his having spent his formative seminary period in the United States for ten years. He had only recently returned to Vietnam.

Discussions with Marines about ARVN forces have been interesting. Over the past two years some Marines have told me they "wanted no part of the ARVN," that they were completely unreliable. Others have told me the ARVN fight well once they get moving, but they prefer to avoid or delay a fight if they can. Still others

* In South Vietnam, it is estimated that 8 per cent of the total population is involved in fighting the war. (About 1.5 per cent of the population of the United States is under arms or in reserve.) Since Nguyen Van Thieu's election as President, a new mobilization plan has been established. Sixty thousand troops are to be added to the 640,000 already under arms as of late 1967.

have been outspoken in praising the ARVN. These same mixed responses came from the hundred and sixty-five officers and men I talked with on Okinawa. These were men who had just left Vietnam. There were men there who indicted the ARVN vehemently, as opposed to others who had nothing but generous praise to offer.

The *Congressional Record* of October 2, 1967 carries some well-chosen remarks by Senator Gale W. McGee about the ARVN forces. Senator McGee particularly stresses the fact that the American press is understandably interested in reporting the activities of American men to the American public. He adds that most servicemen will naturally describe the ARVN in terms of their own personal experiences. Any man who has been critically wounded because someone else failed in a responsibility will be bitter. A man whose life has been saved will be generous in his praise. Mr. McGee quotes a serviceman who had completed eighteen months in the delta with a South Vietnamese unit: "I want you to know that I didn't cringe for one minute, knowing that my life depended on what the guy next to me was going to do or not do. I'd like to have a chance to tell the people this."

Senator McGee makes the point that much of the fighting that the ARVN and other Vietnamese units are assigned to is unglamorous and difficult. Their job is to provide security in rough paddy areas. Unlike big unit fighting, where there are occasional breathers, they must live with uncertainty twenty-four hours a day.

While there have been periods when more American than Vietnamese deaths have been reported, the death and casualty rates of Vietnamese forces are much higher than ours. In the first six months of 1967 the ARVN lost more than 4,000 dead and 7,000 wounded; the Regional forces and Popular Forces lost 3,300 killed and 5,300 wounded. Whatever criterion one uses, this is a lot of dead for forces alleged to be cowardly or apathetic. As Senator McGee put it, you have to be in the middle of something "if you're going to get shot up."

Brigadier General James D. Hittle, USMC (Ret.), points out that the South Vietnamese report only the most seriously wounded of their military casualties. Therefore, comparisons based on their reports can be misleading. Nonetheless, they report some 50,000 South Vietnamese troops killed since 1960. General Hittle notes that if that figure of 50,000 is projected into our U.S. population (about twelve times that of Vietnam), it would amount to the equivalent of 600,000 combat dead for the United States. Anyone quick with figures will realize that this means, proportionately, that the military-combat death rate in Vietnam is three times greater than ours in World War I, double that of ours in World War II, and close to fifteen times ours in Korea. From the beginning of 1966 through the first quarter of 1967, 12,000 South Vietnamese troops were killed in combat. Again proportionately, General Hittle observes, this is equivalent to 144,000 U. S. dead —more than our total deaths in World War I. These figures were reported in the *San Diego Union*, September 18, 1967.

At any rate, my personal impression in October of 1967, gleaned from talking with American Marines in I Corps, was that there has been a substantial increase in respect for Vietnamese forces.

Problems of leadership in the military forces are matched by problems of leadership in the hamlets. According to the State Department, between 1958 and October of 1967, 14,000 civilians have been assassinated and another 44,200 kidnapped by the Viet Cong. Viet Cong strategy is to start assassinations and/or kidnappings with hamlet leaders or others in authority. They not only rob an area of its here-and-now leadership; their actions are intended as a warning to future leaders. Between February and June of 1967, 81 Revolutionary Development workers were killed, 99 wounded, and 13 kidnapped. During the same period the Viet Cong killed 31 Chieu Hoi (defectors from the Viet Cong), wounded 22, and kidnapped 10. All this means, rather obviously, that only the exceptionally courageous will dare to attempt leadership or thwart the Viet Cong. I wonder how a small-town mayor in the United States would react?

Lieutenant General Walt tells a story that may help explain the problems of a people confronted by the Viet Cong.

"One afternoon in July of 1965, I sat down with an elderly couple—they were about seventy years old—in a village from which we had driven the Viet Cong. In fact, it was the first village that we had freed. I sat down with an interpreter and talked to these people for about three hours, and asked them to tell me what had happened to their village. They had been there from the time that the French controlled South Vietnam through the twelve years when the Viet Cong had controlled their village, and of course, they were still there when we came in.

"Their story was a very simple story and one I would like to relate to you, because what happened to their village is exactly what has happened to half of the villages in the I Corps area where I was, and probably happened to half the villages in Vietnam.

"They said they were not very happy under the French or with the French government, but they were getting along. The French did not treat them very well, but, on the other hand, they left them pretty much alone. The French extracted heavy taxes from them, but they were small taxes compared to what they had to pay to

the Viet Cong. In the mid-1950's, strangers started moving
into their little village. They moved in and became good
neighbors. They participated in the village activities and
social activities, government, and so forth. And then suddenly, things started to happen.

"The first thing that happened was that the village
chief, their mayor, was killed. His council was told that
if they didn't disband, the same thing would happen to
them or to their families. So the first thing that happened
was the destruction of the village government. The school
was destroyed. The church was destroyed. The young
people were taken out of the village, and both boys and
girls were sent to North Vietnam for training and indoctrination in Communism. There were two roads leading into this little village, both of which passed over a
river. The Communists destroyed both of the bridges
and replaced them with a single footbridge. People
could not leave the village without a written pass from the
Viet Cong leader, and they had to go over the new bridge
one at a time. They could never take more than half of
their family with them when they went. They always
had to leave half their family in the village as hostages.

"The people were not allowed to have any kind of
civic organization or civic movement. They were not allowed to have any organization that might endanger the
grip of the Communist forces. Actually, there were only
about twenty Viet Cong in this village of eight hundred
to a thousand people, but they controlled these people because they were the only ones who had an organization
and they were the only ones who had any weapons in the
village. They held the people as virtual slaves in the village.
They collected taxes from the people. Fifty per cent of
what they made was paid in taxes, either in money or in
rice, or in whatever they happened to be growing. They
forced the people to work two days a week to build

fortifications in the village for Viet Cong use. Later on, the villagers had to work four days a week on fortifications. The Viet Cong forced the people to help them supply the military forces by carrying the heavy loads over the trail. The Viet Cong were not too popular in the village. People feared them. The elderly couple I talked to had only one child left. They had started out with five sons and daughters, and the only one left in the family besides themselves was a little girl about seven years old, their granddaughter. They couldn't account for the rest of their family.

"When our forces came into the village, we routed the Viet Cong. We kept a few Marines in that village and they protected the people. The people elected a mayor and a council, and they started to rebuild their community. We gave them materials, and they built a school, a church, and a marketplace. We helped rebuild the two bridges that had been blown up. And we gave the people food and medical care, which they needed very badly. Today, that little village is thriving. The mayor or the chief of that village today is a man who was in the Viet Cong. He came back to his village and left the Viet Cong. There are many of them doing that these days. They have had their fill of the VC. Their mayor is a very good chief to have because he understands the tactics of the Viet Cong and he is, like most converts, really anti-Communist.

"But what has happened in that village is the same thing that has happened in other villages; what we have done there has to be done for all the other villages that the Viet Cong have taken over. This has to be done before this war is going to be over in Vietnam. It takes a long time. The anti-guerrilla part is a most difficult part of the war. The guerrilla is so hard to identify. He's so hard to destroy. Because of his terrorist tactics, the people are constantly under an umbrella of fear; and until we have given them positive protection, so that they know that if they help us they are not going to get their throats cut some night—and this has happened many times—until they know that we have positive security for them, they are afraid to help us. But once that positive security is established, then they voluntarily, eagerly, help us get rid of the Viet Cong."

Another story the General tells poignantly is of visiting a hamlet where he talked with the mother and father of seven children. The parents were gravely alarmed. One of their little boys had been missing for four days. As they talked with the General, the little boy came into sight. Both his hands had been cut off. Around his neck was a sign: "If you dare to vote, this, or worse, will happen to all of you."

If this is a politically indifferent people, I have yet to meet a nation of patriots.

As I write at this moment, with the memories of my recent visit to this tragic and courageous land still fresh, I am moved by a CBS report:

*"The survey shows that contrary to a widely held belief outside South Vietnam, its people are not so exhausted and numbed by the war that they no longer care which side wins. They do care very much. They want peace, but not at any price."**

---

* A Public Opinion Survey conducted by the Opinion Research Corporation of Princeton, New Jersey, on behalf of the Columbia Broadcasting System. It is dated March 13, 1967, and formed the basis of a special hour-long television program on March 21, 1967.

12

ALIENATION OF

MORAL AFFECTION

*O*UR DECLARATION OF INDE-
pendence insists on respect for the opinions of mankind.
This concept is rooted in our "American doctrine of the
just war." In mankind at large there is a moral sense of the
rightness and wrongness of things. Fifty million French-
men *can* be wrong, but if all mankind abhors an action,
then that action is certain to be horrendous!

I believe that our national concern about the opinions
of mankind should center upon official opinion—as expressed in the public forums of the nations of the world,
rather than upon private and "unofficial" views as expressed in purely private comments by officials. Those
who want their opinions respected should express them
publicly and unequivocally. As a nation we cannot afford
to be bemused by the veiled ambiguities of those "unim-
peachable" but never-identified spokesmen who pretend
to do us a service by giving us the "inside word" in the
outside corridor.

Tan Sri Ong Yoke-Lin is the Malaysian Ambassador
to the United States. The *Reader's Digest* of November
1967, reports an interview with the Ambassador conducted by Carl T. Rowan. First, the Ambassador makes
it clear that should the United States withdraw from South
Vietnam under present circumstances, this would put
Malaysia in serious trouble. He goes on to assert that our
stand in Asia has given confidence and hope to millions

of Asians who would have otherwise submitted to Communist aggression. He emphasizes the rebellion of the people of Indonesia in crushing the Communist coup attempt in 1965, with a courage largely born of their belief that we would not abandon Asia to communist tyranny. For the first time, Asian economic and social cooperation has been made possible by the stabilizing security provided by U. S. presence.

"No fair-minded Asian," the Ambassador said, "believes that the United States has any ulterior, economic, or territorial motives." He cites, as evidence that "no amount of propaganda can distort," our return of territories occupied in World War II. The vast sums of money we have spent rebuilding them; the fact of our giving independence to the Philippines; our aid to Japan in its progress toward prosperity; our sacrifices in Korea: all this has helped our image.

Major General M. W. J. M. Broekmeijer, Director of the Netherlands Defense Study, reported that he had driven for hundreds of miles across the countryside in Vietnam, and had been mistaken for an American. According to an account in *U.S. News and World Report*, October 1967, everywhere he went, children rushed to take his hand, adults gave cordial welcomes. "From now on," he stated, "I don't believe a single word of the stories of the 'hated Americans.' "

It is often forgotten that many of our allies are supporting South Vietnam, and for the same reasons we are. Thirty-one nations have assisted South Vietnam with military aid, troops, economic and technical assistance, and military training. To argue that our having to "go it alone" in Southeast Asia demonstrates that the world disapproves is to ignore the fact that there are more Allied troops in South Vietnam today, apart from American forces, than there were in Korea. Five nations have sent troops (four of these are SEATO members). When he pleaded for Allied help in Vietnam in coalition with the United States prior to Geneva, Mr. Eisenhower made it clear that small, token forces would be enough to give moral justification for intervention in the Vietnam conflict. Ten countries in Asia, ten in Europe, eight in the Western Hemisphere, and two in Africa have sent help in one form or another.

Surely, other non-Communist nations in the same area would be clamoring for our withdrawal if our cause were as unpopular as it has been called. We have already seen the fear expressed by Thailand's Foreign Minister, Thanat Khoman. Well aware that American unity and resolution in Vietnam would assure cooperation and stability in Southeast Asia, he expressed concern that we might vacillate because of domestic dissension, and he made it clear he was alarmed about Thailand's survival if its people lost confidence in us.

Singapore's Prime Minister Lee Kuan Yew, often thought of as critical of U.S. foreign policy, has repeatedly stated his conviction that a non-Communist South Vietnam is essential to keeping Southeast Asia free, and it is the presence of the United States that is making it all possible.

On September 28, 1966, former President Radhakrishnan of India stated:

> With Hanoi standing pat on its obdurate position, there remains only one hopeful and effective quarter to which peace appeals may be directed. This is the Soviet Union. The United States has recently made strenuous and public efforts to call upon Moscow to face up to its great power responsibilities. . . . So far the

Soviet Union's role has been to stand on the sidelines and help stiffen Hanoi's will to resist. A more positive interest on its part to see that peace prevails in the region is the objective towards which all with influence in Moscow must now work.

Only a year after President Radhakrishnan's remarks, Prime Minister Indira Gandhi, as quoted by Bernard D. Nossiter in the *Washington Post*, October 21, 1967, had an interesting comment on China: "Whatever else has changed in the last five years, China's aggressive posture has not stopped."

Other non-Communist nations in the area have been accused of expressing their reluctance to support the war; they have sent only token troops. Mr. Eisenhower considered this "morally" adequate. So do I. If you are morally opposed to a conflict, how can you morally help at all? How can you send one soldier who might kill somebody, if you are morally convinced of the intrinsic injustice of the cause? How can you, morally, supply advisors, weapons, or any other materials to support the cause?

There may be another side to the story of "unwillingness" on the part of our allies. Correspondent William R. Frye reported from the United Nations that Asian diplomats have a reply to those who ask them to carry a larger share of the fighting. They complain that we have a "superman complex" and don't really want their help. They say we prove this by our unwillingness to give them good weapons and training, because we have no confidence in Asian fighting ability. But, paradoxically, it is also their belief that the North Vietnamese have proved themselves in this war, and the South Koreans, once trusted and trained, proved themselves in the Korean war. If we invested trust, training, and weapons, say the Asians at the United Nations, according to Mr. Frye, in the *Evening Star*, Washington, D.C., October 6, 1967, scores of thousands of Asians would be willing to join the fight. After returning from a recent visit to Vietnam, Senator Percy, of Illinois, echoed something of the same accusation in objecting to our not having supplied the South Vietnamese with the new M-16 rifle. This was early in January 1968. Some units do have this weapon now.

Perhaps there is merit in this argument, but whatever the case, sufficient support has been forthcoming from Asians to leave no doubt about their belief in the cause being upheld by the United States. The repeated public statements of Thailand, Malaysia, Korea, and other countries in the area leave no question about their fear of Communist intent and their recognition of the critical need for the American presence. I think we tend to take far too seriously the rumors about what U.N. diplomats are allegedly saying "in private" about our loss of face. Some of the comments in the press are nothing less than ludicrous. I could hardly believe that a correspondent was writing with a straight face when she recently warned us that our involvement in Vietnam has seriously threatened our status in the eyes of Yugoslavians.

Thailand's Foreign Minister, Thanat Khoman, puts his finger on a vital point: "If you are confused about the righteousness of your own cause in South Vietnam, how can it be possible for the people of Southeast Asia to have faith in you? . . . The United States offers a picture of confusion and self-doubt . . . America's position in international affairs is affected by domestic politics."

His statement was made in an interview with the *Bangkok Post*, as quoted in the *Washington Post*, August 20, 1967. It is necessary for us to remember that we are winning friends and developing trust in many areas.

What I consider a peculiar twist in the argument about our alienating other nations is a point made by Norman Cousins, writing in *The Saturday Review*, February 16, 1966. Mr. Cousins summarizes the accusations of a number of critics in discussing bombings of Vietnam. He argues that bombing can do nothing but alienate us further from Asians, who are historically bitter about white discrimination against yellow men and brown men. Referring to Hiroshima and Nagasaki, he maintains that the primary Asian criticism was levied, not at the *use* of the weapon in itself, but at the fact we used it against people of another race, whereas we would never have used it against *white men*.

This seems a specious argument at best. Our advisors, living as intimately as they do with Vietnamese troops (some of whom fought against the French), do not report that they are resented because they are white. Vietnamese from every walk of life have responded to our presence with warmth.

As a matter of fact, I found the South Vietnamese amazingly friendly. I remember one day, when new in Vietnam, I drove into the marketplace in Danang on some business. In the middle of hundreds of people bargaining over everything from fish to straw mats, my jeep stopped dead. With no knowledge of the language at the time, I could make my plight known only through sign language. But immediately the throngs gathered around, laughing, good-humoredly ridiculing my jeep as "number 10"—the only English they knew, and the ultimate in disparagement. I couldn't count them, but at least fifty youngsters must have swarmed around, offering to push. I accepted. They got me to the nearest gas station, looking for all the world like a maharajah with royal entourage.

Unfortunately, I wasn't simply out of gas—the problem was more serious. So push again they did, to the nearest mechanic. I learned I would have to leave the jeep for repair. Then it became a matter of contacting my base. Along came a policeman on a bicycle, courteous, pleasant, and—most important—fluent in French. Would he help me contact my base? Of course he would, if I would simply follow him. We went off several blocks to the nearest telephone, where the obliging policeman put through the call. Then I had to wait for several hours in the marketplace. Would I have a cup of tea? Something to eat? Would I care to come inside a shop, to sit in the shade? All the offers were in sign language, of course— and with smiles, polite bows, to this utter stranger in their midst. Rarely did I meet an opposite reaction. Indeed, in many a "white" nation I have been greeted with a lot less friendliness.

If there were any initial fears among the Vietnamese, they seem to me to be anxieties aroused by the arrival of strangers as strangers, not by strangers as white men.

Certainly a mother whose child has just been killed in cross fire between American and Viet Cong forces may be bitter against Americans—but she is likely to be equally bitter against the Viet Cong, and probably, at the moment, bitter against the human race. This is not alienation based on color.

Villagers who have lost relatives, homes, land through bombing may well be bitter against Americans who have bombed. Or they *may* be bitter against Ho Chi Minh and the Viet Cong, instead. To assume that they are totally ignorant of their own position vis-à-vis the Viet

Cong and Americans is to assume a great deal, indeed. This is the type of assumption, it seems to me, that clouds our efforts to make intelligent moral judgments. Refugees with whom I talked, though they certainly didn't like being bombed by anyone, seemed quite clear in their understanding about who provoked the bombing—the Viet Cong. What is there in the charge of alienation on the grounds of "white men" bombing yellow or brown men that can be demonstrated? Can it be more than a gratuitous assumption?

Let's reflect for a moment on the use of the atom bomb at Hiroshima and Nagasaki. Can this be construed in any way—validly—as a "white man-colored man" situation, As a matter of very cold and very hard fact, Professor Albert Einstein related that he made his decision to contact President Roosevelt and advise him about the potential and development of an atom bomb only after he, Einstein, learned that the Nazis had been given the key to the bomb. And President Roosevelt made his decision to develop the bomb when he realized what it could mean if the Nazis made one first. There was no question in anyone's mind that white Nazis would use the atom bomb on white Americans or white British, or white whomsoever.

How in the world can the United States be construed as fighting a white-man–yellow-man war, when we are fighting and dying side by side with yellow men—the South Vietnamese? And why, if there are such obvious racial overtones in this war, has Thailand so strongly supported the United States and expressed great fear of a U.S. withdrawal? Why did Cambodia's Sihanouk say, in a letter to *The New York Times*, June 4, 1965: "I concede again that after the disappearance of the USA from our region and the victory of the Communist camp, I, myself, and the People's Socialist Community that I have created would inevitably disappear from the scene"? And why was President Marcos, of the Philippines, as quoted in the *Congressional Record*, September 14, 1966, so anxious to claim, "It was only the American presence in Vietnam, I feel, which prevented the fall of the Indonesian Government into Communist hands. Not only Indonesia, but also other countries."

And why did the President of Korea say, in speaking of North Vietnam's aggressive acts: "Any aggression against the Republic of Vietnam represented a direct and grave menace against the security and peace of free Asia, and therefore directly jeopardized the very security and freedom of our own people"? This sounds much more like yellow men against yellow men, than yellow against white. Or why did the President of Malaysia warn his people that if the United States pulled out of South Vietnam, it would go to the Communists, and after that, it would be only a matter of time until they moved against neighboring states?

Robert Shaplen and Richard M. Nixon, both writing in the September 1967 issue of *Foreign Affairs*, feel that an unrealized benefit of the Vietnam war has been the development of awareness on the part of Asian leaders that the United States has "bought time" for other southeast Asian nations to band together to avoid another Vietnam. Partly because of confidence derived from the U. S. stand in Vietnam, the non-Communist nations in Asia have begun regional cooperation in the new Asian and Pacific Council. Both Mr. Shaplen and Mr. Nixon believe that the Communist debacle in Indonesia resulted in part from the American presence in Vietnam, which "provided a shield behind which anti-Communist forces found courage."

If there is even the smallest grain of merit in the conclusions of these two observers, I find it very difficult to see how anyone can support the "alienation" charge based on color.

However, racial arguments are by no means the only ones offered by those who maintain we are alienating the world at large by our moral insensitivities. Jean Lacouture is often cited as a leading authority on the conflict in Vietnam. In his *Vietnam: Between Two Truces*, Lacouture bitterly attacks the United States for escalating the war and for offering totally fallacious arguments for intervention. Lacouture charges that B-52 bombing attacks on the Mekong delta are terror operations, rather than discriminate attacks on military objectives, and asks what could be less selective than the use of napalm, defoliation, and "temporarily disabling" gas.

Even on the surface, this is a highly speculative and subjective evaluation. Lacouture offers no figures, dates, places; no numbers of bombers, attacks, areas and houses destroyed, or peaceful citizens killed. Just alone, *temporarily disabling* as used with quotations in reference to gas is misleading. Secretary of State Rusk pointed out, in a *State Department Bulletin*, April 21, 1965, that our forces had used *tear* gas—radically different from the gases that kill and maim. It is also radically different from the gases prohibited by the Geneva Convention of 1965. Tear gas *is* temporarily disabling; there is no reason for tongue-in-cheek quotation marks. Rather than an inhumane instrument of warfare, the tear gas used is that commonly used by police forces of the world in riot control, to *prevent* maiming and killing, (and permanent disablement), with the least exertion of force. Secretary Rusk cites an example of its use: A village was held by the Viet Cong; they were holding the villagers hostage and using them as protection to fire through them at the mixed crowds outside the village. The decision to employ tear gas against the Viet Cong was made in the name of humaneness—to avoid the necessity of force, which could have destroyed both the Viet Cong and the villagers.

Since references to napalm are so common—and sound so terrifying—it is interesting to read the report of Dr. George R. Holswade, New York surgeon, who went with eight other American physicians to Vietnam, under the auspices of the American Medical Association's Volunteers for Vietnam program:

> I found these reports [that many Vietnamese civilian casualties had resulted from American bombing] were highly exaggerated. Especially in regard to napalm wounds among children. I personally did not see one, and neither did the eight other American physicians who went there with me . . . I saw three civilians burned by American weapons. One was a small boy who found a U.S. rocket in a field and managed to set it off. The others were a man and a woman burned by white phosphorous smoke. The Allies send up light planes to draw enemy ground fire. When shot at, the planes mark the enemy gunners' positions with white phosphorous. The man and woman must have been close to the point of explosion to get their burns. About 90% of my work involved war injuries. And of the war-wounded, about 75% were civilians, including women and many children, who had blundered into Viet Cong booby traps. Many youngsters had lost arms, legs, and, in some

cases, eyes. A common wound was caused by a
Viet Cong booby trap called a toe-popper. It's
a spring-type device that splits the victim's foot.
Some cases required amputation of the foot, but
we could patch up most of the wounds.

Dr. Howard A. Rusk, M.D., reported on the napalm
burn charges in *The New York Times*, October 1, 1967.
He says that a "distinguished team of American physicians
has written what should be the last clarifying chapter in
the Vietnamese napalm burn reports." Dr. Rusk quotes
the team, which reported to President Johnson:

> Prior to leaving the United States, the team was
> aware of exceptional public interest in the num-
> ber and type of civilian burn cases in Vietnam.
> Throughout our visit, individual team members
> paid particular attention to burns. The cases
> were relatively limited in relation to other in-
> juries and illnesses, and we saw no justification
> for the undue emphasis which had been placed
> by the press upon civilian burns caused by na-
> palm. A greater number of burns appeared to
> be caused by the careless use of gasoline in
> stoves which were not intended for gasoline.
> Probably most burns occurred from this source.

This particular medical team carries rather reasonable
credentials. Its chairman, Dr. F. J. L. Blasingame, is executive vice-president of the American Medical Association.
Its members include a professor of pediatrics at the University of California School of Medicine, the executive
vice-president of the American Hospital Association, an
associate professor of orthopedic surgery at the University of Tennessee College of Medicine, the general

director of Massachusetts General Hospital, and the vice-president of the University of Kentucky.

Finally, Dr. Rusk adds that the team's conclusions confirmed his own, when he reported on a visit made to Vietnam in March 1967.

The Community Association of the Pacific School of Religion is quoted in the *Congressional Record* for September 12, 1966 as stating that more than 1,000 Vietnamese civilians are killed each month by our bombing and burning of villages, or die of hunger due to our destruction of crops.

I do not see how such figures can be based on anything but assumptions and generalizations.

In looking at the war as a whole it is necessary to question the morality of the conflict in Vietnam on the basis of methods we use to wage it. The morality of means used in the war is an integral factor in determining the morality of *exercising* our rights.

A long list can be added to accusations such as using "gas" warfare or overuse of napalm: acts of inhumanity in general, including torturing of prisoners, devastation of fields and crops, destruction of innocent peoples and territories by bombing; the ultimate damage to our own economy; the danger of escalating to a global war and a nuclear holocaust. Such charges, particularly intermeshed, as they so often are, seem to indict the U.S. involvement in Vietnam as morally indefensible—a grotesque Goliath spewing destruction upon David.

In listening carefully to the expressed fears of the "man in the street," I suspect that these touch upon his basic concern, rather than the legal and political problems we have been discussing thus far. Coupled with these are his anxieties about the tragic loss of life involved, and particularly the "waste" of American lives. These, too, I think, are the anxieties of the average sincere "protesters" or peace marchers. Caught up in a surge of anguish, feeling almost a desperate sense of futility and their own inability to stem the tide of disaster, they feel morally compelled to protest, to do whatever they can to stop this war, and to drive out the evil of war altogether.

It would be a manifest absurdity, of course, to deny the tragic facts—that many thousands of lives have been lost, that much destruction has taken place, that the dangers of escalation are always with us, that tremendous resources are being poured into war—that war is grim, bitter, and evil. No one in his right mind chooses war when intelligent alternatives are available. No one in his right mind, embarked upon war, wants the war to continue, when it is reasonably possible to end it. But thus far, who has provided us with demonstrably workable alternatives, or reasonable terminations?

We must, then, as rationally as possible, look at the way we are waging this war. It is important that we look at war emotionally, and never let it become a cold-blooded expedient. But if our viewpoint is entirely emotional, we forget that war *can be* a rational, though bitter, choice of the lesser of several evils. Within this context, certain methods used are morally justifiable. It is the old story of means and ends. Obviously, to drive a knife into a man's side under normal circumstance is immoral. To drive the same knife into his side to remove a diseased appendix is a different matter.

What are some representative arguments that charge us with immorality of method? Dr. John Bennett, a well-known Protestant clergyman, presents a summation of moral objections under the title, "Christian Realism in Vietnam," in *America*, April 30, 1966.

Dr. Bennett says that he rejects our government's arguments in support of our military actions in Vietnam, first off, because we are involved in *morally intolerable* acts of inhumanity. He maintains that we have been more reckless in bombing South Vietnamese than in bombing North Vietnamese, we have poisoned rice crops, and, through our South Vietnamese allies, tortured prisoners. Even though these actions are morally intolerable, he goes on to say, he might have to consider them acceptable in certain circumstances—as by-products of actions designed to overcome greater evils. But we have not demonstrated, he argues, that such actions *are* necessary, even as by-products, to overcome greater evils. On the contrary, he claims, we are probably defeating ourselves both morally and politically by what we are doing and permitting. We may be destroying the very country we purport to be saving. We may so undermine the strength of Vietnam, that it can no longer act as a brake on Chinese power. We may become masters of a country we do not understand. As a white nation, Dr. Bennett maintains, we would be cast in the role of imperialists, and, in our proximity to China, would be a constant reminder to China of its habitual humiliation by the white West. While we would not tolerate Chinese military power gathered on our borders, we treat Chinese protests against our presence as evidence of their aggressiveness.

Dr. Bennnet also accuses us of imposing conditions for negotiation that the other side could not possibly accept. He adds that we have not adequately emphasized the role of such agencies as the United Nations. Our policy-makers still seem to be obsessed by the idea that a Communist regime is the worst fate that can befall a nation, and that Communism is still a monolithic power. Only as we abandon our "anti-Communism obsession," he says, and recognize that it would not be the worst possible outcome of the war for the people of Vietnam to have their own brand of national communism—only then can we come to an intelligent settlement. The potential of Chinese expansionism is a problem for China's Asiatic neighbors, not for the United States.

Next, Dr. Bennett rejects any suggestion that Vietnam is a test case of what the Communists call "wars of national liberation," and that if this Communist effort is not stopped in Vietnam, such wars will be more likely to succeed throughout the world, particularly in Asia and Latin America. In South Vietnam, he says, we have to create a nation. Furthermore, he argues, Communism is not primarily a military threat, it is a political and social threat. Any analogy between the current situation in Vietnam and World War II and Munich is misleading, since Hitlerism was primarily a military threat.

Pastor Ralph Moellering uses the same arguments and adds others in an article, "I Stand Opposed," in *Lutheran Witness*, June 1966. Noting that war is always deplorable, he draws particular attention to the situation of the Vietnamese peasant caught between the cross fire of contending forces, after having endured Japanese imperialism and French colonialism. We make Vietnam the martyr for the free world in exercising our right to draw a dividing line somewhere across it, on the basis of defeating Communism there, rather than in Seattle.

Even the most optimistic appraisals of what can be gained from this war, says Pastor Moellering, could not compensate for the toll in men and materials. He protests the price that Vietnamese peasants must pay for the death of Communist troops and the capturing of their weapons. The misery generated by burned villages, the use of napalm, chemically destroyed crops—this can hardly be erased by promises of pacification and ultimate reconstruction.

Claiming that we are lost in the rice paddies of Vietnam

and know that we are in a weak position militarily, La-couture, in *Between Two Truces*, maintains that we de-liberately escalate the war in a policy of "brinkmanship," because, once it spreads, we become again the great world power that can talk with a loud voice in the diplomatic halls of the world—a role in which we feel superior.

Our bombers are engaged, he says, not in tactical ef-forts to prevent what *we* call "aggression," but in terror operations, using totally unselective methods, such as na-palm, defoliation, and "temporarily disabling" gas. We bomb and destroy houses, rather than underground installa-tions of the Viet Cong. In other words, we are involved in a blind battering of an entire country and are on a road imperiling peaceful coexistence, the future of the West and of American democracy, and the equilibrium of Asia itself.

Peace in Vietnam, scoring wanton destruction of crops and fields, quotes a dramatic interview with a village priest, reported by Jean Larteguy in *Paris Match*, October 2, 1965. The substance of the priest's anguished remarks is that poor mountain people in the destroyed area have been forced to live like wild boars in a forest. Before the bombing, loud speakers told them to stay in their huts. They did as they were told, only to have their huts bombed. The people whose huts were not bombed were forced to come out into the open by the Viet Cong, who then machine-gunned them. The priest's people were burned up by napalm; bodies of women and children were blown to bits, and villages were razed to the ground. Bursting into tears, the priest cursed the war and its hor-rors. He "railed at the Americans . . . as if they were there to hear him . . ."

Describing the tenacity of the Viet Cong and the North Vietnamese, *Peace in Vietnam* maintains that the price of victory means burning villages because they may be potential guerrilla strongholds, destroying rice crops by spraying poisons from the air, dropping grenades in tunnels that may be filled with women and children, bribing children to reveal hideouts, and torturing prisoners for information.

Similar fears and accusations were expressed during the course of the Senate hearings by Senator Pell, former Ambassador George Kennan, and Senator Fulbright. Senator Fulbright added the reminder that we are now, in fact, at war. We are at war without having made a national decision, a national commitment, or a declaration of war.

Neil Sheehan, in *The New York Times Magazine* of October 9, 1966, in an article entitled "Not a Dove, But No Longer a Hawk," begins with the familiar accusation that the war in Vietnam is a civil conflict, not between north and south, but between differing elements of the Vietnamese people. He, too, accuses us of "conniving" with Diem and says we are responsible for prolonging what is basically a civil war. Idealism and dedication, he says, belong largely to the enemy, not to the South Vietnamese, and he concludes that Vietnamese die more willingly for a Communist regime, because it is genuinely nationalistic, than for the regime in South Vietnam, which is largely the creation of Washington. Vietnamese with influence prosper; peasants suffer. Civilian casualties are appalling—we are not actually receiving the true figures of civilian dead and wounded, only fractions thereof. Mr. Sheehan claims that civilian deaths and casualties result largely from American and Vietnamese bombing, artillery, and naval gunfire; that by comparison the gun and knife of the Viet Cong are selective weapons; and that the numbers assassinated by the Viet Cong altogether total far less than the number of civilian victims lost in the war each year. Most refugees told him, Mr. Sheehan says, that although the Viet Cong taxed them they could at least live with the Communists. They had left their homes because they could no longer bear American and South Vietnamese bombs and shells. Refugees are woefully neglected by the government.

Over and above this dreary recital, Mr. Sheehan feels the American presence has had a corrosive effect in many ways, but certainly economically and culturally. The moral degeneration caused by the G.I. culture has mushroomed, he says: bars and bordellos prosper, thousands of young Vietnamese women become prostitutes, gangs of hoodlums abound, and children sell their older sisters and steal wherever they can. Finally, Mr. Sheehan admits, he cannot help worrying that we are corrupting ourselves, in the waging of this war.

On April 7, 1965, the French Catholic newspaper *La Croix* published an article called "The War Which Is Becoming the Best Ally of Communism" (reprinted in *The Viet-Nam Reader*). The article is noteworthy for the intensity with which it expresses most of the accusations just listed. It adds that there are Catholic refugees for whom this war has become a crusade. Blinded by their hatred of Communists, they approve any means whatsoever, says *La Croix*, to achieve widespread destruction. In the end, the number of dead will ironically become Communism's best ally.

A reading of certain issues of the *Congressional Record* will provide an excellent summary of the major objections to our involvement in Vietnam. I refer, in particular, to the remarks of Alaska's Senator Gruening in the Senate, together with the various published articles that he asked be reprinted in the *Record* (September 19, 1966, pp. 22125–22134); those of Senator Morse, in discussing "The Philippine President and U.S. Policy in Asia" (*Congressional Record*, September 19, 1966, pp. 22156–22158); the *Republican White Paper* (*Congressional Record*, September 20, 1966, pp. 22376–22386); again the views of Senator Morse, in commenting on Ambassador Goldberg's address before the United Nations, of September 2, 1966 (*Congressional Record*, September 26, 1966, pp. 22904–22906); and to the remarks of Representative Edwards in the House, on September 13, 1966, concerning the statement of the Community Association of the Pacific School of Religion (*Congressional Record*, September 12, 1966, A4784–A4785).

Throughout 1967 similar arguments are presented in various issues of the *Congressional Record*. However, the articles cited here for 1966 probably represent an adequate cross-section of opinion of those opposed to the war.

Two of these arguments have already been answered; evidence submitted by wholly reliable medical teams takes care of the question of wanton and indiscriminate burning of civilians by napalm. Secretary Rusk has replied to those who accuse us of using "temporarily disabling" gas.

One of the better-written presentations of the "positive" side of the morality argument is, in my opinion, that of Professor Paul Ramsay, Protestant divine. Professor Ramsay replies directly to Dr. Bennett's article on "Christian Realism." In his article "Farewell to Christian Realism" in the magazine *America*, on April 30, 1966, Professor Ramsay first takes Dr. Bennett to task for suggesting that political or military action can be "intolerably evil in itself" and at the same time acceptable under certain circumstances. The question posed is: Is something that is "evil in itself" acceptable if it revolves around an effort to overcome an even greater evil? Professor Ramsay points out this argument is virtually saying that the end justifies even an "intrinsically evil" means.

Confusion of the moral and the political is quite common today among many secular and religious liberals, and is basic to Dr. Bennett's argument. This is not to say that the two do not belong together—but an *ethical* judgment about the "inherent evil" of what we are doing as a nation is not the same as a political conviction that what we are doing is leading us into a tragic blind alley, or vice versa. In other words, one's own political conclusions about the wisdom of specific policy decisions cannot interfere with an objective, ethical analysis of the moral right or wrong that led to making such decisions. Professor Ramsay says that no one has the right to do what Dr. Bennett and so many others do—to use a sweeping moral judgment to buttress one's own policy recommendations.

Professor Ramsay points out that Dr. Bennett fails to examine the nature of the violence used by the insurgent forces in South Vietnam. Terror cannot be justified because it is used selectively. It is not justified because its users may also happen to win the people through other appeals or by the use of a program of national liberation, even if that program is sincere. The use of terror only minimally, or even upon carefully selected people, does not mean that it is *discriminative* in comparison, for example, with American bombing. (The principle of discrimination is rooted in the concept of discriminating between the guilty and the innocent. Militarily we use force against the enemy—not the civilians.) Professor Ramsay says, in effect, that Viet Cong use of warfare in terrorizing the civilians —even though only a few are terrorized as an example to others—is total war as opposed to discriminate war.

One cannot determine whether or not an act of war

is "intrinsically evil" on the basis of a body count. Disembowling only a specifically designated number, or a "reasonable" number of villagers, teachers, and local officials, in order to discourage others from allegiance to the government, is a moral absurdity, a moral contradiction. There is no such thing as a "reasonable" number of deliberate or designed atrocities, regardless of the purpose.

American military strategy is concerned with military targets. By design, guerrilla war strikes civilians in order to subvert them. It avoids striking legitimate military targets as far as possible. This is immoral by its very nature—regardless of its intent in terms of social revolution.

Professor Ramsay acknowledges that in the end only social, economic, and political reforms can defeat insurgency, but the need for military force still confronts us. If the guerrilla chooses to fight behind the populace, it is he, not the counter-guerrilla, who enlarges the legitimate target and brings unavoidable death and destruction upon innocent civilians.

Combat destruction is legitimate—the degree to which unavoidably associated civil damage takes place is up to the guerrilla. Professor Ramsay likens the situation to that in which an enemy places nuclear-warhead missile sites in the heart of his own cities and then assumes immunity from attack because it would be immoral for us to risk killing the innocent civilians living around the missile sites. The enemy thus deliberately enlarges the potential of devastation to the population. The burden of responsibility for unavoidable destruction of civilian lives and property cannot be shifted from the guerrilla to the counter-guerrilla.

In South Vietnam there are, without any question whatever, extensive underground "fortresses." These are in the form of command headquarters, munitions factories, and stores of rice. Intricate, interconnecting tunnels that open into countless peasant huts are used by the guerrilla. (I can certainly vouch for Professor Ramsay's statement on this score. In fact, it was one of the most critical problems I witnessed in our searching operations. I saw many a Marine risk his life exploring underground tunnels, never knowing whether he might confront armed Viet Cong or step on a mine. In most instances, after assuring that a tunnel was empty, the Marine's job would be to block it from future use by dynamiting it. Often these tunnels would lead underground from one hut to another, so that Viet Cong could disappear quickly, if spotted in a hut, then come up into another hut and fire on our troops from behind.) Plainly, then, says the Professor, all these areas are subject to the laws of siege. We did not create these underground fortresses; Mao Tse-tung did. No moralist can rightfully demand that statesmen or military commanders ignore these facts in their plans and policies.

In other words, Professor Ramsay points out, it is unlikely that the main design of the counterinsurgency effort in South Vietnam can validly be considered intrinsically evil, or that we are guilty of morally intolerable use of armed force.

Professor Ramsay is quick to point out that he is not denying that there may well be peripheral acts committed by counterinsurgents that are inherently evil. However, the business of bombing villages to get at the Viet Cong does not fall in this category.

He asserts that the doctrine of the just war is intended to guide political decision-makers in how they are to defend and preserve politically embodied justice, within moral limits.

Professor Ramsay takes to task those who place the

"engines of religion and morality" behind their own particular opinions. A moralist must make it quite clear that he knows someone else can recommend a specific policy even if it is at variance with a policy he has recommended. The moralist is aware that the other person is justified in feeling his recommendation is backed by sound religious and moral doctrine. It is dangerous to indicate doom is inevitable, because one's nation is violating "Christian" principles, when it is quite obvious that other Christians and moralists of other religious faiths interpret the nation's course quite differently. In arguing about ways to prevent a nation's becoming Communist, for example, agreement or disagreement with the government's plans does not make one's arguments more or less "Christian."

Professor Ramsay urges those who criticize our government for its "unclarity" about "unconditional discussions" or accuse it of demanding "unconditional surrender" to ask themselves several questions: Isn't it likely that the Viet Cong believe they can win a "pre-negotiation" victory? Isn't it likely that considerably more force will have to be exerted before the Viet Cong will even come to accept the idea of the NLF being only one of *several* parties in a final settlement rather than the single party, which alone will speak for the peoples of South Vietnam? Professor Ramsay quotes Bernard Fall's insistence that we "do away with the nonsense that there is such an animal as 'unconditional discussions,' let alone 'unconditional negotiations.' Both sides have a pretty good idea about the shape of the future contacts."

The Professor then considers the opinion that national Communism in Vietnam might be the lesser evil than, for example, continuing the war. If anyone thinks so, he suggests they also give careful consideration to General Taylor's statement about the "fierce fighting" which, in such a case, would be needed to save Thailand.

Ramsay urges us to remember the firm stands the United States has taken toward halting Communism in certain crises (for instance, Quemoy and Matsu) and to remember what we gained there. He urges caution about expecting mere replacement of current rulers in Peking to mean a "softer line."

Finally, after reminding us that we have never televised a Viet Cong take-over of a village, but that every day we see on television the "inhumanity" of the war the United States is fighting, Professor Ramsay gives a penetrating analysis of the problems of world power and world responsibility. When attacking the "irresponsible" use of power on the part of the United States, the moralist must remember the fantastic responsibilities inherited by the United States. He asks critics to remind themselves that the capacity of the U.N. Security Council to remove threats of peace was never achieved as originally envisioned, that the peacemaking capabilities of the United Nations have been curtailed by financial crises and the influx of membership, and that when critics demand the admission of Red China so that the United Nations will become a *universal* forum, they must recognize that it will become a forum *only*, and will be, for a long time to come, an even more frustrated and frustrating forum. This leads us to the need for developing a statesmanship that will be required in years to come, and while we are developing that statesmanship, we must recognize the independent initiatives and responsibilities of the United States to try to sustain a just world order. The United States, he says, as her moralistic critics know full well, has inherited both power and responsibility in "imperial" proportions. What is needed is more, not less, realism.

A second source for replying to certain criticisms of

our involvement in the war on moral grounds is J. S. Sebes's *Viet-Nam: An Enigma*. In a chapter titled "Is the U.S. Fighting the Wrong War in Vietnam?," Dr. Sebes takes up a wide range of politico-moral questions.

The first question is, "Can the U.S. fight for democracy by backing undemocratic regimes in Saigon?" (Of course, the question itself assumes that, regardless of how hard they try, the Vietnamese cannot bring about a democratic government in Saigon, an assumption rather difficult to defend, in view of the great strides made during the past two years alone.) But even if the Saigon government is considered completely "undemocratic," how do you establish a tradition of democracy in a country at war? Further, an undemocratic, non-Communist regime can be changed (changes are certainly taking place in South Vietnam, whether or not rapidly enough for American critics). A Communist regime, once entrenched, is relatively permanent, whether or not it becomes modified.

Dr. Sebes asks a number of trenchant questions. For example, "Can Red China and Communism be stopped in Southeast Asia?" He is talking primarily to observers like Walter Lippmann and Hans J. Morgenthau, who argue that Asia is the natural sphere of Chinese influence, as the Western Hemisphere is America's. We are fighting the wrong war, in the wrong place, at the wrong time, say such critics, and cannot hope to check the influence of Red China by militarily defending Thailand and South Vietnam. The situation in Southeast Asia is unlike that in Europe, where dividing lines could be drawn, says Professor Morgenthau, for example, and basically Mr. Lippmann seems to agree.

Dr. Sebes argues that the contrast made so often between Europe and Asia is not nearly so great as believed. In fact, sharp lines have been drawn and can be drawn (e.g., the 38th parallel in Korea, the 17th in Vietnam). The points at which we have stopped Communist aggression in Asia have been no more accidental than those in Europe (Greece, Turkey, Berlin). Ultimately, the defense against aggression must be made at points that are chosen by the Communists—not us.

"Natural sphere" proponents argue that the nature and culture of the Asiatic peoples make them much more amenable to Chinese influence and dominance. Dr. Sebes counters this argument strongly, by pointing out the strength and influence of Buddhism. He notes that not one country of Southeast Asia has given way to Communist political or cultural subversion without military force.

"Do the South Vietnamese care whether they live under Communism or not?" is Dr. Sebes's next question. One of the most frequent assertions I have heard is that the South Vietnamese people want peace at any price; they are hostile to their own government and to us for perpetuating a war in which they are totally uninterested. Dr. Sebes refers to the writings and experience of Professor Patrick J. Honey. Far too many people in South Vietnam are familiar with conditions in North Vietnam. This includes the hundreds of thousands of refugees who fled North Vietnam in 1954 to get away from Communism. Poor as they are in the south, they believe themselves far better off economically than the people in the north. The peasant's attachment to his land, to his rice field, is vital. He wants nothing to do with a system that robs him of his private ownership. Professor Honey points out that the South Vietnamese detest any possibility of Chinese invasion and feel that North Vietnam is under Chinese influence. The South Vietnamese feel they are the only ones holding out against future occupation. Despite their lack of sophistication about ideologies, they are very clear about not wanting Communism, and not wanting to be controlled by the Chinese.

Dr. Sebes takes up, in turn, the following questions: Is Vietnam becoming another Korea? Will increased U.S. intervention bring Russia and Red China together? Will North Vietnam overtly invade South Vietnam? Will Red China intervene? Will Russia intervene? Should Ho Chi Minh be left alone to become the "Tito of Southeast Asia?"

Admittedly, negative responses to these questions must be as speculative as affirmative answers (with the exception of the invasion of the South by North Vietnam, which has unquestionably taken place). However, in considering them, at least some issues can be clarified so that the mere mention of certain possibilities does not overwhelm our moral judgment. The fact that Red China *might* conceivably intervene, that a thermonuclear war *could* conceivably occur, by no means provides an automatic indictment of those actions the United States has taken or may take in regard to Vietnam.

First, Dr. Sebes points out the substantial difference between the Korean situation and the Vietnamese situation. The North Koreans attacked openly from the very beginning, with Chinese backing. During the Korean conflict the Communists enjoyed "privileged sanctuary" beyond the Yalu river. Today, North Vietnam still denies that it is attacking South Vietnam; today, he maintains, our bombing of the North makes it obvious that there will be no privileged sanctuary—as the Secretary of State has repeatedly warned.

A study of North Vietnam–Soviet–Red China relationships of the past few years makes the assertion that increased United States intervention will bring about a

Russo-Chinese détente very questionable. There is a tendency to nod sagely when this question is raised, as though we
can be sure that "blood is thicker than water," and that, by
some sort of mystique, Russia and China would dissolve all
their differences immediately if either were seriously threatened by the United States. This attitude, in turn, seems to be
based on the conviction that all the widely publicized
differences between Russia and Red China are "for show,"
and part of a complex conspiracy to trap the United States.
Surely, some concrete evidence must be presented before
U.S. policy can be attuned to such nebulous speculations.
Dr. Sebes argues that if Russia and China are to unite on
Vietnam, one or the other will have to switch its policy.
For Russia to do so would be to announce to the world
that it has previously been wrong, hence, to risk loss of
prestige with the Communist nations. For Red China to
do so, at least while Mao is alive, is most unlikely.

General Giap, North Vietnam's defense minister, has
stated that if American imperialism can be defeated in
South Vietnam, it can be defeated anywhere in the world:
"South Vietnam is the model of the national liberation
movement of our time. If the special warfare that the
U.S. imperialists are testing in South Vietnam is overcome, then it can be defeated anywhere in the world."
Will he, then, attempt a human wave assault against South
Vietnam, in an all-out and desperate effort to win? (This
would hardly accord either with the basic doctrine of
protracted conflict for which Giap is famous or with
Giap's recent directive to his troop commanders, warning them to prepare for returning from the tactics of
major confrontations to small unit tactics.) Dr. Sebes
cannot concede that all-out war by North Vietnam could
withstand American weaponry and air superiority.

In exploring the possibility of Red Chinese intervention, Dr. Sebes notes that Professor Honey makes much of the traditional hostility of the North Vietnamese toward the Chinese. One of the most intransigent in his hostility is General Giap himself. Ho Chi Minh is. quoted in rather earthy terms: "I would prefer to smell French *merde* for five years than smell the Chinese variety the rest of my life." This gem was forthcoming when Ho was busy pursuading the French to oust the Chinese and take over themselves in 1945. (The Chinese Nationalists had marched into Vietnam with French approval after the Japanese surrender.) Ho knew the French would always be easier to drive out than the Chinese.

But why wouldn't the Chinese come in uninvited? This would give them an opportunity to advance their plan of dominating Southeast Asia. Honey maintains that, over and above all her internal problems, Peking's preparations for war have been primarily defensive. He doubts that, unless Red China is invited by North Vietnam or attacked by the United States, her intervention is likely. Red China's warlike threats, no matter how strong, have always indicated explicitly that she is ready to come to the help of North Vietnam when *asked* or "when the North Vietnamese have need of us." If China intervened without being asked, her first problem would be to pacify the North Vietnamese, a task that would be to the advantage of both South Vietnam and the United States. Finally, he avers, there seems little question that Red China's regular army is needed at home these days, to control its own restive population. She is not in a position to gamble on deploying these forces in North Vietnam or anywhere else at the moment.

As for Soviet intervention, not only would it seem

contrary to Russia's policies toward North Vietnam to date—it would present tremendous logistic problems unless Red China cooperated on a continuing and dependable basis. To elaborate further, comparisons between Tito and Ho Chi Minh simply do not hold up. When Tito broke with Russia, he had a united nation under him and all of Western Europe to turn to, for economic aid and military assistance, together with a 1,100-mile buffer zone separating him from Russia. There is no buffer zone between Ho and Red China, no reliable unity beneath him, no Western Europe to turn to. So, says Dr. Sebes, even if this were a desirable goal—to establish an "independent" Ho Chi Minh, as a "reasonable" man to deal with, à la Tito—it would not be easy at all.

It seems to me that Dr. Sebes is saying throughout his text that, in effect, the burden of proof is on the affirmative. Those who question the morality of our national actions on the basis that we *may* provoke larger dangers certainly do a service by keeping us aware of these dangers. But exaggeration is as dangerous as minimizing the risks. Exaggeration, with the undue and overpowering fears it engenders, can lead to a paralysis of the national will. It can be responsible for encouraging us to renounce our responsibilities to the world at large and can lead to sacrificing our own justifiable self-interest. There is little to prove that any of the dire possibilities mentioned must inevitably become a reality if we continue the course we have been pursuing in Vietnam. Until such proof is available, all the ominous warnings in the world, no matter how sincere, should not be permitted to cloud our moral judgment. Each and every war we are involved in forces us to take calculated risks; such will be the case as long as wars are fought. The fact that results of miscalculation can be fatal does not mean that one abandons the moral right and obligation to calculate. The results of a delicate brain operation or the effort to remove a cancerous growth can also be fatal.

For those who maintain that *we* are the ones who pose impossible requirements and make too much of the necessity of "victory," Dr Sebes quotes General Song Hao, head of the North Vietnamese Army Political Bureau, as reported in *Quan Doi Nanh Dan (Party Daily)*, on April 17, 1965:

> The experience drawn from the revolutionary struggle in our country shows that the imperialists agree to attend a conference and negotiate only when we have a strong military force and actually defeat them on the battlefields. That is why we must be vigilant, must increase our hatred for U.S. imperialism, and fight them more strongly and resolutely to achieve *total victory*. [Italics mine.]

Among the sources quoted as morally objecting to our involvement in the war was a *Sign Magazine* article of August 1966. Under the title "Pacifism and America," a variety of moral viewpoints supporting some form of pacifism were included. The same article, however, presents a number of contrary moral viewpoints. I refer to it briefly as a third source of response to arguments cited previously.

The Very Reverend Francis J. Connell, at the time Dean Emeritus of the Department of Moral Theology at Catholic University in Washington, refers to the Second Vatican Council's "Pastoral Constitution on the Church in the Modern World" and quotes its statement that "Governments cannot be denied the right to legitimate defense, once every means of peaceful settlement has been exhausted." While the Council condemns "indiscriminate" acts of war, Father Connell points out that neither the storing of nuclear weapons nor even the discriminate use of smaller nuclear weapons can be condemned as immoral, in itself.

Michael Novak of Stanford University, an opponent of the war in Vietnam, admits that not even the ultimate terror of nuclear weapons justifies pacifism as a governmental policy for the United States. The use of military force today, he says, is extraordinarily dangerous, but we simply do not have the conditions required for reasonable adjudication and resolution of bitter tensions at the present time. Our policies must recognize the existence of threats of force and violence. They are part of today's real world, even though unidealistic and undesirable. In other words, wishful thinking about the United Nations won't make it so.

The Reverend John F. Cronin, Assistant Director, Social Action Department of the National Catholic Welfare Conference, writing in *Sign Magazine*, makes an interesting reference to the Encyclical of Pope John XXIII, *Pacem in Terris*. This hints that the Communist world might undergo a substantial change for the better. If that is so, Father Cronin says, any lessening of our posture of deterrence, except where we have negotiated arms limitations, might tempt a new generation of adventurers to come forth. He asks, then, whether other so-called free nations would follow the lead of the United States if we were to turn pacifist. (This fond but illusory hope seems implicit in the previously cited plea of Bishop Sheen, that we give the world an example of love for peace by withdrawing from Vietnam.) Father Cronin doubts it, and he suggests we might have more Hungarys and Cubas, more violence and bloodshed, rather than less.

What these writers are getting at, I think, is that as noble as its ideals are, the sort of pacifism that opposes the war in Vietnam simply because it is a war has not clearly justified itself on moral or prudential grounds.

The inevitable conclusion of this chapter must be the conviction that neither the specific nor the general objections to the Vietnamese war as an intrinsic evil have demonstrated that we are acting immorally. Immoral activities have been associated with this war, as with every war —activities ranging from profiteering to atrocities. No one has yet made it clear that any such activities have been a basic design in pursuing the aims of the war. Nor has anyone made it clear that the aim of the war itself is to support such immoral activities. Finally, no one has demonstrated conclusively that this war, despite its associated immoralities and risks, is a greater evil than the evil of inappropriate negotiations. Nor has anyone proved that a course of compromise is worth risking the security of the peoples of South Vietnam or of Southeast Asia. Until that is demonstrated, certainly the Administration is justified in pursuing a course that it sincerely believes is less evil than any of the possibilities inherent in a radical modification of that course.

It seems to me that the policies pursued in general by the United States have been quite consonant with the statement on peace issued by the Roman Catholic Bishops of the United States on November 17, 1966:

> No one is free to evade his personal responsibility by leaving it entirely to others to make moral judgments . . . Citizens of all faiths and of differing political loyalties honestly differ among themselves over the moral issues involved in the tragic conflict . . . While we do not claim

to be able to resolve these issues authoritatively, in the light of the facts as they are known to us, it is reasonable to argue that our presence in Vietnam is justified . . . We share the anguish of our government officials in their awesome responsibility of making life-and-death decisions about our national policy in Vietnam. We commend the valor of our men in the armed forces, and we express to them our debt of gratitude . . . But we cannot stop here. While we can conscientiously support the position of our country in the present circumstances, it is the duty of everyone to search for other alternatives. And everyone—government leaders and citizens alike —must be prepared to change our course whenever a change in circumstances warrants it.

13

TRUTH OR CONSEQUENCES

*I*N AN EARLIER CHAPTER I EX-
pressed my sadness that an important elected official in
the United States would call the President of the United
States a "phony." I consider this a very severe charge.
Much has been made of the right to dissent, and open
debate about our foreign policy has been lauded as a
healthy development. So be it. But is the dissenter free
merely to scorn, to ridicule, to accuse the President of
being a fraud, while offering no data, no facts, no evidence
of fraudulent behavior? Has dissension nothing to do with
truth? If not, then let us expect chaotic consequences. By
what right do we assume or attribute either malice or
stupidity on the part of the President of the United States,
simply because we may disagree with his policy decisions?

I shall devote this final chapter largely to that question,
using as a frame of reference a text that, I believe, unfortunately typifies the implied as well as the expressed
accusation of malice and/or stupidity at Administration
level in the United States. I refer to *Vietnam: Crisis of
Conscience*, which, as mentioned earlier, is the combined
work of Robert McAfee Brown, Protestant clergyman;
Abraham J. Heschel, Jewish rabbi; and Michael Novak,
Catholic layman. This book has been widely distributed
in the United States. It calls the war in Vietnam immoral
—"impossible to justify." It urges: interfaith action to stop
the bombing—unconditionally; negotiation now for peace

without victory; acceptance of the Viet Cong at the negotiation table; preparation for the rebuilding of war-torn Vietnam.

In my opinion, this book not only repeats most of the charges I have discussed previously—and repeats them gratuitously, in many instances; it goes further than many critics in charging the Administration with bad faith. Mr. Novak asks, for example ". . . if we agree that Presidents Eisenhower, Kennedy, and Johnson have acted in good faith, how are we to explain the moral degradation in which we have become involved?" Another reason for treating this particular book in detail is that it is one of the few full-fledged texts that I know of devoted exclusively to the moral aspects of the conflict.

In the following pages, I cite just a few of what I consider the *ad hominem* arguments posed by the authors, as well as the half-truths, the texts out of context, the misquotations.

Mr. Novak begins the book under the title "Stumbling into War and Stumbling Out." Apparently the title is, in part, a reference to Richard N. Goodwin's assertion that it was "almost by accident" that we became involved in Vietnam, and the author indicates that Arthur M. Schlesinger, Jr., supports this thesis. Mr. Novak then goes on to the familiar allegation about the "Eisenhower commitment" and what it supposedly did not involve. This has been thoroughly examined in an earlier chapter. (And if Mr. Eisenhower didn't think SEATO would provide legality for intervention in later years, it is impossible to discover this in his writings. After he had successfully arranged the SEATO Treaty and the Pacific Charter, he stated, with very obvious satisfaction: "The dilemma of finding a moral, legal, and practical basis for helping our friends of the region need not face us again.")

While on Eisenhower quotations, it is interesting to note that Mr. Novak badly mishandles, even more so than others, the famous Eisenhower statement about Ho Chi Minh and elections. Mr. Novak has President Eisenhower saying, vis-à-vis the proposed 1956 elections, not merely that Ho Chi Minh would win 80 per cent of the vote, but 80 per cent of the southern vote! Wrong place, wrong date, wrong party running against Ho.

Perhaps my interpretation is uncharitable, but I do not like what appear to be deliberate juxtapositions such as one found on page 5 of the book. Here Mr. Novak tells us that President Eisenhower "contemplated sending bombers" to defend the beleaguered French at Dien Bien Phu. Then he tells us, immediately, as though this were the rationale for not sending bombers, that Senator Lyndon Johnson "firmly refused to endorse military intervention." I can see no reason for juxtaposing these statements except to discredit Mr. Johnson for having accelerated military intervention after becoming President, as though this action is a damning contradiction of his earlier position. His position has obviously changed with changing circumstances. The whole argument seems to me irrelevant. Even the most superficial reading of *Mandate for Change* shows the military and diplomatic reasons why President Eisenhower did not send bombers. I must wonder how many of those who quote Mr. Eisenhower have read him.

What real use are aphorisms about race, such as those found on pages 14 and 15, where accusations previously discussed—that this is a white man–yellow man war—are repeated with as little supportive evidence? (No more, no less than the other critics cited earlier.) Sympathy with questions about racial discrimination in the United States is one thing. The implications that we have extended deep-rooted racial animosities to the peoples of Asia, or they to us, is very different. Much more proof of such a thesis is needed. Clichés and platitudes, however pious, simply won't do.

On page 25, Mr. Novak refers to Senator Mc-Govern, who questioned why the United States supported French colonialism. But it is precisely, very precisely, on this point that Mr. Eisenhower was so emphatic. His insistence on forming a regional coalition, his continuing review of the question of intervention, his efforts toward getting "world approval," his urging France to take the Indochina conflict to the United Nations, his repeated urging that France give full freedom to the Associated States, and finally, his demand that France announce publicly that the battle was against *Communism* and Communist expansion—all this was in great part to *avoid* supporting French colonialism! Mr. Eden's descriptions of the Eisenhower efforts in this regard (*Full Circle*) complement those of Mr. Eisenhower himself (*Mandate for Change*).

On page 28, Mr. Novak calls on the repeatedly used quotation of President Kennedy's, of September 1963: "In the final analysis, it is their war. We can help them . . . but they have to win it . . ." Yet Mr. Novak fails to do what so many others who quote Mr. Kennedy fail to do—complete the text. In the very same CBS interview in which President Kennedy made the statement cited above, he concluded his remarks with: ". . . I don't agree with those who say we should withdraw. That would be a great mistake. That would be a great mistake. I know people don't like Americans to be engaged in this kind of effort . . . but this is a very important struggle even though it is far away."

On the same page 28, the author discovers that we made a mistake in choosing Diem as "our man in Saigon." Diem, he says (as others have said), took no part in the struggle for independence in Vietnam; he was busy making friends in Washington. We call once more on Professor Bernard Fall, who can hardly be called a pro-Diem man. It will be recalled that Fall describes Diem as a well-known patriot, popular with the people, famed for resisting both the French and the Viet Minh. Mr. Novak continues, however, with the traditional charges about Diem's dictatorship, his cruelty, his murders. At risk of being thought a "Diemophile," I suggest again a reading of the report to the U. S. Senate Committee on the Judiciary, February 17, 1964.

Included in other testimony quoted in this report is that of Ambassador Fernando Volio Jimenez, of Costa Rica, who served as a member of the U.N. fact-finding mission to examine the charges against Diem. Ambassador Volio says that on the basis of stories in the world press, he had been prepared to vote in the United Nations to condemn Diem, but when Diem invited the United Nations to send observers, he held off. After two weeks of intensive investigation in Vietnam, he says, he concluded that the charges made against Diem in the General Assembly of the United Nations had not been sustained. This finally contradicted a statement made by sixteen governments who had charged that the Vietnamese government had been guilty of "a serious violation of human rights." If sixteen governments could be wrong, Mr. Novak's error is understandable. Incidentally, the Senate report referred to here quotes Miss Marguerite Higgins' interview with the famous South Vietnamese Buddhist leader Thich Tri Quang. Miss Higgins says Thich Tri Quang told her:

"We cannot get an arrangement with the north until we get rid of Diem." This is quite a commentary on the political motives of those who led the Buddhist agitation.

On page 32, Mr. Novak repeats the accusation that before 1965 the United States treated the war in Vietnam as predominantly a civil war but that our decision to commit large numbers of troops demanded a new theory —"aggression." I refer once again to the many Eisenhower statements on "aggression," "Communist expansion," and so on, to say nothing of those of Mr. Kennedy—long before 1965. (See *Background Information*, previously cited, and Chapters 3 and 4 of this book.) Mr. Novak does not support his scholarliness by quoting the patently erroneous statement of Richard N. Goodwin (p. 41), who says he is in "doubt if you will find China mentioned in the statement of any American President on Vietnam until the last six or eight months. It was a forbidden word." Mr. Eisenhower's *Mandate for Change* sets the record straight on this error very quickly.

Mr. Novak tells us (p. 47): "There does not seem to be a single good reason why this war must go on, except the need of the Americans to find an honorable peace" (or what he calls, in the end, "saving face"). But it is perhaps not surprising that Mr. Novak would not know why the war continues, since he calls it "amazing" (p. 18) that so few of the revolutions and wars since 1945 have proved serious or widened into conflagrations. Mr. Novak might not find it amazing at all if he reflected a bit upon the "honorable" use of American power. President Marcos, quoted previously, can fill in the details.

Space does not permit detailed attention to the sections of *Vietnam: Crisis of Conscience* written by Rabbi Heschel and Dr. Brown. But a few passages really should be noted. For example, Rabbi Heschel tells us on p. 53 (in the section entitled, "The Moral Outrage of Vietnam"): "We are killing the Vietnamese because we are suspicious of the Chinese." The Rabbi says this—nothing but this. Nothing about Viet Cong terrorism, atrocities, subversion— nothing at all. We defer again to Professor Fall's description of Viet Cong activities. Rabbi Heschel goes on to another definition of our procedures, in the same paragraph. "The aim is to kill the elusive Viet Cong, yet *to come upon one soldier, it is necessary to put an end to a whole village, to the lives of civilians, men, women and children.*" (Italics mine.) Who can fail to respect Rabbi Heschel's sincerity or intensity? But who can accept such generalizations?

Or who can, with the best of goodwill toward Rabbi Heschel's intent, fail to raise an eyebrow over so bland and definitive a conclusion as: "The state of cold war between the U. S. and Soviet Russia *has given place* to a quest of friendly understanding"? (Italics mine.)

And whence comes the authority to assert bluntly: "It is a war we can never win"?

I think a brief look at this idea is in order. What do we mean when we say we can never win the war? Rabbi Heschel means, apparently, that we can not win morally and spiritually—that, regardless of military victories, we shall have lost the people in tears, hatred, rage.

I believe we can win and are winning. The observations I have recorded in Chapter 1 of this book, my personal experiences in Vietnam and that of many chaplains, previous comments about the feelings of Asians—these convince me that, bit by bit, we are winning the trust, not the hostility, of the peoples of South Vietnam. Before March 1965 and the insertion of our military forces at high levels, an election in South Vietnam, once the Diem regime fell, would have been impossible. On September 12,

1967, in an editorial on the elections, the *Kansas City Star* recalled Korea. The *Star*, citing the *London Economist*, reminded us that only about twelve of the nearly seventy independent Asian and African countries have risked holding elections with any significant degree of choice. It then pointed out that among these twelve nations is South Korea, where, in 1948, some 75 per cent of eligible voters braved Communist threats as did the South Vietnamese, and for the same reason—the United States was guaranteeing their basic security.

I think that Rabbi Heschel, justifiably outraged by the horrors of war, is one of those whose judgment about our involvement and the attitudes and future of Vietnam is clouded by this outrage. Once again, we *all* feel the bitter anguish of the problem. The solution, however, certainly does not lie in wishing that there were no war or in accusing ourselves of having "fossilized consciences" and "mortgaged souls." I repeat emphatically that I have found no evidence, nor do I think Rabbi Heschel offers any, that the people of South Vietnam feel about us as the Rabbi thinks they do.

If everything we are doing is so abhorrent, how can the Rabbi justify his insistence on the one hand that "military victory in Vietnam would be a tragic moral defeat" (p. 53) and, on the other, tell us we have a clear choice, to decide in favor of further escalation or in favor of "gradual disengagement followed by negotiation" (p. 54)? If everything we are doing is unspeakably evil, what moral right do we have to *gradual* disengagement? We must stop *now*, immediately. I have no right whatever merely to tone down my torturing, *reduce* the number of atrocities I perform, burn *fewer* children with napalm! I must cease immediately anything as barbaric as the Rabbi seems to think our actions are. Indeed, he tells us explicitly (p.

58) that this war "cannot be waged within the terms of civilized rules of warfare."

On pages 54 and 55 Rabbi Heschel invokes the common charge that we are fighting social revolution with military power and, therefore, cannot win. Howard K. Smith answers this accusation in the *Washington Evening Star*, October 8, 1967. Mr. Smith points out that today political and military actions are inextricably interwoven. If the Communists depended on political means without military force, they would have long since disappeared. If we laid aside our arms today while trying to help South Vietnam build a nation, Southeast Asia would collapse to the Communists.

Finally, when Rabbi Heschel tells us that leading American authorities on international law maintain that we are violating the U.N. Charter, SEATO, the Geneva Accords, international law and the Constitution of the United States, he fails to note the American Bar Association resolution that says exactly the opposite of all this. (*American Bar Association Journal*, May 1966, Volume 52, Number 5.)

Dr. Brown concludes the book with "An Appeal to the Churches and Synagogues." In my opinion, this section shares the faults of the others, with its aphorisms and half-truths. By what authority, for example, can Dr. Brown state: "If the United States is really willing to allow free elections in South Vietnam, for example, the chances are high that South Vietnam will go Communist"? Now I think a statement like this is purely arbitrary. It completely contradicts the reality of events in South Vietnam, as we have already seen.

This, I believe, is the trouble with the entire book. Hundreds of statements, laid one upon another, often ringing with apocalyptic tones, denunciatory, prophetic, anguished, tragic—all together produce a most impressive effect. If the authors want readers to feel the agony of war, the personal responsibility each of us shares for the suffering in the world, to pray for forgiveness for our human treacheries, to engage in continuing reappraisal of our national policies and responsibilities, they succeed in their highly laudable objective. But since they, themselves, make much of the principle that evil means may not be used to procure a good end, I, for one, must question the morality of their method. They bombard the emotions with half-truths, which, though multiplied by the hundreds, never become whole. They "hit and run"— throw the most shattering statements on their pages, then rush on, without reasoned demonstration, clear evidence, scholarly support for their charges. The average reader can hardly be expected to have the personal background or experience to question their dogma—and dogma it is, more often than historic fact. He knows he is reading the work of sincere and reputable men, men who have proved themselves in the marketplace of modern ecumenism, who are dedicated to truly noble causes and unselfish public service. Since their book is one of the very few detailed treatments of the moral dimensions of the war in Vietnam, the unprepared reader has a right to be impressed and strongly influenced.

This is one of the reasons I have given so much time to this book. It is almost singular in topic and typical, I think, of many attitudes. Indeed, the book does a service in bringing together a great number of the arguments opposed to our involvement in Vietnam.

However, I honestly consider it a highly misleading book. And what is doubly disappointing, to me, is that the book begins by asserting its awareness that dissent does not mean insincerity and that it certainly intends to condemn no one. But, on the contrary, in my opinion, its basic premise is that the U.S. administration and the military are stupid, deceptive, and acting in bad faith and that everyone in a significant position in Saigon is completely corrupt. It seems to me that its method is to replace reasoned argument and documented evidence with rhetorical questions and clichés. Its tone is judgmental to the point of being morally apodictic. I think it a bad book.

I would like to cite just a few more illustrations at random from Dr. Brown's section of this book, then leave it, giving this section less space than the others only because I think that most of Dr. Brown's arguments have been treated in sufficient detail in my earlier chapters, in one form or another.

On page 69, Dr. Brown quotes Arthur M. Schlesinger, Jr., to the effect that, by the end of 1966, we had dropped more bombs on North and South Vietnam than on Germany during all of World War II. Now this is quoted apparently to tell us of the stupidity of our tactics— tactics to prolong the war and increase its intensity. But nothing is said to compare the destructiveness wrought in Germany by "saturation bombing" with the effects of discriminative bombing in Vietnam. Has there been any attempted obliteration equal to the bombing of Berlin or Frankfurt? Does Dr. Brown realize that it is precisely because of our care, our determined effort to avoid killing the innocent, that we use more bombs and the war is prolonged? But I really fear that the tenor of his writing hardly makes it likely that he would accept any act of the administration as sincere.

For example, pages 85 to 97 of Dr. Brown's section are devoted to questions of negotiations, alternatives to the status quo, credibility, and allied topics. The recurrent theme of these pages is that every effort on the part of U Thant or other would-be intermediates has been arbitrarily—even rudely—rejected by the administration. Pleas to discuss our foreign policy are answered by the President in "petulant and often angry remarks"; the Vice-President echoes the President's position "with more glowing rhetoric"; the Secretary of State each week repeats a position "increasingly intransigent." Now whose evaluations are these, and what makes them authoritative?

It has been proposed to stop the bombing permanently and unconditionally. But the Administration, Dr. Brown tells us, has not considered the proposals "with utmost seriousness." Where does Dr. Brown's information come from?

Dr. Brown tells us with approval about proposals that we withdraw to a "certain geographical perimeter" and make it clear that we will defend lives within it but will not wage offensive war outside it. In my opinion, this proposal suggests a misunderstanding of the nature of the war, the topography and structure of Vietnam, the history of the French-Viet Minh conflict, the debacle of Dien Bien Phu, and the problems experienced in places like Khe Sanh and Con Thien. Dr. Brown tells us this type of de-escalation would "not endanger military and civilian personnel."

This is, of course, a military question, about which I probably have no more professional competence than Dr. Brown. But I object to the implication that the Administration shrugs off such proposals because of its own intransigence. This is a totally unjust assumption. The Administration has the constant advice of military professionals, who frequently differ in their opinions. The President must make the final decisions. These must often be agonizing decisions to make, but who can validly charge that they are made lightly or in total disregard of contrary opinions? I would like to see if the critics feel as definitive about "enclaves" after they have read Gen-

eral Giap's *People's War, People's Army*—the strategy of
protracted conflict. And speaking of withdrawal within
certain geographical perimeters, wasn't that the idea of
the 17th parallel?

One more. Dr. Brown urges that we make it un-
ambiguously clear that we are willing to use any and all
international organizations in searching for peace, including the United Nations, the International Control Commission, and others. He then tells us how Secretary of
State Dean Rusk has "succeeded in discouraging all hopes
that there can be any negotiations soon," that Ambassador Goldberg "it is reported" was shocked by Rusk's
tone and comments. I feel we have discussed the whole
business of negotiations sufficiently in earlier chapters and
refer to the subject here only as further illustration of
what I consider the ill-founded assumptions in this book.
(But it is worth recalling that the same innuendoes were
bandied about in Ambassador Stevenson's time. "It is reported" that Mr. Stevenson disagreed with the Administration. But, as we have seen, such innuendoes were
denied by Mr. Stevenson while alive and by his son after
the Ambassador died.)

In conclusion, I would like to discuss briefly certain
questions that I think have important moral ramifications
and add a few comments about questions previously discussed.

There is, first, the question of a declaration of war.
Some critics have considered the President to have trans-
gressed his authority, particularly in using the "Tonkin
Gulf" resolution of the Senate, to wage full-fledged war.
The constitutionality of his actions here has been ques-
tioned. The legal aspects of this issue, I think, have been
adequately discussed by members of the American Bar
Association in earlier chapters. But what of the morality?

I feel that arguments presented by the State Department provide a sound basis for a moral judgment (*Position Paper* of November 19, 1965). In terms of international considerations, it is argued that a declaration of war would be undesirable for several reasons: It might broaden the conflict, through misunderstanding of intent or through miscalculation; it could imply dedication to total destruction of the enemy (typical of declared wars in this century); it would reduce flexibility for negotiations; it is not required by international law; the legal rules of international law, such as the 1949 Geneva Conventions for the Protection of War Victims, apply without a declaration of war.

In other words, the interests of good order and justice between nations and for the world at large would appear to be served better by not introducing the psychological dynamics set in motion by a formal declaration of war. Grave though the current conflict is, as a "declared war" it would conceivably be much worse, and the danger of expansion much more serious.

But speaking of potential expansion and the question of Red China's entering the conflict in full strength, certainly anyone in his right mind will maintain an urgent awareness of these and other grave possibilities. But they are, precisely, *possibilities*, not current fact.

It does nothing to end the war, save lives, hasten peace, to mouth such dicta as that "we are no match for the countless hordes of Asia." Is there a pundit available able to assume so assuredly that Red China will enter the war? At the moment, we are a nation of nearly 200 million fighting a nation of less than 10 per cent of that number.

What is accomplished, except the confusion of the gullible, by such statements as that attributed to a distinguished critic: "American casualties have come to exceed the South Vietnamese draft calls?" Precisely what does that mean? Would it improve things if the draft calls exceeded the casualties? As we have seen, the new Saigon government is, in fact, increasing the draft; but, as we have also seen, South Vietnamese are drafted, wounded, and killed at the present time in much higher proportions than Americans are.

One of the most hackneyed criticisms of the attitudes of the South Vietnamese people is that they either have been shameless cowards for harboring or tolerating the Viet Cong for so many years or they are sympathetic to the Viet Cong, who, therefore, must truly represent the South Vietnamese people much more significantly than the government in Saigon does. But if one charges cowardice, one must ask: "Could we be sure that 83 per cent of registered American voters would risk going to the polls if so threatened by terrorists? Would Americans then want the world to believe that the terrorists represented the will of the American people?"

Just in passing, it might be worth noting here that those who have charged that South Vietnamese troops were used to surround villages and intimidate people into voting simply miss the point. Of course the South Vietnamese troops were used—to provide security for those who wanted to vote. One need simply ask again, was the National Guard used in Gary, Indiana, in November 1967 to force people to vote?

How deceptive the "simple" can be. If the Viet Cong or the National Liberation Front represent a significant number of people, why weren't they elected when 83 per cent of the eligible voters expressed their will in September of 1967? Why did they do everything conceivable to prevent people from voting in 1967? Why are more and more of the people exposing the Viet Cong? Why has the number of Viet Cong defectors almost doubled within the past year? Why, after so many years of using every tactic from give-away programs to murder have the Viet Cong been unable to take over South Vietnam?

This leads me to a final remark I should like to make concerning negotiations with the Viet Cong, or the National Liberation Front. I personally believe the United States has made crystal clear its willingness to negotiate at any time, in any place, and with any parties with whom negotiations can be rationally carried out. Many critics of American policy do not believe this. Determined, apparently, that our government deals exclusively in deceit and duplicity and that North Vietnam and the Viet Cong have refused to negotiate because we impose impossible terms, the critics keep demanding that we negotiate on *any* terms, and, particularly, that we give the National Liberation Front a major role in such negotiations.

Now to me, this insistence implies two things— one, that we forget that to negotiate does not mean to capitulate. The other is that Hanoi as represented by the National Liberation Front in South Vietnam has been dramatically successful in convincing a number of Americans that the Viet Cong are true nationalists and that they represent the will of a significant number of the peoples of South Vietnam. Both Hanoi in the north and the National Liberation Front in the south have repeated frequently and violently that the National Liberation Front is the *sole* representative of the peoples of South Vietnam. But by insisting on this, they have been able to get their foot in the door, by having us believe that the Viet Cong and the National Liberation Front *must* represent at least *some* of the people, and probably a large number. Thus is our American sense of fairness used adroitly against us. The argument seems so simple and convincing.

Whose computer has determined that we are "exhausting" our national resources in Vietnam when currently we are spending little more than 3 per cent of our gross national income on the conflict?

Where have clichés such as "We can never win a military victory in Vietnam" come from? Why can't we? Who says we can't? Certainly Hanoi is finding this difficult to believe. The Viet Cong are hardly convinced of it. What Hanoi and the Viet Cong *do* believe, of course, is that *we* shall come to believe that we can't win, and withdraw.

Who thinks he can fabricate peace by cutting out of whole cloth the figures about civilian casualties in South Vietnam—that "we have killed far more civilians by our bombing and shelling than have been killed by the Viet Cong"?

What criteria have been used by those who assure us that this is the first "unpopular" war in American history? Was Valley Forge popular? How many Americans raised vehement voices against risking war with England? What about the conflict between Jefferson and Adams on questions of "national honor" in relation to the Barbary Coast pirates? How many people in the North were opposed to the Civil War? When was the plea for "isolationism" stronger than at the outset of World War II? What was "popular" about Korea? But *should* a war be popular? If this means that the people *want* war—this is savagery, at its worst. If we are talking about the will of the people to do what they are convinced must be done, then it seems to me that this war is as popular as any other. Rapid communications and multiple news media spread the word much more quickly and widely

than ever before. Televised pictures of combat almost
while it's happening are brought directly into the living
room. Should we be surprised by Congressional debate,
expression of public interest and concern, the voice of
dissent? There has been resistance to conscription in every
war America has ever fought. There have been disagreements with method, pleas for greater restraint, for broader
destruction, for negotiating peace at any price, for demanding unconditional surrender.

To me the disagreements merely validate the need
for what I suggested at the outset of this book—the critical need that we read in *depth*, think, study, try to analyze
carefully the data available on the conflict in Vietnam.
To deny the right of dissent would be foolish, indeed.
But to demand that we know wherein we dissent and
why, to dissent on the basis of fact, and not fancy, to
dissent because of reasoned conviction and not because
it's fashionable, to speak when we know whereof we
speak, to be able to support our statements with reasonable evidence, to evaluate the rightness or wrongness of
the war on its own merits, not in relation to poor housing or racial conflicts or satellite programs or medical
research—certainly to demand this is merely to demand
responsible behavior.

God willing, we Americans will always question our
right and our obligation to engage in conflict, will always
examine critically, if not caustically, our methods of waging war, will always demand that our elected officials
do everything reasonable to avoid war, and if unsuccessful
in this, seek ardently and intensely the road to peace. For,
as I remarked before, in a very definite sense every war
is the wrong war, in the wrong place, at the wrong time.
This is because every war means pain and suffering and
sacrifice, and because no war is ever "good."

I believe the war in Vietnam is very much the lesser of the many evils that would engulf us if we chose not to fight it. I do not believe in a domino theory if this means that the fall of the people in one nation to the tyranny of Communism means, inevitably, the fall of an adjacent country. I *do* believe, however, that Communistic terror did not merely disappear in the Philippines—it was confronted and destroyed. Communistic terror did not simply die away or crumble in Malaya—it was confronted and destroyed. Regardless of what the "latest" word may be from Indonesia, I believe that our presence in Asia made possible the revolt against a Communist take-over. I believe in the frightful power of the unconfronted "war of liberation." So do Soviet Russia, Red China, Hanoi. I believe such wars could and would destroy the freedoms of nation after nation—including our own—if we permitted it. We have not permitted it in the past. I do not believe it will ever be the "popular" thing for Americans to do in the future.

Rather, I believe strongly, and pray ardently, that the words of Secretary of State Dulles at the ill-fated Geneva Conference of 1954 will prevail, wherever the war, whenever the time:

> Peace is always easy to achieve—by surrender. Your Government does not propose to buy peace at that price. We do not believe that the American people want peace at that price. So long as that is our national will, and so long as that will be backed by a capacity for effective action, our Nation can face the future with that calm confidence which is the due of those who, in a troubled world, hold fast to that which is good.

AFTERWORD

*A*T THE OUTSET OF THIS
book I noted a trend toward possible negotiations for
peace in Vietnam. I suggested then that if negotiations
should come about and if peace terms are arranged, an
honest recognition of historic fact would still be imperative, if peace is to endure.

I am even more convinced today of the importance
of keeping our facts in order.

On Sunday night, March 31, 1968, President Johnson offered for the thirty-first time to negotiate with
Hanoi.

On Wednesday, April 3, 1968, Hanoi replied: "The
Democratic Republic of Vietnam declares its readiness to
appoint its representative to contact the United States
representative with a view to determining with the American side the unconditional cessation of the United States
bombing raids and all other acts of war against the Democratic Republic of Vietnam so that talks may start."

President Johnson responded on the same day: "Now,
as in the past, the United States is ready to send its representatives to any forum, at any time, to discuss the means
of bringing this war to an end.

"Accordingly we will establish contact with the representatives of North Vietnam. Consultations with the government of South Vietnam and our other allies are now
taking place."

While a record 19 million shares were traded on Wall Street, and editorial pages throughout the United States expressed at least cautious jubilation, a number of political analysts recalled the Trojan horse and warned against letting Hanoi win through negotiations what it has failed to win on the battlefield. More than a few reporters remembered that we lost some 12,000 men *during* the Korean truce talks at Panmunjom. So I believe today what I believed when I began work on this book almost two years ago—that the truth remains critically important.

During the past few months some events have occurred that, superficially understood, might seem to disprove completely the basic tenets of this book. Notable among these was the Viet Cong Tet offensive of February 1968. I am well aware—and honestly amazed—that many American observers believe that Hanoi and the Viet Cong achieved a tremendous victory through this offensive.

The Viet Cong lost at least 50,000 men, of whom the majority were their crack guerrillas. To replace these men, trained as they were in insurgency, in politics, in guerrilla tactics, intimately familiar as they were with the villages and hamlets, the jungles and rice paddies of South Vietnam, will take at least two or three years.

Psychologically, in terms of what the Viet Cong had been promised by their leaders and what they expected, their Tet offensive was disastrous. Captured documents and the testimony of captured Viet Cong demonstrated unquestionably that the rank and file of the Viet Cong had been assured by their leaders and by Hanoi of all-out support by the South Vietnamese armed forces and the South Vietnamese people. The radio constantly informed them that masses of South Vietnamese were rising up to support the Viet Cong, their "liberators," and that the South Vietnamese armed forces were joining the Viet

Cong in fighting to drive out the forces of the United States. The enthusiastic directives given the VC were familiar: "Liberate the 14 million people of South Vietnam and fulfill our revolutionary task. . . . This will be the greatest battle in Vietnamese history. It will decide the fate and the survival of the fatherland. We must achieve final victory at all costs."

What actually happened? There were no popular uprisings among the South Vietnamese, no defecting of South Vietnamese security forces. Certainly the people were frightened at first. Then, seeing that the Viet Cong could not sustain the attack, mindful that their sacred holiday (the lunar New Year) had been grossly violated, the sacred city of Hue profaned, that treachery, destruction, brutality, and terrorism were everywhere, they turned against the Viet Cong in anger and bitter resentment.

Monsignor Jim Killeen, one of my closest friends, a Navy chaplain in Saigon, wrote to me on February 6, 1968, and summarized in a single anecdote the attitude of the South Vietnamese peoples after the Tet attack. "One of the Vietnamese ladies who work in our compound came back to work yesterday and, with hatred in her eyes, spat on the ground, saying, 'VC number 10!' "

One of the newspaper columnists made great sense to me when he pointed out that had the United States lost 600,000 men in an all-out offensive that failed to achieve its objective, the defeat would have been heralded as the most catastrophic in U.S. history. Proportionately, this is what happened to the Viet Cong. And many call it a Viet Cong victory!

Captured documents and prisoners reveal that the Viet Cong came to stay. They honestly believed they were going to take and hold the cities and "liberate"

South Vietnam. They were unable to hold even a single city.

True, Hanoi has since boasted almost daily that the Tet offensive was intended to prove that the Viet Cong could strike at will, whenever, wherever, however they choose, against the South Vietnamese and highly vaunted American forces. I do not believe the Tet offensive was designed to prove this at all. I think it was an attack made either in sheer desperation or in gross miscalculation. In my opinion, history may well record the defeat of the Viet Cong during Tet in terms as decisive as those that recorded the defeat of the French at Dien Bien Phu.

As I conclude this book I feel that I should cite briefly a few other encouraging recent developments.

I was encouraged to see, for example, that those Catholic bishops who had been part of the "Negotiations Now" movement have modified their position to meet objections raised (in part by Bishop John J. Wright, of Pittsburgh) that "Negotiations Now" seemed to seek an end to U.S. bombing without seeking an end to North Vietnam's aggression. A new group, an outgrowth of the "Negotiations Now" movement, is called the "National Committee for a Political Settlement in Vietnam," and appeals for de-escalation by all parties, an end to bombing of the North and troop build-up by the United States, and to Viet Cong terrorism and North Vietnamese aggression against the South. Certainly such a modification of position is a step in the right direction.

I was also encouraged by an Associated Press story that appeared in the *Baltimore Sun* on April 4, 1968— encouraged because I suppose that most people like to have their views supported by authorities, especially if their views are not popularly held. Since the views I have presented about Ngo Dinh Diem in this book differ substantially from those most widely held in the United States, I was naturally very much interested by this item that quoted an expression of feeling about Diem by Frederick E. Nolting, Jr., former Ambassador to South Vietnam. The account states that in an address on April 2, 1968, Mr. Nolting stated that the dilemma in Vietnam started with "the fatal error" of 1963, when the United States, he claimed, undermined President Ngo Dinh Diem.

The news story also reports that Mr. Nolting accused various United States officials of an "abysmal lack of understanding and judgment" during 1963 and that he called Lyndon B. Johnson one of the few advising President Kennedy against undermining Diem. This, according to the report, former Ambassador Nolting stated was "ironic" in light of the situation inherited by President Johnson after Diem's assassination. The report states further that Mr. Nolting blamed himself for failing to persuade the State Department that the overthrow of Diem would be a tragedy for Vietnam and for the United States. Mr. Nolting called it the "miracle of Diem" that he was able to inspire respect in handling problems related to his country. "To me the secret of his success," Mr. Nolting said, "was his moral integrity."

Since I am not a lawyer and have dared to discuss the legal aspects of our involvement in Vietnam, I was naturally encouraged to see the publication of a new book, *Law and Viet Nam*, by Yale Law School graduates Roger Hull and John Novogrod. This book is a very carefully documented work, which concludes quite positively that United States assistance to South Vietnam is legal.

More and more voices are being raised in the warning that withdrawal of the United States from South Vietnam would be disastrous to the world at large, and this, to me, is one of the most encouraging developments of all. The

Washington Post of April 3, 1968, cites what it calls a "cry of anguish from Malaysia [which] surely will jolt thoughtful Americans who have a parochial and insular preoccupation with South Vietnam as a situation apart from the rest of that region of the world." The editorial quotes Malaysia's Prime Minister Tunku Abdul Rahman's statement that: "If the Americans for some reason decided to give up this war in Vietnam and the North decided to take over the South, then it will be the end for all of us." And Field Marshal Sir Gerald Templer, commander of British forces who defeated the Communist guerrillas in Malaya after World War II, is quoted in the *Baltimore Sun* of March 25, 1968, in highly decisive terms: "If the Americans pull out of Vietnam, the Communists will take over the whole of Southeast Asia—and Burma, India, right up to the Caspian Sea would go." Such areas would include the Philippines, Indonesia, Malaysia, Laos, Cambodia, Thailand, Pakistan, Afghanistan, and Iran.

Extremely encouraging, I believe, is the careful internal restructuring taking place in South Vietnam at the direction of the Saigon government. Important officials have been removed in crackdowns on corruption, many province chiefs have been replaced, and steps have been taken toward adding 135,000 men to the armed forces (26,598 men were drafted, and 21,962 enlisted in the past three months).

On April 21, 1967, Senator Gale W. McGee, of Wyoming, addressed the Command and Staff College at Quantico, Virginia (the Marine Base to which I am currently assigned). He talked about how bleak and hopeless the situation had appeared when he had visited Vietnam in 1966, when General Thi's South Vietnamese forces were lined up in a power showdown against General Ky's South Vietnamese forces. It looked as though no one of intelligence would see any sense in continuing to help such a hopelessly confused and internally torn country. But we did not give up, and just a few months later South Vietnam had elected a constitutional assembly, which drafted a constitution that was voted on and adopted. A few months earlier, such a possibility had seemed absurd.

The point that Senator McGee made was that progress has been achieved consistently—slowly, painfully, but unquestionably. He quoted the Foreign Minister of Thailand, Thanat Khoman, whom we have quoted previously in this book: "If the Americans can only prevail in Vietnam, there will be no second Vietnam, there will be no third Vietnam." He also quoted Lee Kuan Yew, Prime Minister of Singapore, the newest republic in Asia: "Because the Americans are in Vietnam, Asia is closer to stability today than ever before in this century."

"All this," maintained Senator McGee, "says that we *are* getting some place, that it *does* make a difference, and that it is desperately important that we not get lost in the minutiae and the detail that we see on the screen and in the headlines every day. Great as our communications media happen to be, we haven't quite yet grown up to them. . . ."

Finally, I am encouraged deeply by the paragraph in President Johnson's March 31, 1968, address—the paragraph ignored by those who think we are preparing to "sell out" for peace at any price. "But let men everywhere know that a strong and a confident and vigilant America stands ready to seek an honorable peace and stands ready tonight to defend an honored cause, whatever the price, whatever the burden, whatever the sacrifice that duty may require."

BIBLIOGRAPHY

American Friends Service Committee. *Peace in Vietnam: A New Approach in Southeast Asia*, rev. ed. New York: Hill & Wang, 1967.

Atlas of South-East Asia. New York: St. Martin's Press, 1964.

Bain, Chester A. *Vietnam: The Roots of Conflict.* Englewood Cliffs, N.J.: Prentice-Hall, 1967.

Ball, George W. *The Issue in Viet-Nam.* Washington: Department of State, 1966. (Pamphlet is an address by Ball.)

Bator, Victor. *Vietnam: A Diplomatic Tragedy.* New York: Oceana Publications, 1965.

Brown, Robert McAfee, Abraham J. Heschel, and Michael Novak. *Vietnam: Crisis of Conscience.* New York: Association Press, 1967.

Bureau of Public Affairs, Department of State. *Concise History of Escalation in Vietnam.* Washington: Office of Public Services, n.d. (Ref. No. 4/32(L)-167BT).

——. *Negotiation Attempts on Vietnam.* Washington: Office of Public Services, Feb. 20, 1965.

——. *The Unending Struggle: Problems of Peace in Viet-Nam.* Washington: Office of Public Services, n.d. (Ref. No. 4/61-567B).

——. *The Viet Cong and the People of South Viet-Nam.* Washington: Office of Public Services, n.d. (Ref. No. 4/55-466B).

Burling, Robbins. *Hill Farms and Padi Fields: Life in Mainland Southeast Asia.* Englewood Cliffs, N.J.: Prentice-Hall, 1965.

Carver, George A. "The Faceless Viet Cong," *Foreign Affairs*, Vol. 44, No. 3 (April 1966), pp. 347–372.

Chinh, Truong. *Primer for Revolt: The Communist Takeover in Vietnam*, with Intro. by Bernard B. Fall. New York: Frederick A. Praeger, 1963.

Collier, Ellen C. *U.S. Policy on Negotiations for a Peaceful Settlement in Vietnam: Its Development Since April 7, 1965,* from the Congressional Record, Vol. 112, No. 52 (March 25, 1966), pp. 6407–6410. Washington: Library of Congress Legislative Reference Service, April 1966.

——. *United States Policy Toward Vietnam: A Summary Review of Its History*. Washington: Library of Congress Legislative Reference Service, March 1966.

Committee on Foreign Relations, U.S. Senate. *Background Information Relating to Southeast Asia and Vietnam*. Washington: GPO, March 1966.

——. *Background Information Relating to Southeast Asia and Vietnam*. Washington: GPO, July 1967.

Committee on the Judiciary, U.S. Senate. *Report of United Nations Fact-Finding Mission to South Viet-Nam*. Washington: GPO, 1964.

Defourneaux, Rene. "A Secret Encounter with Ho Chi Minh," *Look*, Vol. 30, No. 16 (Aug. 9, 1966), pp. 32–33.

Demeter, John. "Ministry of Peace in Time of War," *Report*, Vol. III, No. 11 (Aug. 1966), pp. 16–20.

Department of State. *Aggression from the North: The Record of North Viet-Nam's Campaign to Conquer South Viet-Nam*. Washington: GPO, Feb. 1965.

——. *The Heart of the Problem: Secretary Rusk, General Taylor Review Viet-Nam Policy in Senate Hearings*. Washington: GPO, Feb. 18, 1966.

——. *Legal Basis for United States Action Against North Vietnam*. Memorandum, March 8, 1965.

——. *Quiet Warriors: Supporting Social Revolution in Viet-Nam*. Washington: GPO, April 1966.

——. *Viet-Nam: The Struggle for Freedom*. Washington: GPO, Aug. 1964.

——. *Viet-Nam Information Notes*, No. 6, June 1967. Department of State Bulletin. Jan. 10, 1955, pp. 51–52. May 27, 1957, pp. 851–852. April 27, 1959, pp. 579–583. May 22, 1961, pp. 757–758. Dec. 4, 1961, pp. 920–922. May 11, 1964, pp. 733–736. Feb. 22, 1965, pp. 240–241. March 22, 1965, pp. 403, 419. April 21, 1965, pp. 528–532.

——. *The Pledge of Honolulu*, March 1966.

——. *Viet-Nam: The 38th Day*, March 1966.

Deutsch, E. B. "The Legality of the United States Position in Vietnam," *ABA Journal*, Vol. 52, No. 5 (May 1966), pp. 436–442.

Donlon, Roger H. C. *Outpost of Freedom*. New York: McGraw-Hill, 1965.

Eden, Anthony. *Full Circle*. Boston: Houghton Mifflin, 1960.

——. *Toward Peace in Indochina*. Boston: Houghton Mifflin, 1966.

Eisenhower, Dwight D. *Mandate for Change*. Garden City, N.Y.: Doubleday, 1963.

——. *Waging Peace*. Garden City, N.Y.: Doubleday, 1965.

Fall, Bernard B. *The Two Viet-Nams: A Political and Military Analysis*, 2nd rev. ed. New York: Frederick A. Praeger, 1967.

——. *Viet-Nam Witness: 1953–66*. New York: Frederick A. Praeger, 1966.

Fenrick, Joseph C. *Documents on the Vietnam Issue from the Congressional Record*. Washington: Library of Congress Library Services Division, Sept. 1965.

Finn, James. "The Debate on Vietnam," *The Catholic World*, Vol. 203, No. 1 (May 1966), p. 214.

Fishel, Wesley R., ed. *Problems of Freedom: South Vietnam Since Independence*. New York: The Free Press of Glencoe, 1961.

Fleck, James C. "The Just War Theory: Past, Present, Future," *The Homiletic and Pastoral Review*, Vol. LXVI, No. 10 (July 1966), pp. 819–825.

Giap, Vo Nguyen. *People's War, People's Army*. New York: Frederick A. Praeger, 1962.

Goodwin, Richard N. *Triumph or Tragedy: Reflections on Vietnam*. New York: Random House, 1966.

Gordon, Bernard K. *The Dimensions of Conflict in Southeast Asia*. Englewood Cliffs, N.J.: Prentice-Hall, 1966.

Halberstam, David. *The Making of a Quagmire*. New York: Random House, 1965.

Harrigan, Anthony. *Defense Against Total Attack*. Johannesburg: Nasionale Brehhandel Bepeck, 1965.

Herman, Edward S., and Richard B. DuBoff. *America's Vietnam Policy: The Strategy of Deception*. Washington: Public Affairs Press, 1966.

Higgins, Marguerite. *Our Vietnam Nightmare*. New York: Harper and Row, 1965.

Hoang Van Chi. *From Colonialism to Communism: A Case History of North Vietnam*, with Intro. by P. J. Honey. New York: Frederick A. Praeger, 1964.

Honey, P. J. *Communism in North Vietnam*. Cambridge, Mass.: The M.I.T. Press, 1963.

——. *North Vietnam Today: Profile of a Communist Satellite*. New York: Frederick A. Praeger, 1962.

Hormann, Karl. *Peace and Modern War in the Judgment of the Church*. Westminster, Md.: The Newman Press, 1966.

Hull, Roger, and John Novogrod. *Law and Viet Nam*. 1968.

Humphrey, Robert L. *Fight the Cold War*. Washington: American Institutes for Research, 1966.

Johnson, Lyndon B., Robert McNamara, and Dean Rusk. *Why Vietnam*. Washington: Department of State, Aug. 20, 1965.

Johnson, U. Alexis. *Viet-Nam Today*. Washington: Department of State, 1966. (Pamphlet is an address by Johnson.)

Joy, C. Turner. *How Communists Negotiate*. New York: Macmillan, 1955.

Kahn, Herman. *On Escalation: Metaphors and Scenarios*. New York: Frederick A. Praeger, 1965.

——. *On Thermonuclear War*. Princeton, N.J.: Princeton University Press, 1960.

——. *Thinking About the Unthinkable*. New York: Horizon Press, 1962.

Kastenmeier, Robert, ed. *Vietnam Hearings: Voices from the Grass Roots*. Garden City, N.Y.: Doubleday, 1966.

Labin, Suzanne. *Vietnam: Eye Witness Account*. Arlington, Va.: Crestwood Books, 1964.

Lacouture, Jean. *Vietnam: Between Two Truces*, translated by K. Kellen and J. Carmichael, with Intro. by Joseph Kraft. New York: Random House, 1966.

Lawler, Justus George. *Nuclear War: The Ethic, the Rhetoric, the Reality*. Westminster, Md.: The Newman Press, 1965.

Mansfield, Mike, and others. *The Vietnam Conflict: The Substance and the Shadow*. Washington: GPO, Jan. 6, 1966.

Mecklin, John. *Mission in Torment*. Garden City, N.Y.: Doubleday, 1965.

Morgenthau, Hans. *In Defense of the National Interest*. New York: Alfred A. Knopf, 1951.

——, and others. "Vietnam: What Should We Do Now?" *Look*, Vol. 30, No. 16 (Aug. 9, 1966), pp. 24–31.

Murray, John Courtney, S.J. *We Hold These Truths*. New York: Sheed and Ward, 1960.

Murti, B. S. N. *Vietnam Divided: The Unfinished Struggle*. New York: Asia Publishing House, 1965.

Nagle, William J., ed. *Morality and Modern Warfare*. Baltimore, Md.: Helicon Press, 1960.

Newman, Bernard. *Background to Viet-Nam*. New York: Roy Publishers, 1965.

Nighswonger, William A. *Rural Pacification in Vietnam: 1962–1965*. New York: Frederick A. Praeger, 1966.

Pan, Stephen, and Daniel Lyons. *Vietnam Crisis*. New York: The East Asian Research Institute, 1966.

Pike, Douglas C. *Viet Cong: The Organization and Technique of the National Liberation Front of South Vietnam*. Cambridge, Mass.: The M.I.T. Press, 1966.

Raskin, Marcus G., and Bernard B. Fall, eds. *The Viet-Nam Reader*. New York: Random House, 1965.

Reston, James. *The Artillery of the Press: Its Influence on American Foreign Relations*. New York: Harper and Row, 1967. (Published for the Council on Foreign Relations.)

Rhodes, Alexander de. *Rhodes of Viet-Nam*, translated by S. Hertz. Westminster, Md.: The Newman Press, 1966.

Robinson, Frank M., and Earl Kemp, eds. *Report on the*

Senate Hearings: The Truth About Vietnam. San Diego, Calif.: Greenleaf Classics, 1966.

Sebes, Joseph S. *Viet-Nam: An Enigma.* Washington, D.C., Georgetown University, Nov. 1965. (Prepared for use by Chesapeake and Potomac Telephone Companies.)

Shaplen, Robert. *The Lost Revolution.* New York: Harper and Row, 1965.

Swearingen and Rolf. *Communism in Vietnam.* Chicago: American Bar Association, 1957.

The Vietnam Hearings, with Intro. by J. William Fulbright. New York: Random House, 1966.

Tregaskis, Richard. *Vietnam Diary.* New York: Holt, Rinehart and Winston, 1963.

Tucker, Robert W. *The Just War.* Baltimore, Md.: The Johns Hopkins Press, 1960.

U.S. House of Representatives. "Mutual Security Appropriations," *Hearings Before the House Appropriations Committee, 84th Congress, 2nd Session.* Washington: GPO, 1956, pp. 19–20.

U.S. Mission to the United Nations. Press release No. 4610 (July 30, 1965). Press release No. 4781 (Jan. 5, 1966). Press release No. 4798 (Jan. 31, 1966).

U.S. Senate. *Hearing Before the Committee on Foreign Relations, U.S. Senate, on Vietnam.* Washington: GPO, 1966.

———. *The Legality of U.S. Participation in the Defense of Vietnam.* Congressional Record, March 10, 1966, pp. S5274–5279.